A Warrior's Battlefield
Strategy Devotional

Sheila Holm

A Warrior's Battlefield Strategy Devotional

D1410023

A Warrior's Battlefield Strategy Devotional

ISBN-13: 978-1986535298
ISBN-10: 1986535290

Unless otherwise indicated all scriptures are taken from the
New King James version of the Bible.

Web Site: hisbest.org

Facebook: Sheila Holm Christian Author, HISBest4us

Printed in USA by HIS Best Publishing

DEDICATION

To the Father, the Son and the Holy Spirit for the depth of truth revealed in these days is beyond comprehension.

To Bishop McKinney for standing firm in prayer with me since the day we met in 2000.

To Carol Marfori, for prayerfully seeking deep truth & editing!

To Rebecca King for providing the truth about the glory, the heavenly portals, for the truth is: *Christ gave us the glory before He went to the cross, so we would be one as He and the Father are one.* **John 17:22.**

To President Donald John Trump for his willingness to proceed forward in faith after committing to take on the depth of evil our nation has been encased within for many generations.

To Rodney Howard-Browne for releasing the global truth so all who have ears to hear and eyes to see the plan of the enemy which is unfolding in the world, to realize how to pray and take action for the sake of souls in these days.

To Bill Morford for remaining obedient until the *One New Man Bible Revealing Jewish Roots and Power* was translated direct from the Hebrew and made available to all Christians so believers will see and know the truth: *We are no longer Gentiles, and we are not to do as the Gentiles do!* For providing the book *Fulfillment of Prophecy* by Eliezer Ben-Yehuda for our Father revealed the truth to him: *The two things without which the Jews will not be a nation: The Land and the Language.* A critical stand taken for believers because America is back in the position of not protecting the blessed land GOD provided or the language!

To Mark Taylor for standing firm in truth while sharing the exact words from our Father to the believers around the globe in these days.

To LT, And We Know, for releasing truth so citizens around the globe will personally realize the reason to personally know that they know how to do everything they can to stand firm in faith and retain liberty & freedom.

To Dorothy Spaulding, Channel 49 TV for introducing me to Mark Taylor and for Mark's introductions to Christopher McDonald, McFiles, Omega Man and Sheila Zilinsky media, and Up Front In The Prophetic for the opportunity granted to me to reveal the truth to believers on your programs, aired throughout the world during these unique days in HIStory.

Table of Contents

Prepare:
Pray, Align with the Father's Plan, Put on the Armor of GOD

Romans 12:2. **And do not be conformed to this world, but be transformed by the renewing of your mind, that you may prove what** *is* **that good and acceptable and perfect will of God.**

II Corinthians 2:16. **For** *who has known the mind of the Lord that he may instruct Him?* **But we have the mind of Christ.**

Ephesians 6:10-20 (1-24).

Children and Parents

Children, obey your parents in the Lord, for this is right. 2 *Honor your father and mother,* which is the first commandment with promise: 3 *that it may be well with you and you may live long on the earth.* 4 And you, fathers, do not provoke your children to wrath, but bring them up in the training and admonition of the Lord.

Bond servants and Masters

5 Bond servants, be obedient to those who are your masters according to the flesh, with fear and trembling, in sincerity of heart, as to Christ; 6 not with eye service, as men-pleasers, but as bond servants of Christ, doing the will of God from the heart, 7 with goodwill doing service, as to the Lord, and not to men, 8 knowing that whatever good anyone does, he will receive the same from the Lord, whether *he is* a slave or free. 9 And you, masters, do the same things to them, giving up threatening, knowing that your own Master also is in heaven, and there is no partiality with Him.

The Whole Armor of God

10 Finally, my brethren, be strong in the Lord and in the power of His might. 11 Put on the whole armor of God, that you may be able to stand against the wiles of the devil. 12 For we do not wrestle against flesh and blood, but against principalities, against powers, against the rulers of the darkness of this age, against spiritual *hosts* of wickedness in the heavenly *places.* 13 Therefore take up the whole armor of God, that you may be able to withstand in the evil day, and having done all, to stand. 14 Stand therefore, having girded your waist with truth, having put on the breastplate of righteousness, 15 and having shod your feet with the preparation of the gospel of peace; 16 above all, taking the shield of faith with which you will be able to quench all the fiery darts of the wicked one. 17 And take the helmet of salvation, and the sword of the Spirit, which is the word of God; 18 praying always with all prayer and supplication in the Spirit, being watchful to this end with all perseverance and supplication for all the saints— 19 and for me, that utterance may be given to me, that I may open my mouth boldly to make known the mystery of the gospel, 20 for which I am an ambassador in chains; that in it I may speak boldly, as I ought to speak.

A Gracious Greeting

21 But that you also may know my affairs *and* how I am doing, Tychicus, a beloved brother and faithful minister in the Lord, will make all things known to you; 22 whom I have sent to you for this very purpose, that you may know our affairs, and *that* he may comfort your hearts. 23 Peace to the brethren, and love with faith, from God the Father and the Lord Jesus Christ. 24 Grace *be* with all those who love our Lord Jesus Christ in sincerity. Amen.

Introduction

GOD directed my path to receive three confirmations for a devotional to support our opportunity to OVERCOME each of the tactics of the enemy: Fear, Doubt and Unbelief. Our Father wants us to learn how to thwart all attempts of the enemy to Steal, Kill and Destroy.

Even though I confirmed I was not 'known' so a devotional did not seem like a good 'next step', the confirmations continued. They were intense. Each confirmation provided a specific reason to proceed and they expanded until they became 'like a mighty flood'!

So, finally, I said, *Yes.*

At the same time, I also continued my 'attempts to escape' from Georgia each time I shared the facts with specific people GOD prompted me to share the facts with ... clearly, my plan to prepare so my escape could be accomplished was merely my personal plan!

Personally, I trusted I would not be writing a book, let alone a series of books regarding the vision and word: *For The Sake Of America,* given to the prophets who transitioned to heaven between February 2014 and February 2015.

GOD's sense of humor made a difference!

When HE made it clear that the focus of the devotional would be 'fear not scriptures', and HE provided many confirmations from leaders in the body of CHRIST declaring and repeating the same phrase, *There are 366 fear not scriptures in the bible, one for each day of the year, even Leap Year,* I was excited the devotional 'would be so easy to prepare'!

Truth: There are NOT 366 or 365 'fear not' scriptures!

The statement is repeated, often, but it is not true!

Where did it start?

Perhaps it started with a quote within books by Lloyd Ogilvie as early as 1987. The quote actually took off when it was included within a popular book by John Ortberg, perhaps in part due to the amazing and uplifting title: *If You Want To Walk On The Water You've Got To Get Out Of The Boat.* In fact, the quote became so popular it was part of the film script for the movie, *Facing The Giants.*

The quote was stated by Mark Richt who played himself in the movie. Mark was born in Nebraska (I simply have to include this fact), and later, he became well know as the coach of the Bulldogs or "Dawgs" at the University of Georgia for 15 years. He re-stated the phrase within his quote during the film: *Well, in God's word He said 365 different times, 'Do not fear'. Now if He says it that many times, you know He's serious about it, don't ya?*

In fact, the quote became so popular about the 365 'fear not' scriptures in the bible, the film quote was mis-quoted on the internet and repeated, often by someone 'not related to the film project': *"in God's word He says 'do not fear' 365 times, now if he says it that many times you know he's gonna mean it" -Facing the Giants*

Our Father has prompted me again & again to research, seek the truth for there are so many details shared as facts which are not facts. When we pass on the details which are not facts, we are sharing lies. There are no versions of the truth. Only the truth is the truth!

In fact, in my research, I found a devotional titled: *365 Days of Fear Not* and on my birthday, January 6, 2018, another devotional was released, *Fear Not: A 365 Daily Devotional.*

Through the process of nearly five years while the devotional was 'set aside' due to the four book series focused on the prophetic word and vision *For The Sake Of America,* the decisions regarding 'which scriptures should be included' resulted in a deep, amazing journey which did NOT result in finding 365 fear not scriptures.

First, the search for 'fear' or 'fear not' scriptures barely reached 65, a number clearly short of the goal: 365. Then, after spending a lot more time researching sources who used the headline: *365 Fear Not Scriptures* but, no matter how many times I counted their list of scriptures and matched them with the specific verses I found, the total did not surpass 145. So, it did not seem like the devotional would actually come together.

However, our Father prompted me to share the fact HE wanted me to focus on a devotional regarding fear not during interviews and HE would not do that unless it was important to HIM!

Resting with HIM resulted in HIS input: *Include Doubt and Unbelief.*

Excited because I trusted this would clearly meet or surpass 365!

Wrong! 108 + 145 did not equal 365 or 366. More prayer! Our Father prompted me to add, **Reverential Fear,** which increased the total but, it did not come close to the goal, either.

Then, our Father shared a significant change in the format of the devotional when HE prompted me to go back and re-count the 'fear not' scriptures while confirming the list total was more than 145. When I recounted, there were 146.

Wow! I wanted to laugh because ONE would not help!

However, HE immediately prompted me to scroll through the 145 (now, 146) 'fear not' scriptures and find the one **'in bold'**. The scriptures were not 'in bold' when I prepared the 'cut and paste' copy but, I trusted HE was going to show me 'the answer', and HE did!

When I scrolled through the 'fear not' scriptures one more time, I realized the change to 146 was due to a scripture HE added 'in bold': *The Priestly Blessing.* Then, our Father confirmed the blessing would be inserted on the seventh day each week, on Sabbath, to begin the process of honoring the Sabbath, expanding time to 'rest in HIM' and personally hear HIS truth about your week, your life and HIS plans for you.

In that moment, the LORD was confirming the exact structure of HIS seven day format. It is truly a unique structure for a devotional. HE confirmed the format would be the exact reason why HE wanted me to write this devotional. It is all about living beyond proving the process of countering fear, doubt and unbelief and it would require more than 'fear not' quotes or scripture references.

Immediately, HE prompted me to remember the supernatural vision shared by Lee Benton in 2015 when the producer involved in her meeting confirmed the books were being released on the high holy days as confirmation ... *You have been willing to tell the people the truth ... you are teaching the people to honor the Sabbath ... I am honored to be the one God is speaking through to thank you because it means a lot to me since I am a Messianic Jew ...* (more compliments stated, as he held my hand).

Too Many Leaving, Giving Up, Committing Suicide

Preaching in an area where 18 people committed suicide by hanging within a few months of my arrival. Many suicides in the region, while 18 were actually accomplished 'by hanging'.

Then, while attending a fellowship the confirmation was shared about a few of the members of an Army division newly assigned to the area were requesting prayer. When they were asked about the request for prayer, they confirmed, they wanted to pray as an Army division since 15 within their division committed suicide in a short time frame of 'leaving the field' together. The 15 suicides occurred in less than two months prior to the day of their prayer request. Father had my attention!

The list of confirmations continued with prayers for each person mentioned who committed suicide after becoming overwhelmed by their circumstances, especially when reports of youth committing suicide due to thinking 'no hope, no future, no ability to get married and have a family if global warming means we only have ten or twelve years left. They do not know hope!

Each of the stories of pain and hopelessness fit into the same theme.

Easy to be overtaken by fear, doubt and unbelief when we are away from the word and fellowship with believers because the plan of the enemy is simple: *Cause the people to focus on fear, doubt and unbelief to steal, kill and destroy their plans and their belief in the promise of hope and a future.*

Psalms 34:4.
I sought the Lord, and He heard me,
And delivered me from all my fears.

The full text of **Psalms 34** is so powerful. We often hear only the first part of the verse *Oh taste and see that the Lord is good* while we do not hear the rest of the verse: *Blessed is the man who trusts in Him!*

Psalms 34 is so powerful, I am inserting it because it clearly reveals the only one we are to fear with reverential fear (honor, in awe) is our Father.

Reverential fear is 'standing in awe'!

It is not a fear of what our Father will do to us.

It is actually how we reverence Him and honor who sent us to earth for this exact time in HIStory.

Reverence of who HE is, helps us comprehend TRUTH direct from HIM, for the truth is: **HE is constantly orchestrating our lives, working for us because HE loves us and proceeds with HIS plans 'on our behalf'.**

You will find some days do not have any notes from me and it is because the LORD prompted me to 'not interfere' because He wants you to focus on the scripture with Him and hear direct from our Father regarding how it applies to your life. Standing firm with you in prayer as you review Psalms 34 and allow our Father to reveal His TRUTH direct to you:

Psalms 34.

The Happiness of Those Who Trust in God

A Psalm of David when he pretended madness before Abimelech, who drove him away, and he departed.

I will bless the Lord at all times;
His praise *shall* continually *be* in my mouth.
2 My soul shall make its boast in the Lord;
The humble shall hear *of it* and be glad.
3 Oh, magnify the Lord with me,
And let us exalt His name together.
4 I sought the Lord, and He heard me,
And delivered me from all my fears.
5 They looked to Him and were radiant,
And their faces were not ashamed.
6 This poor man cried out, and the Lord heard *him,*
And saved him out of all his troubles.
7 The angel of the Lord encamps all around those who fear Him,
And delivers them.
8 Oh, taste and see that the Lord *is* good;
Blessed *is* the man *who* trusts in Him!
9 Oh, fear the Lord, you His saints!
There is no want to those who fear Him.
10 The young lions lack and suffer hunger;
But those who seek the Lord shall not lack any good *thing.*
11 Come, you children, listen to me;
I will teach you the fear of the Lord.
12 Who *is* the man *who* desires life,
And loves *many* days, that he may see good?
13 Keep your tongue from evil,
And your lips from speaking deceit.
14 Depart from evil and do good;
Seek peace and pursue it.

15 The eyes of the Lord *are* on the righteous,
And His ears *are open* to their cry.
16 The face of the Lord *is* against those who do evil,
To cut off the remembrance of them from the earth.
17 *The righteous* cry out, and the Lord hears,
And delivers them out of all their troubles.
18 The Lord *is* near to those who have a broken heart,
And saves such as have a contrite spirit.
19 Many *are* the afflictions of the righteous,
But the Lord delivers him out of them all.
20 He guards all his bones;
Not one of them is broken.
21 Evil shall slay the wicked,
And those who hate the righteous shall be condemned.
22 The Lord redeems the soul of His servants,
And none of those who trust in Him shall be condemned.

Father we praise you and thank you for making us joint heirs with Christ, for doing ALL for us, so we can LIVE FREE and do ALL we can each day to bless souls and guide them to YOU! Thank YOU for giving us everything we need to proceed. We know where we are weak, YOU are strong and YOU will strengthen us. Therefore, we will NOT allow the enemy to use his three tactics of fear, doubt and unbelief to gain access to steal, kill and destroy.

<u>FEAR</u>: Genesis 15:1, after the insert (Genesis 4:18-24).

<u>Abram and Melchizedek.</u>

Genesis 4:18-24. Then Melchizedek king of Salem brought out bread and wine; he was the priest of God Most High. 19 And he blessed him and said:

Blessed be Abram of God Most High,

Possessor of heaven and earth;

20 *And blessed be God Most High,*

Who has delivered your enemies into your hand.

And he gave him a tithe of all.

21 Now the king of Sodom said to Abram, *Give me the persons, and take the goods for yourself.* **22 But Abram said to the king of Sodom,** *I have raised my hand to the Lord, God Most High, the Possessor of heaven and earth,* **23** *that I will take nothing, from a thread to a sandal strap, and that I will not take anything that is yours, lest you should say, 'I have made Abram rich'—* **24** *except only what the young men have eaten, and the portion of the men who went with me: Aner, Eshcol, and Mamre; let them take their portion.*

Genesis 15:1. After these things the word of the Lord came to Abram in a vision, saying, *Do not be afraid, Abram. I am your shield, your exceedingly great reward.*

Abraham was presented with options, choices.

The choices confirm the character of Abraham.

Father delivered the enemy to Abraham.

King of Sodom offered to provide a 'worldly reward' if the enemy would be turned over to his command and control.

Abraham confirmed he took the situation to the Father when He responded. His response confirmed he knew our Father delivered the people into his hands; a direct answer to prayer!

The only thing Abraham accepted from the king was enough food for his men. Abraham knew his provision and supply was provided by our Father.

Are the rewards of the world the focus today or the rewards of being a believer, a joint-heir with Christ?

Repentance for _worldly world today_ ?

Adjustment(s) planned? _____

UNBELIEF. Genesis 19:16 (15-22).

When the morning dawned, the angels urged Lot to hurry, saying, *Arise, take your wife and your two daughters who are here, lest you be consumed in the punishment of the city.* 16 And while he lingered, the men took hold of his hand, his wife's hand, and the hands of his two daughters, the Lord being merciful to him, and they brought him out and set him outside the city. 17 So it came to pass, when they had brought them outside, that he said, *Escape for your life! Do not look behind you nor stay anywhere in the plain. Escape to the mountains, lest you be destroyed.*

18 Then Lot said to them, *Please, no, my lords!* 19 *Indeed now, your servant has found favor in your sight, and you have increased your mercy which you have shown me by saving my life; but I cannot escape to the mountains, lest some evil overtake me and I die.* 20 *See now, this city is near enough to flee to, and it is a little one; please let me escape there (is it not a little one?) and my soul shall live.*

21 And he said to him, *See, I have favored you concerning this thing also, in that I will not overthrow this city for which you have spoken.* 22 *Hurry, escape there. For I cannot do anything until you arrive there.*

Therefore the name of the city was called Zoar.

Very interesting negotiation. The plan was set in place for the safety and security of the entire family.

Lot wanted to go in a different direction, to a different location, a different plan which he thought was 'easier' for his family to accomplish.

What is the result of the human choice he made?

Very interesting destination!

Hebrew meaning of Zoar (Tso`ar): <u>insignificance or smallness</u>.

What is your choice today? This week? In life?

- Mountain top perspective with our Father,

- Insignificant / small / easy to humanly manage?

Repentance for _____?

Adjustment(s) planned? _____

DAY THREE

FEAR. Genesis 21:17 (17-18).

And God heard the voice of the lad. Then the angel of God called to Hagar out of heaven, and said to her, *What ails you, Hagar? Fear not, for God has heard the voice of the lad where he is. 18 Arise, lift up the lad and hold him with your hand, for I will make him a great nation.*

TRUTH: Father honored the lineage of both sons of Abraham!

Ishmael fathered 12 sons, princes all.

Same blessing over his lineage, as spoken over Abraham.

Thinking about any 'black sheep' members of the family?

Time to revise the script of your life, the purpose and plan of the members of your family?

Perhaps, today is an opportunity to seek truth from Father about who He sent you to and why, to gain His guidance in changing the script of family life, to no longer think of being or identifying the 'black sheep' of the family?

What led to the departure of Hagar & Ishmael?

Sarah turned against them, changed the plan, after Sarah requested the blessing of a son and set the plan in motion:

Genesis 21:8-16.

Hagar and Ishmael Depart.

So the child grew and was weaned. And Abraham made a great feast on the same day that Isaac was weaned.

9 And Sarah saw the son of Hagar the Egyptian, whom she had borne to Abraham, scoffing. 10 Therefore she said to Abraham, *Cast out this bondwoman and her son; for the son of this bondwoman shall not be heir with my son, namely with Isaac.* 11 And the matter was very displeasing in Abraham's sight because of his son.

12 But God said to Abraham, *Do not let it be displeasing in your sight because of the lad or because of your bondwoman. Whatever Sarah has said to you, listen to her voice; for in Isaac your seed shall be called. 13 Yet I will also make a nation of the son of the bondwoman, because he is your seed.*

14 So Abraham rose early in the morning, and took bread and a skin of water; and putting it on her shoulder, he gave it and the boy to Hagar, and sent her away. Then she departed and wandered in the Wilderness of Beersheba. 15 And the water in the skin was used up, and she placed the boy under one of the shrubs. 16 Then she went and sat down across from him at a distance of about a bowshot; for she said to herself, *Let me not see the death of the boy.* So she sat opposite him, and lifted her voice and wept.

Grateful our Father has arranged an 'unconditional covenant' with us! He does not put a plan in action. Then, change His mind. Cause others to 'align with our ways'.

He wants us to honor the people in our life.

Bottom line: Blessing or cursing, in our thoughts, words and actions! Father planned blessings for ALL mankind!

Have you made a 'covenant' with the Father?

What would life look like if we found a way to align with Father, support & bless each other, aligning with Father's plans?

Repentance for _____?

Adjustment(s) planned? _____

DAY FOUR

FEAR. Genesis 26:24.

And The LORD appeared to him the same night and said, *I am the God of your father Abraham; do not fear, for I am with you; I will bless you and multiply your descendants for My servant Abraham's sake.*

Knowing our Father honors His plans for us, and He is our rear-guard,* what are you willing to do today? This week? In your life?

*Examples: **Isaiah 52:12.**
For you shall not go out with haste,
Nor go by flight;
For the Lord will go before you,
And the God of Israel will be your rear guard.

Before racing forward, the steps are: 1. seek, 2. follow Father's guidance!
Doing all within the 'Faith Walk' to STAND FIRM in truth!

Isaiah 58:8.
Then your light shall break forth like the morning,
Your healing shall spring forth speedily,
And your righteousness shall go before you;
The glory of the Lord shall be your rear guard.

Repentance for _____?

Adjustment(s) planned? _____

18

DOUBT. Genesis 28:15.

Behold, I am with you and will keep you wherever you go, and will bring you back to this land; for I will not leave you until I have done what I have spoken to you.

Father will not leave you or forsake you! What are you willing to do knowing Father will *'keep you wherever you go'*?

Repentance for _____?

Adjustment(s) planned? _____

DAY SIX

REVERENTIAL FEAR. Genesis 28:16-17 (10-22).

Jacob's Vow at Bethel.

Now Jacob went out from Beersheba and went toward Haran. 11 So he came to a certain place and stayed there all night, because the sun had set. And he took one of the stones of that place and put it at his head, and he lay down in that place to sleep. 12 Then he dreamed, and behold, a ladder was set up on the earth, and its top reached to heaven; and there the angels of God were ascending and descending on it.

13 And behold, the Lord stood above it and said: *I am the Lord God of Abraham your father and the God of Isaac; the land on which you lie I will give to you and your descendants.* 14 *Also your descendants shall be as the dust of the earth; you shall spread abroad to the west and the east, to the north and the south; and in you and in your seed all the families of the earth shall be blessed.* 15 *Behold, I am with you and will keep you wherever you go, and will bring you back to this land; for I will not leave you until I have done what I have spoken to you.*

16 Then Jacob awoke from his sleep and said, *Surely the Lord is in this place, and I did not know it.* 17 And he was afraid and said, *How awesome is this place! This is none other than the house of God, and this is the gate of heaven!*

18 Then Jacob rose early in the morning, and took the stone that he had put at his head, set it up as a pillar, and poured oil on top of it. 19 And he called the name of that place Bethel; but the name of that city had been Luz previously. 20 Then Jacob made a vow, saying, *If God will be with me, and keep me in this way that I am going, and give me bread to eat and clothing to put on,* 21 *so that I come back to my father's house in peace, then*

the Lord shall be my God. 22 And this stone which I have set as a pillar shall be God's house, and of all that You give me I will surely give a tenth to You.

Meaning of Bethel in Hebrew: House of El (GOD).

Meaning of Luz in Hebrew: Almond tree/wood

Former royal Canaanite city

Father wants to show you what He has 'in store' for you!

When he shows you, will you align with Him?

Will you receive His word?

What is your vow?

Something which will change your life? Your family? Your extended family?

Repentance for _____?

Adjustment(s) planned? _____

DAY SEVEN

BLESSING. Numbers 6:24-26.
> *The LORD bless you and keep you;*
> *25 The LORD make His face shine upon you,*
> *And be gracious to you;*
> *26 The LORD lift up His countenance upon you,*
> *And give you peace.*

Blessings received: _____

Blessings shared: _____

Declarations/Testimonies: _____

DAY ONE

<u>FEAR</u>. Genesis 35:17 (16-17).
<u>Death of Rachel.</u>
Then they journeyed from Bethel. And when there was but a little distance to go to Ephrath, Rachel labored in childbirth, and she had hard labor. 17 Now it came to pass, when she was in hard labor, that the midwife said to her, *Do not fear; you will have this son also.*

There will be struggles. There will be joy!

There will be strife & defeat. There will be victories!

There will be encouragement from our Father, ALWAYS, to 'carry on'.

Plus, most days 'during our days on earth' do not result in death. Odds are great that we will accomplish our purpose and plan. Are you committed to the plan our Father has for your life?

Repentance for _____?

Adjustment(s) planned? _____

DAY TWO

<u>FEAR</u>. Genesis 43:23 (18-25).
Now the men were afraid because they were brought into Joseph's house; and they said, *It is because of the money, which was returned in our sacks the first time, that we are brought in, so that he may make a case against us and seize us, to take us as slaves with our donkeys.*

19 When they drew near to the steward of Joseph's house, they talked with him at the door of the house, 20 and said, *O sir, we indeed came down the first time to buy food;* **21** *but it happened, when we came to the encampment, that we opened our sacks, and there, each man's money was in the mouth of his sack, our money in full weight; so we have brought it back in our hand.* **22** *And we have brought down other money in our hands to buy food. We do not know who put our money in our sacks.*

23 But he said, *Peace be with you, do not be afraid. Your God and the God of your father has given you treasure in your sacks; I had your money.* **Then he brought Simeon out to them.**

24 So the man brought the men into Joseph's house and gave them water, and they washed their feet; and he gave their donkeys feed. 25 Then

they made the present ready for Joseph's coming at noon, for they heard that they would eat bread there.

The truth was known. In the prior verses, the men were instructed to take with them the money which 'found a way into the mouth of their sacks' during the prior journey. Because they prepared the 'return of the money', their return resulted in an invitation to go to Joseph's home, where a feast was being prepared. Joseph honored the men.

The men also prepared and honored Joseph.

Resolved with all being forgiven without words shared.

Repentance for _____?

Adjustment(s) planned? _____

DAY THREE

<u>FEAR</u>. **Genesis 46:3 (1-7).**
<u>Jacob's Journey to Egypt</u>.
So Israel took his journey with all that he had, and came to Beersheba, and offered sacrifices to the God of his father Isaac. 2 Then God spoke to Israel in the visions of the night, and said, *Jacob, Jacob!*

And he said, *Here I am.*

3 So He said, *I am God, the God of your father; do not fear to go down to Egypt, for I will make of you a great nation there. 4 I will go down with you to Egypt, and I will also surely bring you up again; and Joseph will put his hand on your eyes.*

5 Then Jacob arose from Beersheba; and the sons of Israel carried their father Jacob, their little ones, and their wives, in the carts which Pharaoh had sent to carry him. 6 So they took their livestock and their goods, which they had acquired in the land of Canaan, and went to Egypt, Jacob and all his descendants with him. 7 His sons and his sons' sons, his daughters and his sons' daughters, and all his descendants he brought with him to Egypt.

The call upon your life. Your purpose and plan. Known?

Potential of being 'uprooted' and sent to another region.

Would you feel overwhelmed? Would you resist the opportunity to proceed?

If you are going to leave the 'familiar' to go into the 'unknown', would you be willing?

22

What would we be willing to sacrifice?

Would the sacrifice outweigh the reward?

What would be sacrificed by ignoring the prompting?

Corrie Ten Boom quote:
Never be afraid to trust an unknown future to a known God.

Repentance for _____?

Adjustment(s) planned? _____

DAY FOUR

<u>**DOUBT.**</u> **Exodus 3:12 (9-14).**
Now therefore, behold, the cry of the children of Israel has come to Me, and I have also seen the oppression with which the Egyptians oppress them. **10** *Come now, therefore, and I will send you to Pharaoh that you may bring My people, the children of Israel, out of Egypt.*

11 But Moses said to God, *Who am I that I should go to Pharaoh, and that I should bring the children of Israel out of Egypt?*

12 So He said, *I will certainly be with you. And this shall be a sign to you that I have sent you: When you have brought the people out of Egypt, you shall serve God on this mountain.*

13 Then Moses said to God, *Indeed, when I come to the children of Israel and say to them, 'The God of your fathers has sent me to you,' and they say to me, 'What is His name?' what shall I say to them?*

14 And God said to Moses, *I AM WHO I AM.* **And He said,** *Thus you shall say to the children of Israel, 'I AM has sent me to you.'*

Are we restricting ourselves from accomplishing our purpose and plan with a list of excuses, reasons, weaknesses, etc.?

If Father can send Moses, a man who expressed anger to the point of committing murder ... a man who 'hid out' in the desert for decades ... and yet, Moses faced his fears and experienced true intimacy with our Father to accomplish so much for the people, the multitude enslaved in Egypt, 'before Christ' ...

Since we are each Ambassadors for Christ while 'on earth', knowing who we represent and praying as He taught us to pray, as one servant (with the potential of beginning the process at an earlier age than Moses) what can we accomplish for the kingdom while we are here?

23

Repentance for _____?

Adjustment(s) planned? _____

DAY FIVE

UNBELIEF. Exodus 4:1.

Then Moses answered and said, _But suppose they will not believe me or listen to my voice; suppose they say, 'The Lord has not appeared to you.'_

Are we leaning upon the input from other 'humans' or GOD?

Are we allowing 'mere mortals' to impact our destiny?

Father knows the end from the beginning!

When we make our decision, will it confirm we trust Him?

Repentance for _____?

Adjustment(s) planned? _____

DAY SIX

REVERENTIAL FEAR. Exodus 14:31.

Thus Israel saw the great work which the Lord had done in Egypt; so the people feared the Lord, and believed the Lord and His servant Moses.

How fortunate are we to serve a GOD who never leaves or forsakes us? Evidence of His divine protection again and again when the people held Him in 'reverential fear', when they prayed, aligned together, praised our Father and proceeded as GOD directed.

What are you are hearing from our Father today?

What has our Father shared with you over time, words from our Father which you are prompted to hear again today?

Repentance for _____?

Adjustment(s) planned? _____

BLESSING. Numbers 6:24-26.
> *The LORD bless you and keep you;*
> *25 The LORD make His face shine upon you,*
> *And be gracious to you;*
> *26 The LORD lift up His countenance upon you,*
> *And give you peace.*

Blessings received:_____

Blessings shared:_____

Declarations/Testimonies: _____

WEEK THREE

DAY ONE

FEAR. Genesis 50:19 (15-19).
Joseph Reassures His Brothers.
When Joseph's brothers saw that their father was dead, they said, *Perhaps Joseph will hate us, and may [c]actually repay us for all the evil which we did to him.* 16 So they sent messengers to Joseph, saying, *Before your father died he commanded, saying,* 17 *'Thus you shall say to Joseph: "I beg you, please forgive the trespass of your brothers and their sin; for they did evil to you." '* Now, please, forgive the trespass of the servants of the God of your father. And Joseph wept when they spoke to him.

18 Then his brothers also went and fell down before his face, and they said, *Behold, we are your servants.*

19 Joseph said to them, *Do not be afraid, for am I in the place of God?*

When prior events, especially deeds 'done in secret', are about to be revealed and dealt with, and it appears the specifics hoped to be 'left in the past' are about to be disclosed, how will the situation be resolved? In truth? Within a plan, a strategy, a scheme or a cover up?

Repentance for _____?

Adjustment(s) planned? _____

FEAR. Genesis 50:21 (20-21).

But as for you, you meant evil against me; but God meant it for good, in order to bring it about as it is this day, to save many people alive. [21] *Now therefore, do not be afraid; I will provide for you and your little ones.* **And he comforted them and spoke kindly to them.**

Ah, to be 'in the room' when the revelation of truth is shared!

Very different if the revelation uncovers something 'unresolved' from the past. Often the resolution, request for forgiveness, repentance of 'past stuff' results in full restoration.

What is burdening your heart?

Our Father will reveal the 'depths of the details' when He is brought 'into the situation'. Then, he will 'be with you' while the forgiveness and restoration take place.

What needs to be forgiven, spoken after repented for, so restoration can take place in your life and the life of any other people involved?

Repentance for _____?

Adjustment(s) planned? _____

DAY THREE

UNBELIEF. Exodus 4:8-9.

Then it will be, if they do not believe you, nor heed the message of the first sign, that they may believe the message of the latter sign. 9 And it shall be, if they do not believe even these two signs, or listen to your voice, that you shall take water from the river and pour it on the dry land. The water which you take from the river will become blood on the dry land.

10 Then Moses said to the Lord, O my Lord, I am not eloquent, neither before nor since You have spoken to Your servant; but I am slow of speech and slow of tongue.

11 So the Lord said to him, Who has made man's mouth? Or who makes the mute, the deaf, the seeing, or the blind? Have not I, the Lord? 12 Now therefore, go, and I will be with your mouth and teach you what you shall say.

Ah, Moses! At the moment of choice, he deferred with reasons and excuses.

Suppose the slow of speech meant that he stuttered?

Moses was chosen since he had 'history' in the palace.

Due to his concerns, an option was provided by GOD: Aaron was approaching and our Father offered for Moses to prepare Aaron to speak.

Seeking the resources, the sources to complete the task while encouraging each other to keep on, keepin' on until DONE!

To continue to assist through discipleship, one to another, sharpening each other in truth as iron sharpens iron and NOT allowing an 'offense' to be taken during the 'training phase' will reap rewards! Discipleship is a process which is not easily accepted. However, it is the goal. Few will allow discipleship and even fewer will disciple others when our Father provides the truth. The field is WHITE (saved souls) for harvest but, the laborers are few!

John 4:34-36 confirms: **Jesus said to them,** *My food is to do the will of Him who sent Me, and to finish His work.* **35** *Do you not say, 'There are still four months and then comes the harvest'? Behold, I say to you, lift up your eyes and look at the fields, for they are already white for harvest!* **36** *And he who reaps receives wages, and gathers fruit for eternal life, that both he who sows and he who reaps may rejoice together.*

Will you seek to follow the prompting of our Father when He directs you to the people ready for discipleship? Will you be willing to strengthen believers in the truth as directed by our Father? Hopeful, because the 'field is white' with saved souls ready to be discipled!

Repentance for _____?

Adjustment(s) planned? _____

DAY FOUR

<u>DOUBT</u>. Exodus 12:14 (12-17).

For I will pass through the land of Egypt on that night, and will strike all the firstborn in the land of Egypt, both man and beast; and against all the gods of Egypt I will execute judgment: I am the Lord. **13** *Now the blood shall be a sign for you on the houses where you are. And when I see the blood, I will pass over you; and the plague shall not be on you to destroy you when I strike the land of Egypt.*

14 *So this day shall be to you a memorial; and you shall keep it as a feast to the Lord throughout your generations. You shall keep it as a feast by an everlasting ordinance.* **15** *Seven days you shall eat unleavened bread. On the*

27

first day you shall remove leaven from your houses. For whoever eats leavened bread from the first day until the seventh day, that person shall be cut off from Israel. 16 On the first day there shall be a holy convocation, and on the seventh day there shall be a holy convocation for you. No manner of work shall be done on them; but that which everyone must eat—that only may be prepared by you. 17 So you shall observe the Feast of Unleavened Bread, for on this same day I will have brought your armies out of the land of Egypt. Therefore you shall observe this day throughout your generations as an everlasting ordinance.

When our Father presents a huge assignment, do you doubt Him? Do you truly think He is worried about worldly restrictions? Do you think He worries even one ounce about what might 'not be possible' for you to accomplish? Do you think He is not able to prove to us that ALL things (not some) are possible through Him?

EVERLASTING ORDINANCE of divine protection! WOW!

Repentance for _____?

Adjustment(s) planned? _____

DAY FIVE

FEAR. Exodus 14:13.
Moses answered the people, '*Do not be afraid. Stand firm and you will see the deliverance the Lord will bring you today. The Egyptians you see today you will never see again.*

Wow! The enemy we 'will never see again'. Remembering the enemy is the evil spirits within the people. Which spirits have become familiar spirits? When they are identified, do you see a pattern? Does it appear they show up wherever you are?

Repentance for _____?

Adjustment(s) planned? _____

DAY SIX

REVERENTIAL FEAR; also FEAR. Exodus 20:20.

And Moses said to the people *'Do not fear; for God has come to test you, and that His fear may be before you, so that you may not sin.'*

Worry used to show up for me when it appeared the LORD was asking my intentions about a matter.

At the time I was unaware of the option to proceed with prayers of repentance, clearing the slate (aka 'become an empty vessel') and it was not a consideration that our Father may choose to 'check on the choices' when He is prepared to share a new assignment. NO DISCIPLESHIP from man, only GOD.

Then, a discipled believer shared the truth and helped me realized our Father ALREADY KNOWS ALL (not some; not a small list, not a few facts or limited to what I was sharing in my prayers) and His plans are BIG!

When we are willing to 'let go of all that is holding us back', to forgive and repent for ALL brought to mind so we will be available to be sent by our Father, the prior days have no way of comparing to the glory our Father has 'in store' for all who love Him! Confirmed in scripture:

Spiritual Wisdom. I Corinthians 2:9 (6-9).
However, we speak wisdom among those who are mature, yet not the wisdom of this age, nor of the rulers of this age, who are coming to nothing. **7** *But we speak the wisdom of God in a mystery, the hidden wisdom which God ordained before the ages for our glory, 8 which none of the rulers of this age knew; for had they known, they would not have crucified the Lord of glory.*
9 But as it is written:
Eye has not seen, nor ear heard,
Nor have entered into the heart of man
The things which God has prepared for those who love Him.
There is NOTHING that can compare with the journey we are on with our Father!

Every portion of the travel has been blessed with the scripture in **I Corinthians 2:9.** Lately, I've not quoted it. When it came to mind right now, I actually opened the bible to **II Corinthians 2:9.** Right chapter and verse but the wrong book! However, our Father had a reason for prompting me to go to the chapter and verse to see the words and share them with you: **II Corinthians 2:9.** *For to this end I also wrote, that I might put you to the test, whether you are obedient in all things.*

Repentance for _____?

Adjustment(s) planned? _____

DAY SEVEN

BLESSING. Numbers 6:24-26.
"The LORD bless you and keep you;
25 The LORD make His face shine upon you,
     And be gracious to you;
26 The LORD lift up His countenance upon you,
     And give you peace." '

Blessings received:_____

Blessings shared: _____

Declarations/Testimonies: _____

DAY ONE

FEAR. **Leviticus 26:6 (1-6)**.

Promise of Blessing and Retribution.

'You shall not make idols for yourselves; neither a carved image nor a sacred pillar shall you rear up for yourselves; nor shall you set up an engraved stone in your land, to bow down to it; for I am the Lord your God.

2 You shall keep My Sabbaths and reverence My sanctuary: I am the Lord.

3 'If you walk in My statutes and keep My commandments, and perform them, 4 then I will give you rain in its season, the land shall yield its produce, and the trees of the field shall yield their fruit.

5 Your threshing shall last till the time of vintage, and the vintage shall last till the time of sowing; you shall eat your bread to the full, and dwell in your land safely.

6 I will give peace in the land, and you shall lie down, and none will make you afraid; I will rid the land of evil beasts, and the sword will not go through your land.

Father desires to be our first love and we are HIS treasure!

What draws more attention, gains more importance and takes your full focus during the day? Is there something, a topic, a program, etc., which causes your daily life to be 'out of balance'?

Repentance for _____?

Adjustment(s) planned? _____

DAY TWO

DOUBT. **Numbers 11:21-23**.

And Moses said, *The people whom I am among are six hundred thousand men on foot; yet You have said, 'I will give them meat, that they may eat for a whole month.'* **22** *Shall flocks and herds be slaughtered for them, to provide enough for them? Or shall all the fish of the sea be gathered together for them, to provide enough for them?*

23 And the Lord said to Moses, *Has the Lord's arm been shortened? Now you shall see whether what I say will happen to you or not.*

This reminds me of the response from our Father to Job when Job did not realize he was questioning the Father! The response is staggering! In fact, it is a stop us in our tracks staggering moment because the truth is who, but GOD,

31

knows how it ALL works? There is ONLY one Creator. Imagine being Job in the moment: **Job 38:1.** *Then the Lord answered Job out of the whirlwind, and said: ...* Do we believe in HIM? Do we really believe in HIM for ALL things, for ALL reasons, at ALL times?

Repentance for _____?

Adjustment(s) planned? _____

DAY THREE

<u>FEAR</u>. Numbers 14:9 (1-9).
Israel Refuses to Enter Canaan.
So all the congregation lifted up their voices and cried, and the people wept that night. 2 And all the children of Israel complained against Moses and Aaron, and the whole congregation said to them, *If only we had died in the land of Egypt! Or if only we had died in this wilderness! 3 Why has the Lord brought us to this land to fall by the sword, that our wives and children should become victims? Would it not be better for us to return to Egypt?* **4 So they said to one another,** *Let us select a leader and return to Egypt.*

5 Then Moses and Aaron fell on their faces before all the assembly of the congregation of the children of Israel.

6 But Joshua the son of Nun and Caleb the son of Jephunneh, who were among those who had spied out the land, tore their clothes; 7 and they spoke to all the congregation of the children of Israel, saying: *The land we passed through to spy out is an exceedingly good land. 8 If the Lord delights in us, then He will bring us into this land and give it to us, 'a land which flows with milk and honey.' 9 Only do not rebel against the Lord, nor fear the people of the land, for they are our bread; their protection has departed from them, and the Lord is with us. Do not fear them.*

Wow! They are 'at the destination'! They are 'at the border' and yet, they are asking if they should choose a different leader and return to Egypt? ALL were talking against the plan to enter into the land!

IF everyone around you directed you to turn around and return to where they were comfortable with you and you felt 'comfortable', would you?

This status could be a current day headline.

You have journeyed, witnessed miracles, experienced ALL being provided and you have hindsight to know what it took to have the sea part AFTER you put your foot in the water with ALL being saved from the mighty army speeding behind you with horses and chariots. Will you participate in what is required to go forward OR will you turn around and return to where you were comfortable instead of aligning with the plan our Father has laid out before you?

Repentance for _____?

Adjustment(s) planned? _____

DAY FOUR

FEAR. Numbers 21:34 (33-35).
King Og Defeated.
And they turned and went up by the way to Bashan. So Og king of Bashan went out against them, he and all his people, to battle at Edrei. 34 Then the Lord said to Moses, *Do not fear him, for I have delivered him into your hand, with all his people and his land; and you shall do to him as you did to Sihon king of the Amorites, who dwelt at Heshbon.* **35 So they defeated him, his sons, and all his people, until there was no survivor left him; and they took possession of his land.**

Important to know and heed the voice of our Father.

He announced what would happen.

Moses proceeded as guided.

Victory was announced before the battle and it was obtained.

This is exactly what happened for Abraham, also. The enemy was delivered to him!

When our Father announces a plan which appears to be 'too huge to be possible', will you trust that ALL THINGS ARE POSSIBLE and proceed without hesitation?

Repentance for _____?

Adjustment(s) planned? _____

DAY FIVE

FEAR. Matthew 17:7 (1-8).
Jesus Transfigured on the Mount.
Now after six days Jesus took Peter, James, and John his brother, led them up on a high mountain by themselves; 2 and He was transfigured

before them. His face shone like the sun, and His clothes became as white as the light. 3 And behold, Moses and Elijah appeared to them, talking with Him. 4 Then Peter answered and said to Jesus, *Lord, it is good for us to be here; if You wish, let us make here three tabernacles: one for You, one for Moses, and one for Elijah.*

5 While he was still speaking, behold, a bright cloud overshadowed them; and suddenly a voice came out of the cloud, saying, *This is My beloved Son, in whom I am well pleased. Hear Him!* 6 And when the disciples heard it, they fell on their faces and were greatly afraid. 7 But Jesus came and touched them and said, *Arise, and do not be afraid.* 8 When they had lifted up their eyes, they saw no one but Jesus only.

Out of order and yet, Father prompted this position due to powerful moments in time. Experiencing the supernatural, operating in the supernatural.

When our Father prompted me to move the scripture in Matthew to this position after keeping the scripture structure 'in order', it seemed odd. However, it is powerful to realize the destiny plan for Moses immediately after the rebellion he experienced as a leader who reached the border but, did not enter into the promised land.

The message from our Father is the same for us, from that day to this day!

Moses & Elijah! Confirmation that all of the resistance Moses dealt with in the prior scripture reference did NOT stop him from aligning with the Father. People did not place Moses on a different path than our Father laid out before him!

Do you desire to be fully aligned with the Father's plan for you and STAND FIRM no matter how much resistance you are experiencing 'in the world'?

Repentance for _____?

Adjustment(s) planned? _____

DAY SIX
REVERENTIAL FEAR. Deuteronomy 4:10-11 (7-11).
For what great nation is there that has God so near to it, as the LORD our God is to us, for whatever reason we may call upon Him? 8 And what great nation is there that has such statutes and righteous judgments as are in all this law which I set before you this day? 9 Only take heed to yourself, and diligently keep yourself, lest you forget the things your eyes have seen, and lest they depart from your heart all the days of your life. And teach them to your

children and your grandchildren, **10** *especially concerning the day you stood before the* LORD *your God in Horeb, when the* LORD *said to me, 'Gather the people to Me, and I will let them hear My words, that they may learn to fear Me all the days they live on the earth, and that they may teach their children.'*

This message is the same today and it aligns with the Proverbs scripture reminding us to raise up a child in the way they should go so they will not depart from it. The training structure is specifically identified on the Faith Monument, the plan to help us remain living in Liberty & Freedom.

The plan is for all to be with the Father 'as children'. In your interactions with 'GOD's children'. are you helping to train them up (disciple them) so they learn how to hear the Father's voice and do not depart from the plan He has for them?

Repentance for _____?

Adjustment(s) planned? _____

DAY SEVEN

BLESSING. Numbers 6:24-26.
> *The* LORD *bless you and keep you;*
> **25** *The* LORD *make His face shine upon you,*
> *And be gracious to you;*
> **26** *The* LORD *lift up His countenance upon you,*
> *And give you peace.*

Blessings received: _____

Blessings shared: _____

Declarations/Testimonies: _____

WEEK FIVE

DAY ONE

FEAR. Deuteronomy 1:17.
You shall not show partiality in judgment; you shall hear the small and the great; you shall not be afraid in any man's presence, for the judgment is God's. The case that is too hard for you, bring it to me, and I will hear it.'

Interesting! Judgment 'without the e' is final. Considering points can result in a human judgment of a person or a 'thing'. Doing this OR participating in this results in creating, participating in and spreading 'gossip' (LIES). Over time, by spreading 'news that is not news' a person who is innocent is charged 'in the media' and it is actually changing our due process procedures of justice from the rules of law to a mob/lynching mentality of declaring guilt before the facts are known. As our Father desires us to process 'not in part' and 'do not show partiality' no matter who is 'in the room or listening to the message'.

Repentance for _____?

Adjustment(s) planned? _____

DAY TWO
FEAR. Deuteronomy 1:21.
Look, the LORD your God has set the land before you; go up and possess it, as the LORD God of your fathers has spoken to you; do not fear or be discouraged.

Remember, it was known as the land of milk and honey. However, when the 12 leaders entered into the land they saw the giants! Only Joshua and Caleb retained faith and hope regarding the future!

Father has provided all, supplied all, and sent HIS SON to 'take care of all sin' so we are able to live FREE and carry out our purpose and fulfill our destiny, encouraged and without fear!

Repentance for _____?

Adjustment(s) planned? _____

DAY THREE
FEAR. Deuteronomy 1:29 (1:29-33).
Then I said to you, *'Do not be terrified, or afraid of them. 30 The Lord your God, who goes before you, He will fight for you, according to all He did for you in Egypt before your eyes, 31 and in the wilderness where you saw how the Lord your God carried you, as a man carries his son, in all the way that you went until you came to this place.' 32 Yet, for all that, you did not believe the Lord your God, 33 who went in the way before you to search out a*

place for you to pitch your tents, to show you the way you should go, in the fire by night and in the cloud by day.'

It is our journey. Father is our rear-guard! Aligned with HIM 'what can mere mortals do to us'! We are watching this 'in real time' in our nation right now. We are in a spiritual war. Until the war 'heated up' we thought all who claimed Christianity were Christians. Now, we are realizing we need discernment for the battles always have a wilderness element! This reminds me of the great need for discernment, and a very special quote from my earthly father when the court battle was so intense (filled with fraud and corruption; attorneys and judges, plus the people who filed the case) regarding my corporation: *It does not matter how many people jump into the fox hole with you. Until the shooting starts, you will not know who has your back.*

It was life-altering when I realized how much I needed to learn about discernment! Trust was granted 'so freely' before the experiences in and out of the courthouse, even with the people (curiosity seekers vs. warfare prayer partners; many faded away) who wanted to attend the court sessions with me!

Repentance for _____?

Adjustment(s) planned? _____

DAY FOUR

DOUBT. Deuteronomy 7:17-19.
If you should say in your heart, *'These nations are greater than I; how can I dispossess them?'*— 18 you shall not be afraid of them, but you shall remember well what the Lord your God did to Pharaoh and to all Egypt: 19 the great trials which your eyes saw, the signs and the wonders, the mighty hand and the outstretched arm, by which the Lord your God brought you out. So shall the Lord your God do to all the peoples of whom you are afraid.

Father knows the plans He has for us, to prosper us and provide more than enough for us. Whatever the world does 'to a generation', our Father has changed the leadership OR brought the people OUT of the situation to flourish once again.

When I was reminding our Father about the 'dark cloud' people noticed over me during the toughest phases, He actually laughed! I was shocked. Then, He merely stated it was during those times that I 'shut down', became dis-heartened (remember Christ resides in our hearts – he brought this up again, after this example) and in those times I actually stopped RECEIVING!

He sent people to tell me the story (a FEW times!) about the person who went to heaven and saw the warehouse of beautiful white boxes with large red bows which were still 'on the shelf' waiting to be delivered but, the person was not ready to receive them, yet.

The story was shared so many times when I was feeling isolated, without realizing it – I stopped listening to the words.

Truly, I want to RECEIVE all our Father has but, it was 'filling up the cloud as RAIN (darkened the cloud), waiting for me to re-align. Father, let it rain! I ACCEPT all You have laid out before me in assignments and blessings!

Repentance for _____?

Adjustment(s) planned? _____

DAY FIVE
REVERENTIAL FEAR. Deuteronomy 6:13.
You shall fear the Lord your God and serve Him, and shall take oaths in His name.

Perfect moment to think about ANY THING which has become an idol, any oath taken to ANY society, especially the fraternal, secret societies!

Our Father LOVES us unconditionally and does NOT want us to take an oath to ANY THING, ANY GROUP, ANY Organization, ANY Society.

Important to NOT have 'conflicts' between us and our Father.

Anything coming between you and Father today? In life? At work?

Repentance for _____?

Adjustment(s) planned? _____

DAY SIX

REVERENTIAL FEAR. Deuteronomy 6:13-15.

You shall fear the Lord your God and serve Him, and shall take oaths in His name. **14** *You shall not go after other gods, the gods of the peoples who are all around you* **15** *(for the Lord your God is a jealous God among you), lest the anger of the Lord your God be aroused against you and destroy you from the face of the earth.*

It was not comfortable to remain on the 'speaker circuit' as the 'idols' were talked about, sports or celebrities or even mega church pastors. When I stated (back in the 1990's), *The church and nation are becoming a Sodom & Gomorrah,* I was told, *These are the end times and we are not going to be able to do anything to turn it around.* It was a complete shock to me that nobody would listen because our Father was showing me how life could change on this night as it did within a moment in time in Sodom and Gomorrah: **Genesis 19.** All was destroyed in the brimstone and fire as soon as Lot escaped and was safe.

Repentance for _____?

Adjustment(s) planned? _____

DAY SEVEN

BLESSING. Numbers 6:24-26.
"The LORD bless you and keep you;
25 *The LORD make His face shine upon you,*
And be gracious to you;
26 *The LORD lift up His countenance upon you,*
And give you peace." '

Blessings received:_____

Blessings shared: _____

Declarations/Testimonies: _____

WEEK SIX

DAY ONE

FEAR. Deuteronomy 3:2. And the Lord said to me, 'Do not fear him, for I have delivered him and all of his people into your hand; you shall do to him as you did to Sihon king of the Amorites, who dwelt in Heshbon.

Deuteronomy 3:22. *You must not fear them, for the Lord your God Himself fights for you.*

Who or what do you fear in the fight? Do you remember a time when you knew that you knew your Father in heaven was fighting with and for you?

Repentance for _____?

Adjustment(s) planned? _____

DAY TWO

REVERENTIAL FEAR. Deuteronomy 4:10-11 (7-11)
For what great nation is there that has God so near to it, as the LORD our God is to us, for whatever reason we may call upon Him?

8 And what great nation is there that has such statutes and righteous judgments as are in all this law which I set before you this day?

9 Only take heed to yourself, and diligently keep yourself, lest you forget the things your eyes have seen, and lest they depart from your heart all the days of your life. And teach them to your children and your grandchildren, 10 especially concerning the day you stood before the LORD your God in Horeb, when the LORD said to me, 'Gather the people to Me, and I will let them hear My words, that they may learn to fear Me all the days they live on the earth, and that they may teach their children.'

11 Then you came near and stood at the foot of the mountain, and the mountain burned with fire to the midst of heaven, with darkness, cloud, and thick darkness.

There were many changes before the nation united. It was only after so many died and after Moses did NOT enter in. Will you revere Him and allow Him to guide you through the changes required to draw you even closer to Him?

Repentance for _____?

Adjustment(s) planned? _____

DAY THREE

FEAR. Deuteronomy 7:18 (17-19).
If you should say in your heart, 'These nations are greater than I; how can I dispossess them them?' - 18 you shall not be afraid of them, but you shall remember well that the LORD your God did to Pharaoh and to all Egypt: 19 the great trials which your eyes saw, the signs and the wonders, the

mighty hand and the outstretched arm, by which the LORD your God brought you out. So shall the LORD your God do to all the peoples whom you are afraid.

This was 'before Christ' however, the same option – Father guiding you, strengthening you where and when you are feeling weak, means you are greater than any person or thing coming against you! Now, 'after Christ', HE who is IN YOU is greater than ANY PERSON or THING in the world!

Repentance for _____?

Adjustment(s) planned? _____

DAY FOUR

REVERENTIAL FEAR. Deuteronomy 10:20-21.
You shall fear the Lord your God; you shall serve Him, and to Him you shall hold fast, and take oaths in His name. 21 He is your praise, and He is your God, who has done for you these great and awesome things which your eyes have seen.

Remaining aligned with our Father in ALL things for it is through Him that ALL things are possible. What appears to be impossible today? In life?

Repentance for _____?

Adjustment(s) planned? _____

DAY FIVE

DOUBT. Deuteronomy 16:1.
Observe the month of Abib, and keep the Passover to the Lord your God, for in the month of Abib the Lord your God brought you out of Egypt by night.

In the ancient Hebrew calendar the month of Abib or Aviv is the first month of the ecclesiastical calendar, which generally covers the end of March and early part of April. The Nisan reference in modern Hebrew reflects the capture by the Assyrians since the month of Nisan has the same definition.

41

The key to this portion of the chapter confirms the Passover is a time of sacrifice and no leaven (within the bread; Christ referred to it 'in the words', lies) during the days!

When I introduce the Passover meal to people wherever I am at that time of year, I am grateful they choose to involve their family and prepare the meal each year after they are introduced to and become aware of the honoring during the feast and festival. Now, I receive testimonies from the families and they are always about souls saved, people delivered with lives and relationships healed.

In the personal note 'just between us', I have inserted a photo of the Passover plate. Fortunate to find them at local grocery stores since they sell the food and specific items to celebrate each of the feasts and festivals which Christ observed while He was 'on earth'.

Repentance for _____?

Adjustment(s) planned? _____

DAY SIX

<u>FEAR</u>. **Deuteronomy 20:3 (2-4).**
So it shall be, when you are on the verge of the battle, that the priest shall approach and speak to the people. 3 And He shall say to them, _'Hear, O Israel: Today you are on the verge of battle with enemies. Do not let your heart faint, do not be afraid, and do not tremble or be terrified because of them; 4 for the LORD your God is He who goes with you, to fight for you against your enemies, to save you.'_

This is the battle stance, especially when we remember to invite our Father into the situation (whatever we are facing), for our goal is to be aligned with Him, being guided by Him, knowing He is with us and He will fight for us. The problems increase when 'we think we know, so off to the races we go' before consulting with and obtaining our Father's wisdom!

The first line of **Hosea 4:6** is often quoted:

> *My people are destroyed* (some translations: perish) *for lack of knowledge.*

Rare that we ever hear the remainder of this important scripture:

Because you have rejected knowledge,
I also will reject you from being priest for Me;
Because you have forgotten the law of your God,
I also will forget your children.

Yikes. Another reminder:

What are we passing on to the third and fourth generations?
Blessings? Or Curses?

Often I hear people blaming the 'removal of prayer from school classrooms'.

How did it change the lives of believers?

Why did believers allow (without opposing), align with and then blame the decision made for classrooms within the public schools?

The decision did not remove prayer from the homes and family bedrooms.

The person who became the voice and accomplished her plan was Madalyn Murray O'Hair. One person who declared to be an atheist.

Other key Supreme court cases, including abortion, were championed by ONE person!

These cases result in the laws of the land!

If ONE atheist can do this and push and push to take down crosses from battlefields and lands obtained through mighty battles, imagine what can by done by ONE believer let alone a dozen GOD-fearing believers who become A VOICE for truth and justice!

Will we 'possess until Christ returns'?

President John F Kennedy proceeded immediately within a press conference at the State Department after the Supreme Court decision that prayer would be removed from schools.

His message for all believers is clear: pray more & pray with our families.

His specific message: https://www.youtube.com/watch?v=F0sPUpj7Fac

Repentance for _____?

Adjustment(s) planned? _____

BLESSING. Numbers 6:24-26.
> *"The LORD bless you and keep you;*
> *25 The LORD make His face shine upon you,*
> *And be gracious to you;*
> *26 The LORD lift up His countenance upon you,*
> *And give you peace." '*

Blessings received: _____

Blessings shared: _____

Declarations/Testimonies: _____

DAY ONE

<u>DOUBT</u>, also <u>FEAR</u>. Deuteronomy 20:1.
Principles Governing Warfare.
When you go out to battle against your enemies, and see horses and chariots and people more numerous than you, do not be afraid of them; for the Lord your God is with you, who brought you up from the land of Egypt.

We are in a spiritual war!

What seems 'too big to handle'? Whatever it is, is our Father invited to join?

What appears to be overwhelming today, over time, for a long time?

No matter how many are involved in a conflict or how big the situation appears, remember who you are aligned with, He is with you and He is your rear-guard!

Repentance for _____?

Adjustment(s) planned? _____

DAY TWO

<u>FEAR</u>. Deuteronomy 31:6 (3-6).
(Moses confirmed he will not be crossing over the Jordan) *The LORD your God Himself crosses over before you; He will destroy these nations* (people) *from before you, and you shall dispossess them. Joshua himself crosses over before you, just as the LORD has said. 4 And the LORD will do to them as He did to Sihon and Og, the kings of the Amorites and their land, when He destroyed them. 5 The LORD will give them over to you, that you may do to them according to every commandment which I have commanded you. 6 Be strong and of good courage, do not fear nor be afraid of them; for the LORD your God, He is the One who goes with you. He will not leave you nor forsake you.*

When our Father guides, the enemy is defeated. It will be done BEFORE.

As with the Crossing of the Jordan. NOTHING happened until feet were in the water. Faith expressed, the crooked (impossible) made straight (possible).

Are you ready to step forward in faith, willing to be guided?

Repentance for _____?

45

Adjustment(s) planned? _____

DAY THREE

FEAR. Deuteronomy 31:8 (7-8).

Then Moses summoned Joshua and said to him in the presence of all Israel, *Be strong and courageous, for you must go with this people into the land that the Lord swore to their ancestors to give them, and you must divide it among them as their inheritance. 8 The Lord himself goes before you and will be with you; he will never leave you nor forsake you. Do not be afraid; do not be discouraged.*

What is your purpose?

Are you ready to posses and enter into your plan, your land, your destiny?

How is the current assignment related to your purpose?

The good news is, our LORD will not leave or forsake you.

The truth: He goes before you!

Repentance for _____?

Adjustment(s) planned? _____

DAY FOUR

FEAR. Joshua 1:9 (1:7-9).

Be strong and very courageous. Be careful to obey all the law my servant Moses gave you; do not turn from it to the right or to the left, that you may be successful wherever you go. 8 Keep this Book of the Law always on your lips; meditate on it day and night, so that you may be careful to do everything written in it. Then you will be prosperous and successful. 9 Have I not commanded you? Be strong and courageous. Do not be afraid; do not be discouraged, for the LORD your God will be with you wherever you go.

Whatever the assignment is, be strong and courageous for it is the reason why you are here.

Remain in truth, aligned with the Father. You will be prosperous and successful.

Father has a plan specifically prepared for you!

Repentance for _____?

Adjustment(s) planned? _____

DAY FIVE

<u>REVERENTIAL FEAR</u>. Joshua 4:24 (19-24).

Now the people came up from the Jordan on the tenth _day_ **of the first month, and they camped in Gilgal on the east border of Jericho. 20 And those twelve stones which they took out of the Jordan, Joshua set up in Gilgal. 21 Then he spoke to the children of Israel, saying:** _When your children ask their fathers in time to come, saying, 'What are these stones? 22_ **then you shall let your children know, saying,** _'Israel crossed over this Jordan on dry land'_; **23** _for the Lord your God dried up the waters of the Jordan before you until you had crossed over, as the Lord your God did to the Red Sea, which He dried up before us until we had crossed over,_ **24** _that all the peoples of the earth may know the hand of the Lord, that it is mighty, that you may fear the Lord your God forever._

The stones of remembrance.

The focus of the first chapter of _For The Sake Of America III_.

Current day status: Stones were left 'in a pile' in the middle of a town named Baldwin, a word which stands for stone pile! However, the web site for the town mentions the pile of stones left by the Cherokee who lived abundantly upon the land until their departure on the Trail of Tears; since the Cherokee are gone, the mystery about the pile of stones is lost forever.

Do we remember what was done for us?

Do we share truth with all who have ears to hear and eyes to see truth?

Praying the world will not keep us from accomplishing our purpose and plan for these days while we here, available to do ALL our Father has laid out before us!

Remember to invite our Father into all situations and especially to hear and know the truth: What is your legacy which you are here for and what are you going to pass on to the third and fourth generations?

Repentance for _____?

Adjustment(s) planned? _____

DAY SIX

UNBELIEF. II Kings 7:2 (6:33-7:2).
Famine in Samaria
II Kings 6:33. And while he was still talking with them, there was the messenger, coming down to him; and then *the king* **said,** *Surely this calamity is from the LORD; why should I wait for the LORD any longer?*

II Kings 7:1-2. Then Elisha said, *Hear the word of the Lord. Thus says the Lord: 'Tomorrow about this time a seah of fine flour shall be sold for a shekel, and two seahs of barley for a shekel, at the gate of Samaria.'*

2 So an officer on whose hand the king leaned answered the man of God and said, *Look, if the Lord would make windows in heaven, could this thing be?*

And he said, *In fact, you shall see it with your eyes, but you shall not eat of it.*

Blaming the LORD for the famine, a drought, a tough status.

Oh ye of little faith!

When even a king says 'enough is enough', blames GOD and turns his back on the LORD!

Any situations come to mind when it seemed like it was not going to happen even though it was declared to you that it would happen?

Do you want answers 'in your time' or 'in the perfect timing of the LORD'?

Time after time in the scriptures, when leadership aligns with the LORD, praises the LORD for the victory BEFORE the battle, the enemy is handed over!

Will you depart from the LORD when you do not get what you want, when and how you want it?

Or, will you remain in thanksgiving, praising your Father for ALL that you have, all that He supplies and provides, until ...

Repentance for _____?

Adjustment(s) planned? _____

BLESSING. Numbers 6:24-26.
> *"The LORD bless you and keep you;*
> 25 *The LORD make His face shine upon you,*
>   *And be gracious to you;*
> 26 *The LORD lift up His countenance upon you,*
>   *And give you peace." '*

Blessings received: _____

Blessings shared: _____

Declarations/Testimonies: _____

WEEK EIGHT

DAY ONE

FEAR. Joshua 8:1 (1-2).
The Fall of Ai
Now the LORD said to Joshua: *Do not be afraid, nor be dismayed; take all the people of war with you, and arise, go up to Ai. See, I have given into your hand the king of Ai, his people, his city, and his land. 2 And you shall do to Ai and its king as you did to Jericho and its king. Only its spoil and its cattle you shall take as booty for yourselves. Lay an ambush for the city behind it.*

Do you have a current enemy? Whatever you are facing, your Father has a plan for you to live abundantly and prosper. Hearing the voice of your Father provides the plan. To hear HIS voice, it requires silence on our part to listen so well we can hear HIS voice, even when HE whispers! Are you listening?

Repentance for _____?

Adjustment(s) planned? _____

DAY TWO

FEAR. Joshua 10:8 (3-8).
Therefore Adoni-Zedek king of Jerusalem sent to Hoham king of Hebron, Piram king of Jarmuth, Japhia king of Lachish, and Debir king of Eglon, saying, 4 *Come up to me and help me, that we may attack Gibeon, for*

it has made peace with Joshua and with the children of Israel. **5 Therefore the five kings of the Amorites, the king of Jerusalem, the king of Hebron, the king of Jarmuth, the king of Lachish, and the king of Eglon, gathered together and went up, they and all their armies, and camped before Gibeon and made war against it.**

6 And the men of Gibeon sent to Joshua at the camp at Gilgal, saying, *Do not forsake your servants; come up to us quickly, save us and help us, for all the kings of the Amorites who dwell in the mountains have gathered together against us.*

7 So Joshua ascended from Gilgal, he and all the people of war with him, and all the mighty men of valor. 8 And the Lord said to Joshua, *Do not fear them, for I have delivered them into your hand; not a man of them shall stand before you.*

Again, our Father delivered HIS people from multiple nations (people)!

So grateful for our salvation, which is ours on top of what our Father provided because HE loves us so much HE sent HIS SON and then, HE sent a comforter, the Holy Spirit! We are so blessed and yet, we are human. Is a conflict affecting your life? Have you invited our Father into the midst of it?

Repentance for _____?

Adjustment(s) planned? _____

DAY THREE

<u>FEAR</u>. **Joshua 10:25 (22-25).**
Then Joshua said, *Open the mouth of the cave, and bring out those five kings to me from the cave.* **23 And they did so, and brought out those five kings to him from the cave: the king of Jerusalem, the king of Hebron, the king of Jarmuth, the king of Lachish, and the king of Eglon.**

24 So it was, when they brought out those kings to Joshua, that Joshua called for all the men of Israel, and said to the captains of the men of war who went with him, *Come near, put your feet on the necks of these kings.* **And they drew near and put their feet on their necks. 25 Then Joshua said to them,** *Do not be afraid, nor be dismayed; be strong and of good courage, for thus the Lord will do to all your enemies against whom you fight.*

Following the counsel of our Father, the enemy was delivered into the hands of Joshua. Who is the enemy in the midst of your battle? What steps are you being prompted by our Father to take so the conflict will be resolved?

Repentance for _____?

Adjustment(s) planned? _____

DAY FOUR

FEAR. Joshua 11:6 (1-6).
And it came to pass, when Jabin king of Hazor heard these things, that he sent to Jobab king of Madon, to the king of Shimron, to the king of Achshaph, 2 and to the kings who were from the north, in the mountains, in the plain south of Chinneroth, in the lowland, and in the heights of Dor on the west, 3 to the Canaanites in the east and in the west, the Amorite, the Hittite, the Perizzite, the Jebusite in the mountains, and the Hivite below Hermon in the land of Mizpah. 4 So they went out, they and all their armies with them, as many people as the sand that is on the seashore in multitude, with very many horses and chariots. 5 And when all these kings had met together, they came and camped together at the waters of Merom to fight against Israel.
6 But the Lord said to Joshua, *Do not be afraid because of them, for tomorrow about this time I will deliver all of them slain before Israel. You shall hamstring their horses and burn their chariots with fire.*

Even when ALL of the enemies from ALL directions are positioned to steal, kill or destroy from you, there is no reason to fear the outcome. When evil plans become evident, it is important to seek the counsel of our Father. HE will provide TRUTH and WISDOM when all seems lost.

Repentance for _____?

Adjustment(s) planned? _____

DAY FIVE

DOUBT. Judges 6:39-40.
Then Gideon said to God, *Do not be angry with me, but let me speak just once more: Let me test, I pray, just once more with the fleece; let it now be dry only on the fleece, but on all the ground let there be dew.*
40 And God did so that night. It was dry on the fleece only, but there was dew on all the ground.

HE is OK with us questioning, testing the spirit, to know it is HE who is prompting us, speaking HIS truth to us! Grateful we have the guidance of the Holy Spirit to help 'speed up' the process, while the TRUTH direct from our Father is critical. HE warned us, the enemy will do everything to 'sound like' the Father so spend time with HIM to know that you know the voice is HIS voice.

Repentance for _____?

Adjustment(s) planned? _____

DAY SIX

REVERENTIAL FEAR. Joshua 24:14.
Now therefore, fear the Lord, serve Him in sincerity and in truth, and put away the gods which your fathers served on the other side of the River and in Egypt. Serve the Lord!

Many were shocked to hear we have become 'enslaved' again. To align with the world plan, to do whatever the world wants and proceed per the success plan in the world separates us from the plans of our Father for HE is the only one who knows the end from the beginning. What we are facing in the nation and globally is a reflection of becoming 'enslaved' without realizing we were on the path to being 'enslaved'. Our Father provides divine protection when we gain and retain reverential fear. There are examples everywhere in the word and for some, life examples are evident in the world. George Washington example is provided within *For The Sake Of America II,* with all ammunition being accurate, not one shot affected him in the battle. Any ammunition or firey darts, or stones aimed at you? What are a few of your 'divinely protected' experiences?

Repentance for _____?

Adjustment(s) planned? _____

DAY SEVEN

BLESSING. Numbers 6:24-26.
"The Lord bless you and keep you;

52

25 *The LORD make His face shine upon you,*
   And be gracious to you;
26 *The LORD lift up His countenance upon you,*
   And give you peace." '

Blessings received: _____

Blessings shared: _____

Declarations/Testimonies: _____

WEEK NINE

DAY ONE

FEAR. Judges 4:18 (12-22)

And they reported to Sisera that Barak the son of Abinoam had gone up to Mount Tabor. 13 So Sisera gathered together all his chariots, nine hundred chariots of iron, and all the people who were with him, from Harosheth Hagoyim to the River Kishon.

14 Then Deborah said to Barak, *Up! For this is the day in which the Lord has delivered Sisera into your hand. Has not the Lord gone out before you?* So Barak went down from Mount Tabor with ten thousand men following him. 15 And the Lord routed Sisera and all his chariots and all his army with the edge of the sword before Barak; and Sisera alighted from his chariot and fled away on foot. 16 But Barak pursued the chariots and the army as far as Harosheth Hagoyim, and all the army of Sisera fell by the edge of the sword; not a man was left.

17 However, Sisera had fled away on foot to the tent of Jael, the wife of Heber the Kenite; for there was peace between Jabin king of Hazor and the house of Heber the Kenite. 18 And Jael went out to meet Sisera, and said to him, *Turn aside, my lord, turn aside to me; do not fear.* And when he had turned aside with her into the tent, she covered him with a blanket.

19 Then he said to her, *Please give me a little water to drink, for I am thirsty.* So she opened a jug of milk, gave him a drink, and covered him. 20 And he said to her, *Stand at the door of the tent, and if any man comes and inquires of you, and says, 'Is there any man here?' you shall say, 'No.'*

21 Then Jael, Heber's wife, took a tent peg and took a hammer in her hand, and went softly to him and drove the peg into his temple, and it went down into the ground; for he was fast asleep and weary. So he died. 22 And then, as Barak pursued Sisera, Jael came out to meet him, and said to him, *Come, I will show you the man whom you seek.* And when he went into her tent, there lay Sisera, dead with the peg in his temple.

Even when the conflict you are facing includes 900 chariots of iron, when our Father is guiding you through the conflict ALL details are 'handled', ALL involved as the opposition will be dealt with and the plan our Father has laid out before you shall come to pass. Knowing the conflict will be handled, what are you being prompted to accomplish?

Repentance for _____?

Adjustment(s) planned? _____

DAY TWO

FEAR. Judges 6:23 (20-24).

The Angel of God said to him, *Take the meat and the unleavened bread and lay them on this rock, and pour out the broth.* And he did so.

21 Then the Angel of the Lord put out the end of the staff that was in His hand, and touched the meat and the unleavened bread; and fire rose out of the rock and consumed the meat and the unleavened bread. And the Angel of the Lord departed out of his sight.

22 Now Gideon perceived that He was the Angel of the Lord. So Gideon said, *Alas, O Lord God! For I have seen the Angel of the Lord face to face.*

23 Then the Lord said to him, *Peace be with you; do not fear, you shall not die.* 24 So Gideon built an altar there to the Lord, and called it The-Lord-Is-Peace. To this day it is still in Ophrah of the Abiezrites.

Often what our Father does, HE does it ONLY for us. When we attempt to help other people realize the powerful things our Father is doing for us, on our behalf, because HE loves us, it is not easy for people, even believers, to comprehend. Why? They were trained to realize 'specific, historical, significant events' and they think they are not witnessing 'specific, historical, significant events'. The event for Gideon was for him alone, as many of the experiences in scripture unfolded. For Gideon, it was private and yet life-altering. He memorialized his experience for all time. What are your life-altering experiences due to receiving assistance, resolution of a conflict whether it is financial or not, and hearing a word 'just for you' from our Father?

Repentance for _____?

Adjustment(s) planned? _____

DAY THREE

DOUBT. Judges 20:22.

And the people, that is, the men of Israel, encouraged themselves and again formed the battle line at the place where they had put themselves in array on the first day.

Who is surrounding you? Who encourages you, supports you in TRUTH, especially when you are questioning yourself and your alignment with the WORD? Would they form a battle line with you? Need to expand your territory?

Repentance for _____?

Adjustment(s) planned? _____

DAY FOUR
FEAR. I Samuel 4:20 (12-22).
Death of Eli
Then a man of Benjamin ran from the battle line the same day, and came to Shiloh with his clothes torn and dirt on his head. 13 Now when he came, there was Eli, sitting on a seat by the wayside watching, for his heart trembled for the ark of God. And when the man came into the city and told it, all the city cried out. 14 When Eli heard the noise of the outcry, he said, *What does the sound of this tumult mean?* And the man came quickly and told Eli. 15 Eli was ninety-eight years old, and his eyes were so dim that he could not see.

16 Then the man said to Eli, *I am he who came from the battle. And I fled today from the battle line.* And he said, *What happened, my son?*

17 So the messenger answered and said, *Israel has fled before the Philistines, and there has been a great slaughter among the people. Also your two sons, Hophni and Phinehas, are dead; and the ark of God has been captured.* 18 Then it happened, when he made mention of the ark of God, that Eli fell off the seat backward by the side of the gate; and his neck was broken and he died, for the man was old and heavy. And he had judged Israel forty years.

19 Now his daughter-in-law, Phinehas' wife, was with child, due to be delivered; and when she heard the news that the ark of God was captured, and that her father-in-law and her husband were dead, she bowed herself and gave birth, for her labor pains came upon her. 20 And about the time of her death the women who stood by her said to her, *Do not fear, for you have borne a son.* But she did not answer, nor did she regard it. 21 Then she named the child Ichabod, saying, *The glory has departed from Israel!* because the ark of God had been captured and because of her father-in-law and her husband. 22 And she said, *The glory has departed from Israel, for the ark of God has been captured.*

Even in the worst moments we could possible imagine, our Father has a plan and all things are possible when we align with HIS plan. No matter how it seems 'in the natural', the plan is unfolding for us whether we align with it or choose to go on our own path. When Christ was on earth, HE confirmed that HE gave us the glory that we would be one (united) as HE and the Father are one! We have the promise of hope and a future. Whose plan are you aligned with?

Repentance for _____?

Adjustment(s) planned? _____

DAY FIVE
REVERENTIAL FEAR. I Samuel 12:18.
So Samuel called to the Lord, and the Lord sent thunder and rain that day; and all the people greatly feared the Lord and Samuel.

When our Father hears the cry of the people and sends the answer, it shocks the people even though they wanted it, prayed for it and said they trusted our Father would do it! Before Christ, people lived with the understanding of reverential fear of the LORD and the knowledge HE provided the answers, the provision whether they were in a battle or they needed rain for the crops. When it was 'not working for them', it would shock them to find out our Father would send someone to reveal HIS TRUTH to them. Samuel was sent! Often, when we follow-up with people who have shared intense prayer requests, they did not send send a testimony of how great is our LORD when they received the answer (often in a miraculous way) and yet, they are surprised we are following up. We pray expecting the confirmation of the hand of our LORD in the situation! We invite him into the situation and thank HIM for HIS resolution. Any testimonies you have not shared to let others know how the LORD answered your cry?

Repentance for _____?

Adjustment(s) planned? _____

DAY SIX
FEAR. I Samuel 12:20 (16-25).
Now therefore, stand and see this great thing which the Lord will do before your eyes: 17 Is today not the wheat harvest? I will call to the Lord, and He will send thunder and rain, that you may perceive and see that your

wickedness is great, which you have done in the sight of the Lord, in asking a king for yourselves.

18 So Samuel called to the Lord, and the Lord sent thunder and rain that day; and all the people greatly feared the Lord and Samuel. 19 And all the people said to Samuel, *Pray for your servants to the Lord your God, that we may not die; for we have added to all our sins the evil of asking a king for ourselves.* **20 Then Samuel said to the people,** *Do not fear. You have done all this wickedness; yet do not turn aside from following the Lord, but serve the Lord with all your heart.* **21** *And do not turn aside; for then you would go after empty things which cannot profit or deliver, for they are nothing.* **22** *For the Lord will not forsake His people, for His great name's sake, because it has pleased the Lord to make you His people.* **23** *Moreover, as for me, far be it from me that I should sin against the Lord in ceasing to pray for you; but I will teach you the good and the right way.* **24** *Only fear the Lord, and serve Him in truth with all your heart; for consider what great things He has done for you.* **25** *But if you still do wickedly, you shall be swept away, both you and your king.*

Amazing to recognize ALL our Father has done for us, beginning with taking our hand and bringing us up and out of the pit! What would it take to become like Samuel and not sin against the LORD so we can pray and help other believers?

Repentance for _____?

Adjustment(s) planned? _____

DAY SEVEN

BLESSING. Numbers 6:24-26.
> *"The LORD bless you and keep you;*
> **25** *The LORD make His face shine upon you,*
> *And be gracious to you;*
> **26** *The LORD lift up His countenance upon you,*
> *And give you peace." '*

Blessings received: _____

Blessings shared: _____

Declarations/Testimonies: _____

WEEK TEN

DAY ONE

FEAR. I Samuel 22:23 (17-23).

Then the king said to the guards who stood about him, *Turn and kill the priests of the Lord, because their hand also is with David, and because they knew when he fled and did not tell it to me.* But the servants of the king would not lift their hands to strike the priests of the Lord. 18 And the king said to Doeg, *You turn and kill the priests!* So Doeg the Edomite turned and struck the priests, and killed on that day eighty-five men who wore a linen ephod. 19 Also Nob, the city of the priests, he struck with the edge of the sword, both men and women, children and nursing infants, oxen and donkeys and sheep—with the edge of the sword.

20 Now one of the sons of Ahimelech the son of Ahitub, named Abiathar, escaped and fled after David. 21 And Abiathar told David that Saul had killed the Lord's priests. 22 So David said to Abiathar, *I knew that day, when Doeg the Edomite was there, that he would surely tell Saul. I have caused the death of all the persons of your father's house. 23 Stay with me; do not fear. For he who seeks my life seeks your life, but with me you shall be safe.*

Whether in the midst of a situation or having fled from a situation, when commanded by someone in the world to kill, whether it is to kill a dream, a plan or a life, or if your plan, your dream or your life was in jeopardy, who would you go to for counsel? Who would you trust? What would you do?

Repentance for _____?

Adjustment(s) planned? _____

DAY TWO
REVERENTIAL FEAR. I Samuel 12:24.
Only fear the Lord, and serve Him in truth with all your heart; for consider what great things He has done for you.

Prompted to think of the life of Smith Wigglesworth, a plumber by trade who was prayed for by the wife of his pastor (Alexander 'Alex' Boddy). When she laid hands upon him, he spoke in tongues. Prior to this day in history, Wigglesworth did not read. From this day forward the Holy Spirit and Wigglesworth's beloved wife Polly assisted him in reading the bible, and only the bible was allowed in their home. When Wigglesworth was in Australia the hosting pastor shared an amazing account of taking Wigglesworth to a high brow restaurant where the wealthy were dining. Wigglesworth tapped a glass and shared some tough words about the people NOT praying, NOT thanking the supplier of their meal. The pastor was a bit embarrassed during the meal. However, he realized the impact of the statement by Wigglesworth after the meal when three separate families stopped by their table and confessed their conversations during the meal focused upon the prayer spoken by Wigglesworth, the fact their lives were not aligned with the Father and they asked for Wigglesworth to pray for their salvation. Multiple souls due to a simple act by Wigglesworth with a prayer resulting in the TRUTH being revealed to people who knew their souls were 'at stake' in that very moment in time. Souls are important to our Father! Will you insert TRUTH in the moment to impact lives and help people realize their soul is at stake?

Repentance for _____?

Adjustment(s) planned? _____

DAY THREE
FEAR. I Samuel 23:17 (14-18).
David in Wilderness Strongholds
And David stayed in strongholds in the wilderness, and remained in the mountains in the Wilderness of Ziph. Saul sought him every day, but God did not deliver him into his hand. 15 So David saw that Saul had come out to seek his life. And David was in the Wilderness of Ziph in a forest. 16 Then Jonathan, Saul's son, arose and went to David in the woods and strengthened his hand in God. 17 And he said to him, *Do not fear, for the hand of Saul my father shall not find you. You shall be king over Israel, and I shall be next to you. Even my father Saul knows that.* 18 So the two of them made a covenant before the Lord. And David stayed in the woods, and Jonathan went to his own house.

David was so close with our Father, he knew he was being 'divinely protected'. He also knew the plans our Father has for Jonathan and it was also confirmed to his heart and mind that Saul knew. Jonathan knew who he could trust, to go to and he knew he could inform David and be protected. All of this unfolded between people who were aligned with our Father even though Saul wanted David to be killed, an act Saul desired for his own purpose. In the midst of the battle, making the covenant before the LORD is the key. Have you made a covenant with the Father?

Repentance for _____?

Adjustment(s) planned? _____

DAY FOUR

FEAR. I Samuel 28:13 (10-19).

And Saul swore to her by the Lord, saying, *As the Lord lives, no punishment shall come upon you for this thing.*

11 Then the woman said, *Whom shall I bring up for you?*

And he said, *Bring up Samuel for me.*

12 When the woman saw Samuel, she cried out with a loud voice. And the woman spoke to Saul, saying, *Why have you deceived me? For you are Saul!*

13 And the king said to her, *Do not be afraid. What did you see?*

And the woman said to Saul, *I saw a spirit ascending out of the earth.*

14 So he said to her, *What is his form?*

And she said, *An old man is coming up, and he is covered with a mantle.* **And Saul perceived that it was Samuel, and he stooped with his face to the ground and bowed down.**

15 Now Samuel said to Saul, *Why have you disturbed me by bringing me up?*

And Saul answered, *I am deeply distressed; for the Philistines make war against me, and God has departed from me and does not answer me anymore, neither by prophets nor by dreams. Therefore I have called you, that you may reveal to me what I should do.*

16 Then Samuel said: *So why do you ask me, seeing the Lord has departed from you and has become your enemy? 17 And the Lord has done for Himself as He spoke by me. For the Lord has torn the kingdom out of your hand and given it to your neighbor, David. 18 Because you did not obey the voice of the Lord nor execute His fierce wrath upon Amalek, therefore the Lord has done this thing to you this day. 19 Moreover the Lord will also deliver Israel with you into the hand of the Philistines. And tomorrow you and your sons will be with me. The Lord will also deliver the army of Israel into the hand of the Philistines.*

Saul sought counsel from a medium, a woman described in that time as a witch ('the witch of EnDor') Saul consulted to conjure up the spirit of Samuel for counsel. Saul could have realigned and sought counsel direct from the Father. It had to be a shock to Saul, to hear that the destiny he questioned was not victory and the enemy was not going to be 'in his hands'. Instead, Saul, his sons and the lives of the army of Israel would be delivered into the hands of the Philistines. Historians have confirmed the Philistines are the 'modern day' Palestinians, conquerors of the land granted to Israel. The land, the future of the nation, is biblical! Back to Saul. He made personal choices as a man and as a king which placed his life, his sons (heirs to the throne) and the entire army 'in jeopardy'. Who are you seeking counsel from? What is the impact of your choices? Any day, we can renew our covenant with our Father and 'choose different'!

Repentance for _____?

Adjustment(s) planned? _____

DAY FIVE

FEAR. II Samuel 9:7 (3-7).

Then the king said, *Is there not still someone of the house of Saul, to whom I may show the kindness of God?*

And Ziba said to the king, *There is still a son of Jonathan who is lame in his feet.*

4 So the king said to him, *Where is he?*

And Ziba said to the king, *Indeed he is in the house of Machir the son of Ammiel, in Lo Debar.*

5 Then King David sent and brought him out of the house of Machir the son of Ammiel, from Lo Debar.

6 Now when Mephibosheth the son of Jonathan, the son of Saul, had come to David, he fell on his face and prostrated himself. Then David said, *Mephibosheth?*

And he answered, *Here is your servant!*

7 So David said to him, *Do not fear, for I will surely show you kindness for Jonathan your father's sake, and will restore to you all the land of Saul your grandfather; and you shall eat bread at my table continually.*

The bold action of Jonathan, seeking counsel of David during a fearful time in his family, his life, resulting in making a covenant with the LORD and now, full restoration of the land of Saul being passed on to the future generation(s). Any prior decisions which need to be clarified in the current generation to ensure the blessings being passed on to the third and fourth generations? Standing firm with you that the correct choices will be made and declared!

Repentance for _____?

Adjustment(s) planned? _____

DAY SIX

<u>**DOUBT.**</u> **I Kings 19:6-8.**
Then he (Elijah) **looked, and there by his head was a cake baked on coals, and a jar of water. So he ate and drank, and lay down again. 7 And the angel of the Lord came back the second time, and touched him, and said,** *Arise and eat, because the journey is too great for you.* **8 So he arose, and ate and drank; and he went in the strength of that food forty days and forty nights as far as Horeb, the mountain of God.**

Amazing. The world dictionary describes the mountain as glowing / heat or 'sun' and Sinai as 'moon'. Subtle? Very interesting to be prompted in this moment to seek the Hebrew meaning of Horeb which is also known as Sinai, and the mountain of GOD, and this is TRUTH. The mountain is one: Horeb / Sinai, and it is NOT the mountain of the 'sun god'! Horeb is actually the same mountain where Moses fasted for 40 days, twice! Powerful to realize Elijah was prepared with one meal delivered direct from the LORD to be able to fast for 40 days. Whether you begin with four hours of resting with the LORD, then 40 hours. The TRUTH revealed is a blessing! If you thinking about a 40 day fast with the LORD, at home or on mount Horeb, I trust our Father would meet you there! What is HE revealing to you now?

Repentance for _____?

Adjustment(s) planned? _____

DAY SEVEN

<u>**BLESSING.**</u> **Numbers 6:24-26.**
"The LORD bless you and keep you;
25 The LORD make His face shine upon you,

And be gracious to you;
26 The LORD lift up His countenance upon you,
And give you peace." '

Blessings received: _____

Blessings shared: _____

Declarations/Testimonies: _____

WEEK ELEVEN

DAY ONE

<u>REVERENTIAL FEAR</u>. I Kings 8:43 (41-43).

Moreover, concerning a foreigner, who is not of Your people Israel, but has come from a far country for Your name's sake 42 (for they will hear of Your great name and Your strong hand and Your outstretched arm), when he comes and prays toward this temple, 43 hear in heaven Your dwelling place, and do according to all for which the foreigner calls to You, that all peoples of the earth may know Your name and fear You, as do Your people Israel, and that they may know that this temple which I have built is called by Your name.

Do those who come receive assistance because they desire the blessings and provision of the nation from heaven and therefore, they have reverential fear of the Father? The dream the devil supposedly provided to Albert Pike in 1871 described the future based upon wars: WWI, WWII and WWIII being the battle between people based upon their faith, specifically the Jews & Christians fighting the Muslims. We are not fully responsible for the plans since they have proceeded since the beginning of the nation and especially since 1871 and we became assets of the corporation established as The United States of America Corporation within the Act of 1871. However, while we are here it is important to disciple to all nations, people, and be the example and voice while we are here. Who are you an example to? Who is hearing the TRUTH from you?

Repentance for _____?

Adjustment(s) planned? _____

<u>FEAR</u>. I Kings 17:13 (8-16).
<u>Elijah and the Widow</u>
Then the word of the Lord came to him, saying, **9** *Arise, go to Zarephath, which belongs to Sidon, and dwell there. See, I have commanded a widow there to provide for you.* **10** So he arose and went to Zarephath. And when he came to the gate of the city, indeed a widow was there gathering sticks. And he called to her and said, *Please bring me a little water in a cup, that I may drink.* **11** And as she was going to get it, he called to her and said, *Please bring me a morsel of bread in your hand.*

12 So she said, *As the Lord your God lives, I do not have bread, only a handful of flour in a bin, and a little oil in a jar; and see, I am gathering a couple of sticks that I may go in and prepare it for myself and my son, that we may eat it, and die.*

13 And Elijah said to her, *Do not fear; go and do as you have said, but make me a small cake from it first, and bring it to me; and afterward make some for yourself and your son.* **14** *For thus says the Lord God of Israel: 'The bin of flour shall not be used up, nor shall the jar of oil run dry, until the day the Lord sends rain on the earth.'*

15 So she went away and did according to the word of Elijah; and she and he and her household ate for many days. **16** The bin of flour was not used up, nor did the jar of oil run dry, according to the word of the Lord which He spoke by Elijah.

When we reach points in time when we feel we 'do not have enough', it helps to be in conversation with a believer whether they are a prophet or not because we need to be reminded that we serve a LORD who is 'more than enough'. Shifting our belief to all provision coming from our Father and not the world can take a little time due to the tempting of the world for a temporary supply forgetting it is only temporary. Our Father has a BIGGER plan:

II Corinthians 4:16-18. <u>Seeing the Invisible</u>. Therefore we do not lose heart. Even though our outward man is perishing, yet the inward *man* is being renewed day by day. 17 For our light affliction, which is but for a moment, is working for us a far more exceeding *and* eternal weight of glory, 18 while we do not look at the things which are seen, but at the things which are not seen. For the things which are seen *are* temporary, but the things which are not seen *are* eternal.

On a scale of 1-10, what is your level of commitment to our Father's plan for you?

Repentance for _____?

Adjustment(s) planned? _____

DAY THREE

<u>FEAR</u>. II Kings 1:15 (5-17).

And when the messengers returned to him (Ahaziah, King of Samaria who sent the messengers to find Baal-Zebub, the god of Ekron, to inquire if he shall recover from his injury), **he said to them,** *Why have you come back?*

6 So they said to him, *A man came up to meet us, and said to us, 'Go, return to the king who sent you, and say to him, Thus says the Lord: 'Is it because there is no God in Israel that you are sending to inquire of Baal-Zebub, the god of Ekron? Therefore you shall not come down from the bed to which you have gone up, but you shall surely die.'*

7 Then he said to them, *What kind of man was it who came up to meet you and told you these words?* **8 So they answered him,** *A hairy man wearing a leather belt around his waist.* **And he said,** *It is Elijah the Tishbite.*

9 Then the king sent to him a captain of fifty with his fifty men. So he went up to him; and there he was, sitting on the top of a hill. And he spoke to him: *Man of God, the king has said, 'Come down!'*

10 So Elijah answered and said to the captain of fifty, *If I am a man of God, then let fire come down from heaven and consume you and your fifty men.* **And fire came down from heaven and consumed him and his fifty. 11 Then he sent to him another captain of fifty with his fifty men.**

And he answered and said to him: *Man of God, thus has the king said, 'Come down quickly!'*

12 So Elijah answered and said to them, *If I am a man of God, let fire come down from heaven and consume you and your fifty men.* **And the fire of God came down from heaven and consumed him and his fifty.**

13 Again, he sent a third captain of fifty with his fifty men. And the third captain of fifty went up, and came and fell on his knees before Elijah, and pleaded with him, and said to him: *Man of God, please let my life and the life of these fifty servants of yours be precious in your sight.* **14** *Look, fire has come down from heaven and burned up the first two captains of fifties with their fifties. But let my life now be precious in your sight.*

15 And the angel of the Lord said to Elijah, *Go down with him; do not be afraid of him.* **So he arose and went down with him to the king. 16 Then he said to him,** *Thus says the Lord: 'Because you have sent messengers to inquire of Baal-Zebub, the god of Ekron, is it because there is no God in Israel to inquire of His word? Therefore you shall not come down from the bed to which you have gone up, but you shall surely die.'*

17 So Ahaziah died according to the word of the Lord which Elijah had spoken. Because he had no son, Jehoram became king in his place, in the second year of Jehoram the son of Jehoshaphat, king of Judah.

Who do you call upon for counsel in ALL things?

Repentance for _____?

Adjustment(s) planned? _____

DAY FOUR

FEAR. 11 Kings 6:16 (8-24).

Now the king of Syria was making war against Israel; and he consulted with his servants, saying, *My camp will be in such and such a place.* 9 And the man of God sent to the king of Israel, saying, *Beware that you do not pass this place, for the Syrians are coming down there.* 10 Then the king of Israel sent someone to the place of which the man of God had told him. Thus he warned him, and he was watchful there, not just once or twice.

11 Therefore the heart of the king of Syria was greatly troubled by this thing; and he called his servants and said to them, *Will you not show me which of us is for the king of Israel?*

12 And one of his servants said, *None, my lord, O king; but Elisha, the prophet who is in Israel, tells the king of Israel the words that you speak in your bedroom.*

13 So he said, *Go and see where he is, that I may send and get him.*

And it was told him, saying, *Surely he is in Dothan.*

14 Therefore he sent horses and chariots and a great army there, and they came by night and surrounded the city. 15 And when the servant of the man of God arose early and went out, there was an army, surrounding the city with horses and chariots. And his servant said to him, *Alas, my master! What shall we do?*

16 So he answered, *Do not fear, for those who are with us are more than those who are with them.* 17 And Elisha prayed, and said, *Lord, I pray, open his eyes that he may see.* Then the Lord opened the eyes of the young man, and he saw. And behold, the mountain was full of horses and chariots of fire all around Elisha. 18 So when the Syrians came down to him, Elisha prayed to the Lord, and said, *Strike this people, I pray, with blindness.* And He struck them with blindness according to the word of Elisha.

19 Now Elisha said to them, *This is not the way, nor is this the city. Follow me, and I will bring you to the man whom you seek.* But he led them to Samaria. 20 So it was, when they had come to Samaria, that Elisha said, *Lord, open the eyes of these men, that they may see.* And the Lord opened their eyes, and they saw; and there they were, inside Samaria!

21 Now when the king of Israel saw them, he said to Elisha, *My father, shall I kill them? Shall I kill them?* 22 But he answered, *You shall not kill them. Would you kill those whom you have taken captive with your sword and your bow? Set food and water before them, that they may eat and drink and go to their master.* 23 Then he prepared a great feast for them; and after they ate and drank, he sent them away and they went to their master. So the bands of Syrian raiders came no more into the land of Israel.

Whether our Father blinds the enemy or makes us invisible so the plan can unfold, divine assistance and protection is a precious gift for us. Thinking about the report from a ministry team serving in Haiti. The supplies are typically confiscated at the port but, they were surprised to be 100% successful in unloading and leaving with their supplies. Within miles, however, a truckload of men with high powered rifles were shooting at their vehicle. Our Father prompted them to pull over to the side of the road. It is not seem feasible however, they were not able to out-run the truck. As the truck passed by, the men aiming their guns were clearly looking for them and did not see them or their vehicle as they raced by them.

This scripture is another example of delivery the enemy into the hands of the righteous. It is another example of divine guidance and protection. Few share the testimonies of the precision realized when the guidance and divine protection 'in the moment' is orchestrated by our Father. Will you share the testimonies of the amazing 'in the moment' experiences you have live through and benefited from?

Repentance for _____?

Adjustment(s) planned? _____

DAY FIVE

UNBELIEF. II Kings 17:14-15.
Nevertheless they would not hear, but stiffened their necks, like the necks of their fathers, who did not believe in the Lord their God. 15 And they rejected His statutes and His covenant that He had made with their fathers, and His testimonies which He had testified against them; they followed idols, became idolaters, and went after the nations who were all around them, concerning whom the Lord had charged them that they should not do like them.

Who are you in covenant with and who do you fully serve?

Repentance for _____?

Adjustment(s) planned? _____

DAY SIX

FEAR. II Kings 19:6 (1-7).

And so it was, when King Hezekiah heard it, that he tore his clothes, covered himself with sackcloth, and went into the house of the Lord. 2 Then he sent Eliakim, who was over the household, Shebna the scribe, and the elders of the priests, covered with sackcloth, to Isaiah the prophet, the son of Amoz.

3 And they said to him, *Thus says Hezekiah: 'This day is a day of trouble, and rebuke, and blasphemy; for the children have come to birth, but there is no strength to bring them forth. 4 It may be that the Lord your God will hear all the words of the Rabshakeh, whom his master the king of Assyria has sent to reproach the living God, and will rebuke the words which the Lord your God has heard. Therefore lift up your prayer for the remnant that is left.'*

5 So the servants of King Hezekiah came to Isaiah. 6 And Isaiah said to them, *Thus you shall say to your master, 'Thus says the Lord: Do not be afraid of the words which you have heard, with which the servants of the king of Assyria have blasphemed Me. 7 Surely I will send a spirit upon him, and he shall hear a rumor and return to his own land; and I will cause him to fall by the sword in his own land.*

When we are told how to compromise with the world plan it is up to us to choose to seek the truth, the guidance of our Father! What examples come to mind regarding how our Father has provided the right words to you and when you proceeded with HIS guidance, HE saved you from a devastating result?

Repentance for _____ ?

Adjustment(s) planned? _____

DAY SEVEN

BLESSING. Numbers 6:24-26.
> *"The LORD bless you and keep you;*
> 25 *The LORD make His face shine upon you,*
> *And be gracious to you;*
> 26 *The LORD lift up His countenance upon you,*
> *And give you peace." '*

Blessings received: _____

Blessings shared:_____

Declarations/Testimonies: _____

DAY ONE

<u>FEAR</u>. II Kings 25:24 (22-26).
<u>Gedaliah Made Governor of Judah</u>
Then he made Gedaliah the son of Ahikam, the son of Shaphan, governor over the people who remained in the land of Judah, whom Nebuchadnezzar king of Babylon had left. 23 Now when all the captains of the armies, they and their men, heard that the king of Babylon had made Gedaliah governor, they came to Gedaliah at Mizpah—Ishmael the son of Nethaniah, Johanan the son of Careah, Seraiah the son of Tanhumeth the Netophathite, and Jaazaniah the son of a Maachathite, they and their men. 24 And Gedaliah took an oath before them and their men, and said to them, *Do not be afraid of the servants of the Chaldeans. Dwell in the land and serve the king of Babylon, and it shall be well with you.*

25 But it happened in the seventh month that Ishmael the son of Nethaniah, the son of Elishama, of the royal family, came with ten men and struck and killed Gedaliah, the Jews, as well as the Chaldeans who were with him at Mizpah. 26 And all the people, small and great, and the captains of the armies, arose and went to Egypt; for they were afraid of the Chaldeans.

Chaldeans are considered Christians today, merging with the Catholics in the 1800's, but their ancient Babylonian religion focused upon worship of a god over thunder, Marduk, and they referred to him as their Lord Bel. It was a unique transition when tens of thousands of Chaldeans, multiple generations of each family, were relocated to San Diego, California. They were introduced as Christians while it was not evident in their daily life or in showing any interest in attending the local churches. Many only remained close with fellow Chaldeans and spoke only in their language so it was not easy to communicate with them. Gedaliah proceeded as the Governor of Judah based upon human wisdom and all who trusted him perished. What is our Father revealing to you about the words you are to share and/or the steps you are to take in these days?

Repentance for _____?

Adjustment(s) planned? _____

DAY TWO
<u>DOUBT</u>. I Chronicles 16:8-13.

> Oh, give thanks to the Lord!
> Call upon His name;
> Make known His deeds among the peoples!
> 9 Sing to Him, sing psalms to Him;
> Talk of all His wondrous works!
> 10 Glory in His holy name;
> Let the hearts of those rejoice who seek the Lord!
> 11 Seek the Lord and His strength;
> Seek His face evermore!
> 12 Remember His marvelous works which He has done,
> His wonders, and the judgments of His mouth,
> 13 O seed of Israel His servant,
> You children of Jacob, His chosen ones!

When 'in doubt', choose to praise, rejoice and give thanks! In doubt?

Repentance for _____?

Adjustment(s) planned? _____

DAY THREE

REVERENTIAL FEAR. I Chronicles 16:25.
For the Lord is great and greatly to be praised;
He is also to be feared above all gods.

Any idols getting in the way? Re-commit & praise, praise, praise!

Repentance for _____?

Adjustment(s) planned? _____

DAY FOUR

FEAR. I Chronicles 22:13 (6-13).
Then he (King David) **called for his son Solomon, and charged him to
build a house for the Lord God of Israel. 7 And David said to Solomon:** *My
son, as for me, it was in my mind to build a house to the name of the Lord my
God; 8 but the word of the Lord came to me, saying, 'You have shed much
blood and have made great wars; you shall not build a house for My name,
because you have shed much blood on the earth in My sight. 9 Behold, a son
shall be born to you, who shall be a man of rest; and I will give him rest from
all his enemies all around. His name shall be Solomon, for I will give peace
and quietness to Israel in his days. 10 He shall build a house for My name,
and he shall be My son, and I will be his Father; and I will establish the*

70

throne of his kingdom over Israel forever.' 11 *Now, my son, may the Lord be with you; and may you prosper, and build the house of the Lord your God, as He has said to you.* 12 *Only may the Lord give you wisdom and understanding, and give you charge concerning Israel, that you may keep the law of the Lord your God.* 13 *Then you will prosper, if you take care to fulfill the statutes and judgments with which the Lord charged Moses concerning Israel. Be strong and of good courage; do not fear nor be dismayed.*

Solomon was the tenth son of King David. Powerful to remind him to ONLY receive wisdom from the ONLY LORD of ALL. Solomon became the second king of ancient united Israel, the twelve tribes, ten tribes in north and two in the south (Judah). He is considered to be the most prosperous and productive king ever to rule over Israel. What would life be like if we ONLY received the wisdom from the ONLY LORD of ALL?

Repentance for _____?

Adjustment(s) planned? _____

DAY FIVE

FEAR. I Chronicles 28:20 (19-21).
All this, said David, *the Lord made me understand in writing, by His hand upon me, all the works of these plans.* 20 **And David said to his son Solomon,** *Be strong and of good courage, and do it; do not fear nor be dismayed, for the Lord God—my God—will be with you. He will not leave you nor forsake you, until you have finished all the work for the service of the house of the Lord.* 21 *Here are the divisions of the priests and the Levites for all the service of the house of God; and every willing craftsman will be with you for all manner of workmanship, for every kind of service; also the leaders and all the people will be completely at your command.*

How powerful to tell sons and daughters to be of good courage, and do it; do not fear nor be dismayed, for the LORD GOD – my GOD – will be with you. He will not leave you nor forsake you … raising up a child in the way they should go so they will not depart from it! For a long time, I was frustrated in thinking 'minimal salvations' since our Father is focused upon souls. Then, HE told me, *If it takes 1000 people to touch one person's heart, you may only be number 575 or 999 so you do not see results. Do not become discouraged, the fact is you touched the heart and that is what matters.*
Are you speaking truth and sharing words of blessing with the people in your life and the people our Father places in your path?

Repentance for _____?

Adjustment(s) planned? _____

DAY SIX

REVERENTIAL FEAR. II Chronicles 6:33 (32-33).

Moreover, concerning a foreigner, who is not of Your people Israel, but has come from a far country for the sake of Your great name and Your mighty hand and Your outstretched arm, when they come and pray in this temple; 33 then hear from heaven Your dwelling place, and do according to all for which the foreigner calls to You, that all peoples of the earth may know Your name and fear You, as do Your people Israel, and that they may know that this temple which I have built is called by Your name.

Sound familiar?

Same message in **I Kings 8:43 (41-43). Week Eleven, Day One.**

Do those who come receive assistance because they desire the blessings and provision of the nation from heaven and therefore, they have reverential fear of the Father?

Another reminder to speak truth to the people who come to the fellowship and gather together with believers. Disciple them in truth with the direct guidance and wisdom provided by our Father.

Who are you an example for? Who is hearing the TRUTH from you?

Repentance for _____?

Adjustment(s) planned? _____

DAY SEVEN

BLESSING. Numbers 6:24-26.
> *"The LORD bless you and keep you;*
> *25 The LORD make His face shine upon you,*
> *And be gracious to you;*
> *26 The LORD lift up His countenance upon you,*
> *And give you peace." '*

Blessings received: _____

Blessings shared: _____

Declarations/Testimonies: _____

WEEK THIRTEEN

DAY ONE

<u>REVERENTIAL FEAR</u>. Malachi 4:2.
>But to you who fear My name
>The Sun of Righteousness shall arise
>With healing in His wings;
>And you shall go out
>And grow fat like stall-fed calves.

Growing fat is not desired while options are: 'live abundantly & prosper'.

Repentance for _____?

Adjustment(s) planned? _____

DAY TWO

(Personal Insert) II Chronicles 7:14.
If My people who are called by My name will humble themselves, and pray and seek My face, and turn from their wicked ways (REPENT), *then I will hear from heaven, and will forgive their sin and heal their land* (RESTORE).

Full repentance = full restoration.

Precious position, to be recognized as HIS people, seeking him 100%!

Repentance for _____?

Adjustment(s) planned? _____

DAY THREE

<u>DOUBT</u>, also <u>FEAR</u>. II Chronicles 20:15 (13-15).
Now all Judah, with their little ones, their wives, and their children, stood before the Lord.
14 Then the Spirit of the Lord came upon Jahaziel the son of Zechariah, the son of Benaiah, the son of Jeiel, the son of Mattaniah, a Levite of the sons of Asaph, in the midst of the assembly.
15 And he said, *Listen, all you of Judah and you inhabitants of Jerusalem, and you, King Jehoshaphat! Thus says the Lord to you: 'Do not*

be afraid nor dismayed because of this great multitude, for the battle is not yours, but God's.

The last phrase is quoted often. However, the lineage leading up to and praying and praising for this status is not mentioned when the phrase is quoted so many who state the phrase as a way of encouraging others are actually confirming they do not have to do anything, *for the battle is not yours, but God's.* That is NOT the truth!

Prayers and praise to the LORD extended for hours, putting all trust and faith in the victory. Our Father confirmed the victory before they proceeded over the hill to view ALL of the armies from ALL of the nations coming against them were dead. ALL warriors were dead!

Important to be in praise and worship with our Father after inviting him into the situation and not stop, turn back, change the plan, until the victory is confirmed.

Repentance for _____ ?

Adjustment(s) planned? _____

DAY FOUR

<u>**FEAR**</u>. **II Chronicles 20:17 (16-17).**
Tomorrow go down against them. They will surely come up by the Ascent of Ziz, and you will find them at the end of the brook before the Wilderness of Jeruel. 17 You will not need to fight in this battle. Position yourselves, stand still and see the salvation of the Lord, who is with you, O Judah and Jerusalem!' Do not fear or be dismayed; tomorrow go out against them, for the Lord is with you.

A famous saying: IF you KNEW you could NOT fail, what would you do, how would you carry out the plan our Father has laid out before you?

Repentance for _____ ?

Adjustment(s) planned? _____

74

DAY FIVE

<u>REVERENTIAL FEAR</u>. II Chronicles 20:29.
And the fear of God was on all the kingdoms of those countries when they heard that the Lord had fought against the enemies of Israel.

Father delivered the enemies into their hands, often. These facts are repeated again and again in scripture. It makes me think of the special quote by Smith Wigglesworth: *If you seek nothing but the will of GOD, HE will always put you in the right place at the right time.*

Repentance for _____?

Adjustment(s) planned? _____

DAY SIX

<u>DOUBT</u>. II Chronicles 32:6-8.
Then he set military captains over the people, gathered them together to him in the open square of the city gate, and gave them encouragement, saying, 7 *Be strong and courageous; do not be afraid nor dismayed before the king of Assyria, nor before all the multitude that is with him; for there are more with us than with him. 8 With him is an arm of flesh; but with us is the Lord our God, to help us and to fight our battles.* And the people were strengthened by the words of Hezekiah king of Judah.

Why were the people in doubt? Assyria took ALL of the people in the ten tribes of Israel captive in 721 BC. King Hezekiah strengthened his people by referring to the Assyian destruction of the north of Israel.

Hezekiah was a 'new king', about one year into his reign in Judah, when the Assyrians destroyed the tribes to the north and took the people captive.

Judah, comprised of the southern tribes of Judah & Benjamin, was more fortunate than the tribes in the north since Judah occasionally experienced a godly king who reformed their government.

The tribes in the north only had evil kings.

Regardless, Judah did not retain their liberty and freedom.

Within about 120 years, Judah was destroyed and the influential people were marched off to assist the Babylonians in Babylon. It is not clear if the Babylonian destruction of Judah resulted in all members of the tribes taken captive, as the Assyrians proceeded in their full capture of ALL of the people in the ten northern tribes.

Government is in the process of being reformed in our nation at this time.

We do not have a 'next option' if liberty and freedom is not retained in our nation. We do not have a nation or 'uninhabited lands' to go to in the future.

The tribes were granted the 'uninhabited lands' in the world. We do not have that option. Father trusts we will unite together, aligned in HIS truth with HIM and HIS purpose and plan for these days. Are we a people who will secure the blessings and pass them on to the third and fourth generation? What is your part in the process with our Father?

Repentance for _____?

Adjustment(s) planned? _____

DAY SEVEN

BLESSING. Numbers 6:24-26.
> *"The LORD bless you and keep you;*
> *25 The LORD make His face shine upon you,*
> *And be gracious to you;*
> *26 The LORD lift up His countenance upon you,*
> *And give you peace." '*

Blessings received: _____

Blessings shared: _____

Declarations/Testimonies: _____

FIRST QUARTER: What is our Father revealing to you, about you?

_____

DAY ONE

FEAR. II Chronicles 32:7 (2-8).

And when Hezekiah saw that Sennacherib had come, and that his purpose was to make war against Jerusalem, 3 he consulted with his leaders and commanders to stop the water from the springs which were outside the city; and they helped him. 4 Thus many people gathered together who stopped all the springs and the brook that ran through the land, saying, Why should the kings of Assyria come and find much water? 5 And he strengthened himself, built up all the wall that was broken, raised it up to the towers, and built another wall outside; also he repaired the Millo in the City of David, and made weapons and shields in abundance. 6 Then he set military captains over the people, gathered them together to him in the open square of the city gate, and gave them encouragement, saying, 7 Be strong and courageous; do not be afraid nor dismayed before the king of Assyria, nor before all the multitude that is with him; for there are more with us than with him. 8 With him is an arm of flesh; but with us is the Lord our God, to help us and to fight our battles. And the people were strengthened by the words of Hezekiah king of Judah.

Confirmation, again, of the reason to unite together as believers for no matter what we face there are more believers than non believers. Our challenge is to be a voice and share truth and not become a silent majority. Exciting days to be a witness to the voices of truth across the nation and around the globe, well known men and women who are sharing their testimonies and waking up tens of thousands at a time! Powerful to hear teenagers confirm the first time they heard the name of Jesus Christ is due to the new 'awakening' in our nation. What is the message our Father is revealing to you to share with fellow believers, words which will impact their lives, the lives of non-believers and those who are unaware of the truth?

Repentance for _____?

Adjustment(s) planned? _____

DAY TWO

UNBELIEF. II Chronicles 32:15.

(Sennacherib, the king of Assyria brags to put fear into the hearts of the people when he states 'no other gods' in any of the other nations protected the people from the capture and captivity by Assyria) *Now therefore, do not let Hezekiah deceive you or persuade you like this, and do not believe him; for no god of any nation or kingdom was able to deliver his people from my hand or the hand of my fathers. How much less will your God deliver you from my hand?'*

The King of Assyria attempted to proceed with a 'fear campaign'. He lied.

When liars state and repeat their lies, will you comply?

Or, will you and your house reject the lies and serve the LIVING LORD?

Repentance for _____?

Adjustment(s) planned? _____

DAY THREE

REVERENTIAL FEAR. Ezra 9:4.
Then everyone who trembled at the words of the God of Israel assembled to me, because of the transgression of those who had been carried away captive, and I sat astonished until the evening sacrifice.

Many, fathers and sons, married outside of their faith during their time away. Now they are returning to Jerusalem with spouses who were Canaanites, Assyrians and Babylonians of other faiths. When they returned and heard the true word of the LORD once again, it shook them to their core. Ezra fasted and prayed through by confessing the sins, the transgressions, the actions which caused distance between the people and the Father, their first love, Yahweh. Is there anything our Father is prompting you to pray about, anything causing distance between you and the Father?

Repentance for _____?

Adjustment(s) planned? _____

DAY FOUR

REVERENTIAL FEAR. Ezra 10:3.

78

Now therefore, let us make a covenant with our God to put away all these wives and those who have been born to them, according to the advice of my master and of those who tremble at the commandment of our God; and let it be done according to the law.

Turned away. To remove the distance between the people and the Father, those who proceed according to other beliefs were 'put away'. What is to be resolved or put away to remove distance between you and the Father?

Repentance for _____ ?

Adjustment(s) planned? _____

DAY FIVE

<u>FEAR</u>. **Nehemiah 4:14 (10-14).**
Then Judah said, *The strength of the laborers is failing, and there is so much rubbish that we are not able to build the wall.*
11 And our adversaries said, *They will neither know nor see anything, till we come into their midst and kill them and cause the work to cease.*
12 So it was, when the Jews who dwelt near them came, that they told us ten times, *From whatever place you turn, they will be upon us.*
13 Therefore I positioned men behind the lower parts of the wall, at the openings; and I set the people according to their families, with their swords, their spears, and their bows. 14 And I looked, and arose and said to the nobles, to the leaders, and to the rest of the people, *Do not be afraid of them. Remember the Lord, great and awesome, and fight for your brethren, your sons, your daughters, your wives, and your houses.*

Amazing! A crisis due to the wall not being complete, the construction not being a solid structure and to protect the families and their homes, all people were to bring their swords, spears, and their bows. It is an issue in these days. Protection of the people and their homes was not a focus for a long time. Now, it is a priority and the wall is being built. The new construction is absolutely a solid structure. We do not have to 'meet at the border' with our swords and spears in these days. What is our Father prompting you to do to retain the protection of the blessings, the homes, the lands for the current and future generations?

Repentance for _____ ?

Adjustment(s) planned? _____

DAY SIX

UNBELIEF. Nehemiah 9:16-17.
> But they and our fathers acted proudly,
> Hardened their necks,
> And did not heed Your commandments.
> 17 They refused to obey,
> And they were not mindful of Your wonders
> That You did among them.
> But they hardened their necks,
> And in their rebellion
> They appointed a leader
> To return to their bondage.
> But You are God,
> Ready to pardon,
> Gracious and merciful,
> Slow to anger,
> Abundant in kindness,
> And did not forsake them.

Realignment. Comparable to 'getting the tires aligned' on your vehicle. When you notice the tires are causing some drifting to the right or the left, you schedule an appointment to re-align the tires. It's the same 'in life'. One of the most profound statements I received from our Father was during the time of questioning my qualifications. Yahweh was NOT questioning me, I was questioning my level of understanding since I am not a bible scholar and I was not a seminary graduate, two items which the world wants to know about us before we are considered credible. Father reminded me of the truth, HE is walking with me (us) today exactly as HE has always walked with believers through ALL situations, ALL crisis moments, NEVER leaving or forsaking us. After HE reveals profound facts to me, HE will reveal the person in the bible who experienced similar concerns or situations and HE provided wisdom for them 'in the moment' exactly as HE guides and shares HIS wisdom with us, today. What is HE revealing to you? Would a re-alignment be beneficial?

Repentance for _____?

Adjustment(s) planned? _____

DAY SEVEN

BLESSING. Numbers 6:24-26.
> *"The LORD bless you and keep you;*
> 25 *The LORD make His face shine upon you,*
> *And be gracious to you;*
> 26 *The LORD lift up His countenance upon you,*
> *And give you peace."* '

Blessings received: _____

Blessings shared: _____

Declarations/Testimonies: _____

WEEK FIFTEEN

DAY ONE

DOUBT. Job 4:3-4 (1-6).
Eliphaz: Job Has Sinned
Then Eliphaz the Temanite answered and said:
2 "If one attempts a word with you, will you become weary?
But who can withhold himself from speaking?
3 Surely you have instructed many,
And you have strengthened weak hands.
4 Your words have upheld him who was stumbling,
And you have strengthened the feeble knees;
5 But now it comes upon you, and you are weary;
It touches you, and you are troubled.
6 Is not your reverence your confidence?
And the integrity of your ways your hope?

Repentance for _____?

Adjustment(s) planned? _____

DAY TWO

FEAR. Job 5:21 (17-27).
Behold, happy is the man whom God corrects;

Therefore do not despise the chastening of the Almighty.
18 For He bruises, but He binds up;
He wounds, but His hands make whole.
19 He shall deliver you in six troubles,
Yes, in seven no evil shall touch you.
20 In famine He shall redeem you from death,
And in war from the power of the sword.
21 You shall be hidden from the scourge of the tongue,
And you shall not be afraid of destruction when it comes.
22 You shall laugh at destruction and famine,
And you shall not be afraid of the beasts of the earth.
23 For you shall have a covenant with the stones of the field,
And the beasts of the field shall be at peace with you.
24 You shall know that your tent is in peace;
You shall visit your dwelling and find nothing amiss.
25 You shall also know that your descendants shall be many,
And your offspring like the grass of the earth.
26 You shall come to the grave at a full age,
As a sheaf of grain ripens in its season.
27 Behold, this we have searched out;
It is true.
Hear it, and know for yourself.

Repentance for _____?

Adjustment(s) planned? _____

DAY THREE

FEAR. Job 11:15 13-20.
If you would prepare your heart,
And stretch out your hands toward Him;
14 If iniquity were in your hand, and you put it far away,
And would not let wickedness dwell in your tents;
15 Then surely you could lift up your face without spot;
Yes, you could be steadfast, and not fear;
16 Because you would forget your misery,
And remember it as waters that have passed away,
17 And your life would be brighter than noonday.
Though you were dark, you would be like the morning.
18 And you would be secure, because there is hope;
Yes, you would dig around you, and take your rest in safety.
19 You would also lie down, and no one would make you afraid;
Yes, many would court your favor.
20 But the eyes of the wicked will fail,
And they shall not escape,
And their hope—loss of life!

Repentance for _____?

Adjustment(s) planned? _____

DAY FOUR

FEAR. Job 21:9 (4-16).
As for me, is my complaint against man?
And if it were, why should I not be impatient?
5 Look at me and be astonished;
Put your hand over your mouth.
6 Even when I remember I am terrified,
And trembling takes hold of my flesh.
7 Why do the wicked live and become old,
Yes, become mighty in power?
8 Their descendants are established with them in their sight,
And their offspring before their eyes.
9 Their houses are safe from fear,
Neither is the rod of God upon them.
10 Their bull breeds without failure;
Their cow calves without miscarriage.
11 They send forth their little ones like a flock,
And their children dance.
12 They sing to the tambourine and harp,
And rejoice to the sound of the flute.
13 They spend their days in wealth,
And in a moment go down to the grave.
14 Yet they say to God, 'Depart from us,
For we do not desire the knowledge of Your ways.
15 Who is the Almighty, that we should serve Him?
And what profit do we have if we pray to Him?'
16 Indeed their prosperity is not in their hand;
The counsel of the wicked is far from me.

Repentance for _____?

Adjustment(s) planned? _____

DAY FIVE

REVERENTIAL FEAR. Job 25:2.
Dominion and fear belong to Him;
He makes peace in His high places.

Value the definition of REPENT: Return to the high place with GOD!

Repentance for _____?

Adjustment(s) planned? _____

DAY SIX

REVERENTIAL FEAR. Job 37:23-24.
As for the Almighty, we cannot find Him;
He is excellent in power,
In judgment and abundant justice;
He does not oppress.
24 Therefore men fear Him;
He shows no partiality to any who are wise of heart.

With all injustices witnessed in these days, it would bless many to align with and seek the wisdom of our Father! HE lifts us up, HE encourages us, HE has laid out a plan before us, HE will never leave or forsake us and the best news is: HE knows the end from the beginning!

Repentance for _____?

Adjustment(s) planned? _____

DAY SEVEN

BLESSING. Numbers 6:24-26.
"The LORD bless you and keep you;
25 The LORD make His face shine upon you,
And be gracious to you;
26 The LORD lift up His countenance upon you,
And give you peace." '

Blessings received: _____

Blessings shared: _____

Declarations/Testimonies: _____

DAY ONE

REVERENTIAL FEAR. Psalm 2:11.
    Serve the Lord with fear,
    And rejoice with trembling.

Serve with honor.

Praise and rejoice in worship to the ONLY LORD.

What is our Father prompting you to remember in this moment?

Repentance for _____?

Adjustment(s) planned? _____

DAY TWO

REVERENTIAL FEAR. Psalm 2:11-12.
    Serve the Lord with fear,
    And rejoice with trembling.
    12 Kiss the Son, lest He be angry,
    And you perish in the way,
    When His wrath is kindled but a little.
    Blessed are all those who put their trust in Him.

Whatever battle or conflict you are entering into on this day, honor, praise and rejoice in worship to our Father and be sure to bless and acknowledge your loved ones when you depart from them. The blessings which are the protection on the journey are available to all who put their trust in Him. Is there anything you are holding on to instead of trusting the final outcome to our Father?

Repentance for _____?

Adjustment(s) planned? _____

DAY THREE

FEAR. Psalm 3:6 (1-6).

Lord, how they have increased who trouble me!
Many are they who rise up against me.
2 Many are they who say of me,
There is no help for him in God. Selah
3 But You, O Lord, are a shield for me,
My glory and the One who lifts up my head.
4 I cried to the Lord with my voice,
And He heard me from His holy hill. Selah
5 I lay down and slept;
I awoke, for the Lord sustained me.
6 I will not be afraid of ten thousands of people
Who have set themselves against me all around.

Selah means to praise, to reflect upon what is being stated.

Once we bring it ALL to our Father, we can rest in HIM, and await HIS prompting, HIS purpose to be revealed to us so we know that we know the truth about our concerns and how we are to proceed. Can you release the 'ten thousands of people who are operating against you from all angles?

Repentance for _____?

Adjustment(s) planned? _____

DAY FOUR

FEAR. Psalm 4:8 (1-8).
Hear me when I call, O God of my righteousness!
You have relieved me in my distress;
Have mercy on me, and hear my prayer.
2 How long, O you sons of men,
Will you turn my glory to shame?
How long will you love worthlessness
And seek falsehood? Selah
3 But know that the Lord has set apart for Himself him who is godly;
The Lord will hear when I call to Him.
4 Be angry, and do not sin.
Meditate within your heart on your bed, and be still. Selah
5 Offer the sacrifices of righteousness,
And put your trust in the Lord.
6 There are many who say,
Who will show us any good?
Lord, lift up the light of Your countenance upon us.
7 You have put gladness in my heart,
More than in the season that their grain and wine increased.
8 I will both lie down in peace, and sleep;
For You alone, O Lord, make me dwell in safety.

Counsel in the world is 'for naught'. ALL truth is revealed direct from our Father. In the quiet moments with Father, what is HE revealing to you today?

Repentance for _____?

Adjustment(s) planned? _____

DAY FIVE

REVERENTIAL FEAR. Psalm 5:7.
But as for me,
I will come into Your house in the multitude of Your mercy;
In fear of You I will worship toward Your holy temple.

Grateful for HIS mercy.

Grateful HE sent HIS son to 'tabernacle' with us, disciple us so would learn how to become the church with CHRIST as the Chief Cornerstone with the apostles and prophets, supporting and encouraging the efforts of the pastors, teachers and evangelists while the fellowship grows in HIS glory!

As Christ confirmed in **John 17** HE gave us the glory 'on purpose'!

John 17:20-23.
Jesus Prays for All Believers
I do not pray for these alone, but also for those who [j]will believe in Me through their word; 21 that they all may be one, as You, Father, are in Me, and I in You; that they also may be one in Us, that the world may believe that You sent Me. 22 And the glory which You gave Me I have given them, that they may be one just as We are one: 23 I in them, and You in Me; that they may be made perfect in one, and that the world may know that You have sent Me, and have loved them as You have loved Me.

How has HE shown HIS mercy to you in your life?

Repentance for _____?

Adjustment(s) planned? _____

DAY SIX

FEAR. Psalm 16:9 (5-9).
O Lord, You are the portion of my inheritance and my cup;
You maintain my lot.
6 The lines have fallen to me in pleasant places;

Yes, I have a good inheritance.
7 I will bless the Lord who has given me counsel;
My heart also instructs me in the night seasons.
8 I have set the Lord always before me;
Because He is at my right hand I shall not be moved.
9 Therefore my heart is glad, and my glory rejoices;
My flesh also will rest in hope.

When your heart instructs in the night season is the voice due to Christ residing in your heart?

Twice the inheritance is confirmed and appreciated! Are you seeking the inheritance from sources in the world or are you grateful for the heavenly inheritance our Father has prepared for you because you love HIM?

Praising, blessing the LORD for HIS counsel?

What is HIS counsel for you today, in your life?

Repentance for _____ ?

Adjustment(s) planned? _____

DAY SEVEN

BLESSING. Numbers 6:24-26.
"The LORD bless you and keep you;
25 The LORD make His face shine upon you,
And be gracious to you;
26 The LORD lift up His countenance upon you,
And give you peace." '

Blessings received: _____

Blessings shared: _____

Declarations/Testimonies: _____

DAY ONE

DOUBT. Psalm 22:4-5.
Our fathers trusted in You;
They trusted, and You delivered them.
5 They cried to You, and were delivered;
They trusted in You, and were not ashamed.

Are family members delivered? Are you trusting, crying out to the LORD?

Repentance for _____?

Adjustment(s) planned? _____

DAY TWO

REVERENTIAL FEAR. Psalm 22:23.
You who fear the Lord, praise Him!
All you descendants of Jacob, glorify Him,
And fear Him, all you offspring of Israel!

HE resides in the praises of HIS people.

When fear enters, praise HIM!

What are you praising HIM for today, in your life?

Repentance for _____?

Adjustment(s) planned? _____

DAY THREE

FEAR. Psalm 23:4 (4-6).
Yea, though I walk through the valley of the shadow of death,
I will fear no evil;
For You are with me;
Your rod and Your staff, they comfort me.
5 You prepare a table before me in the presence of my enemies;
You anoint my head with oil;
My cup runs over.
6 Surely goodness and mercy shall follow me

All the days of my life;
And I will dwell in the house of the Lord
Forever.

No fear.

Not even in the presence of enemies!

Goodness & mercy follows!

Knowing truth, where are you willing to walk in faith today and who are you willing to share truth with today?

Repentance for _____?

Adjustment(s) planned? _____

DAY FOUR

FEAR. Psalm 27:1 1-2.
The Lord is my light and my salvation;
Whom shall I fear?
The Lord is the strength of my life;
Of whom shall I be afraid?
2 When the wicked came against me
To eat up my flesh,
My enemies and foes,
They stumbled and fell.

Because of salvation and the strength of the LORD, we are stable in our ways and our enemies and foes will stumble and fall.

Therefore, who shall you fear?

Repentance for _____?

Adjustment(s) planned? _____

DAY FIVE

FEAR. Psalm 27:3.
Though an army may encamp against me,
My heart shall not fear;
Though war may rise against me,

In this I will be confident.

With our LORD all things are possible, even the ability to proceed with confidence when an army encamps against us or a war rises up against us. Knowing this, what is the new perspective on the challenge(s) you are facing?

Repentance for _____?

Adjustment(s) planned? _____

DAY SIX

FEAR. Psalm 29:11 8-11.
The voice of the Lord shakes the wilderness;
The Lord shakes the Wilderness of Kadesh.
9 The voice of the Lord makes the deer give birth,
And strips the forests bare;
And in His temple everyone says, "Glory!"
10 The Lord sat enthroned at the Flood,
And the Lord sits as King forever.
11 The Lord will give strength to His people;
The Lord will bless His people with peace.

Powerful testimony of Prophetess Nancy Haney of Alaska. The day I met her, she shared a testimony which has blessed so many people and it aligns with the vision our Father gave me at the conclusion of the search for Wigglesworth. Nancy suffered a full body debilitating stroke. No ability to speak, eat, use her limbs. The Doctors could not get it across to her since she had commitments, a full schedule to proceed upon!

Immediately after the lecture by her physicians, she used every ounce of strength to move her legs to the side of the bed to stand up and within seconds she was a blob on the floor, unable to do anything. Hospital staff rushed in and helped her get back on the bed.

She was in tears! Realizing her condition was much worse than she thought, she immediately repented for her actions. Amidst her tears and intense repentance, she felt a jolt in her body as though they brought the blue cart and tried to revive her. Her body rose above the bed several inches while she was

91

shouting, **WHAT?** She heard her voice, her arms were working and her legs were working. She jumped out of bed and started dancing and praising the Father. The Doctor returned and was amazed while Nancy continued to rejoice.

This happened on the THIRD DAY in the hospital and Father confirmed it was RESURRECTION POWER. He instructed Nancy to go to Niagara Falls. Long story short, the LORD confirmed the power in each of us because Christ resides in our hearts, is MORE than in Niagara Falls. GOD prompted me to research how much power in the falls and it is enough to light up more than 3.8 million homes and HE said HIS people are not even tapping into it.

The vision after the search for Wigglesworth was an Emergency room entrance at a hospital with ambulances lining up and revealing each patient was a church that flat-lined.

In this moment, the LORD confirmed the truth: *IF Christ resides in our hearts, how could we flat-line?* He wants us to use the RESURRECTION POWER of Christ, since HE resides in our hearts, to restore each other.

Whose heart will you restore today or tomorrow?

Repentance for _____?

Adjustment(s) planned? _____

DAY SEVEN

BLESSING. Numbers 6:24-26.
"The LORD bless you and keep you;
25 The LORD make His face shine upon you,
And be gracious to you;
26 The LORD lift up His countenance upon you,
And give you peace." '

Blessings received: _____

Blessings shared: _____

Declarations/Testimonies: _____

DAY ONE

REVERENTIAL FEAR. Psalm 33:8-9.
> *Let all the earth fear the Lord;*
> *Let all the inhabitants of the world stand in awe of Him.*
> *9 For He spoke, and it was done;*
> *He commanded, and it stood fast.*

It would be an amazing day with ALL the earth living in reverential fear of the LORD!

Unity in truth.

Peace would be evident.

Unity and peace which HE gave to us.

He created ALL when HE spoke!

What is the plan HE has created with and for you?

What is HE saying to you?

Repentance for _____?

Adjustment(s) planned? _____

DAY TWO

DOUBT. Psalm 42:11.
> *Why are you cast down, O my soul?*
> *And why are you disquieted within me?*
> *Hope in God;*
> *For I shall yet praise Him,*
> *The help of my countenance and my God.*

Even in the worst moments, HE is only ONE BREATH away for every fresh new breath is LIFE from HIM!

When we gather it is the greeting: *May ALL be well with your soul!*

Why? Our well-being, our health, our thoughts are all linked to the status of our soul.

May our Father reveal to you ANY THING in your life, your thoughts, your beliefs, ANY THING which is affecting your soul so it can be dealt with, confessed and repented for, so ALL will be well with your soul!

What is our Father revealing to you?

Repentance for _____?

Adjustment(s) planned? _____

DAY THREE

<u>FEAR</u>. **Psalm 46:2 (1-3).**
God is our refuge and strength,
A very present help in trouble.
2 Therefore we will not fear,
Even though the earth be removed,
And though the mountains be carried into the midst of the sea;
3 Though its waters roar and be troubled,
Though the mountains shake with its swelling. Selah

If we have no earth, no place to stand, then will we remember the perspective of our Father?

We are seated in heavenly places, **Ephesians 2:6!**

Ephesians 2:4-10.
<u>By Grace Through Faith</u>
But God, who is rich in mercy, because of His great love with which He loved us, 5 even when we were dead in trespasses, made us alive together with Christ (by grace you have been saved), 6 and raised us up together, and made us sit together in the heavenly places in Christ Jesus, 7 that in the ages to come He might show the exceeding riches of His grace in His kindness toward us in Christ Jesus. 8 For by grace you have been saved through faith, and that not of yourselves; it is the gift of God, 9 not of works, lest anyone should boast. 10 For we are His workmanship, created in Christ Jesus for good works, which God prepared beforehand that we should walk in them.

During this moment in time, a moment to pause and reflect upon the message to gain understanding, it is clear that no matter what changes in our life today or tonight, even if nothing resembles life tomorrow, we know where our very present help in trouble comes from! What are you seeking help with today?

Repentance for _____?

Adjustment(s) planned? _____

DAY FOUR

FEAR. Psalm 49:16 (16-17).
Do not be afraid when one becomes rich,
When the glory of his house is increased;
17 For when he dies he shall carry nothing away;
His glory shall not descend after him.

A good reminder that the focus is not upon THINGS,

Focus is always upon SOULS.

Are you prompted to list a few names, a few lives / souls to impact?

Or, wherever your journey takes you today will you seek souls to impact?

Repentance for _____?

Adjustment(s) planned? _____

DAY FIVE

FEAR. Psalm 56: 3-4 (1-4).
Be merciful to me, O God, for man would swallow me up;
Fighting all day he oppresses me.
2 My enemies would hound me all day,
For there are many who fight against me, O Most High.
3 Whenever I am afraid,
I will trust in You.
4 In God (I will praise His word),
In God I have put my trust;
I will not fear.
What can flesh do to me?

Love the confirmation in the scriptures, the what can flesh do to me is often

quoted as: *What can mere mortals do to me?*

Is there anything wearing upon your heart or mind?

Knowing 'mere mortals' can do nothing to you, what is our Father guiding you to say or do regarding the situation, the challenge(s) you are facing today, in your life?

Repentance for _____?

Adjustment(s) planned? _____

DAY SIX

REVERENTIAL FEAR. Psalm 56:4.
> *In God (I will praise His word),*
> *In God I have put my trust;*
> *I will not fear.*
> *What can flesh do to me?*

Another reminder.

Flesh, mere mortals, are not able to do anything to you!

Knowing this, what is your plan?

What is our Father revealing to you?

What are you prompted to do today?

Repentance for _____?

Adjustment(s) planned? _____

DAY SEVEN

BLESSING. Numbers 6:24-26.
> *"The LORD bless you and keep you;*
> *25 The LORD make His face shine upon you,*
> *   And be gracious to you;*
> *26 The LORD lift up His countenance upon you,*
> *   And give you peace." '*

Blessings received: _____

Blessings shared: _____

Declarations/Testimonies: _____

DAY ONE

<u>FEAR</u>. Psalm 56:11 (8-11).
You number my wanderings;
Put my tears into Your bottle;
Are they not in Your book?
9 When I cry out to You,
Then my enemies will turn back;
This I know, because God is for me.
10 In God (I will praise His word),
In the Lord (I will praise His word),
11 In God I have put my trust;
I will not be afraid.
What can man do to me?

Father puts our tears in a bottle! This scripture has always blessed me, to realize the depth of care and compassion our Father has for each of us!

Remember, whatever the plan is for your life there is NOTHING man can do to you, to impact the health of your soul!

He would not limit the bible by excluding your journeys with him! Since only a few facts are inserted about the lives identified within the bible, what would your book in the bible include about your life?

Repentance for _____?

Adjustment(s) planned? _____

DAY TWO

<u>REVERENTIAL FEAR</u>. Psalm 64:9.
All men shall fear,
And shall declare the work of God;
For they shall wisely consider His doing.

CHRIST confirmed, HE only did what HE saw our Father do and said what HE heard our Father say!

John 5:

<u>Honor the Father and the Son</u>

16 For this reason the Jews persecuted Jesus, and sought to kill Him, because He had done these things on the Sabbath. 17 But Jesus answered them, *My Father has been working until now, and I have been working.*

18 Therefore the Jews sought all the more to kill Him, because He not only broke the Sabbath, but also said that God was His Father, making Himself equal with God. 19 Then Jesus answered and said to them, *Most assuredly, I say to you, the Son can do nothing of Himself, but what He sees the Father do; for whatever He does, the Son also does in like manner. 20 For the Father loves the Son, and shows Him all things that He Himself does; and He will show Him greater works than these, that you may marvel. 21 For as the Father raises the dead and gives life to them, even so the Son gives life to whom He will. 22 For the Father judges no one, but has committed all judgment to the Son, 23 that all should honor the Son just as they honor the Father. He who does not honor the Son does not honor the Father who sent Him.*

Similar word in **John 8: 27-30. They did not understand that He spoke to them of the Father. 28 Then Jesus said to them,** *When you lift up the Son of Man, then you will know that I am He, and that I do nothing of Myself; but as My Father taught Me, I speak these things. 29 And He who sent Me is with Me. The Father has not left Me alone, for I always do those things that please Him.* **30 As He spoke these words, many believed in Him.**

And in **John 12:42-50.**
<u>Walk in the Light</u>
Nevertheless even among the rulers many believed in Him, but because of the Pharisees they did not confess Him, lest they should be put out of the synagogue; 43 for they loved the praise of men more than the praise of God.

44 Then Jesus cried out and said, *He who believes in Me, believes not in Me but in Him who sent Me. 45 And he who sees Me sees Him who sent Me. 46 I have come as a light into the world, that whoever believes in Me should not abide in darkness. 47 And if anyone hears My words and does not believe, I do not judge him; for I did not come to judge the world but to save the world. 48 He who rejects Me, and does not receive My words, has that which judges him—the word that I have spoken will judge him in the last day. 49 For I have not spoken on My own authority; but the Father who sent Me gave Me a command, what I should say and what I should speak. 50 And I know that His command is everlasting life. Therefore, whatever I speak, just as the Father has told Me, so I speak.*

We are joint heirs. CHRIST prepared the way for us. HE taught us how to pray and how to disciple. HE gave us the glory so we would unite in TRUTH and be one together as HE and the Father are ONE.

What are you seeing our Father do and say for the sake of souls today?

Repentance for _____?

Adjustment(s) planned? _____

DAY THREE

REVERENTIAL FEAR. Psalm 67:7.
God shall bless us,
And all the ends of the earth shall fear Him.

Aligned with the Father, living in reverence of who HE is for us, all people to the ends of the earth then realize who HE is they will choose HIM.

Powerful to witness this TRUTH while I was in Ghana, West Africa.

The miraculous way our Father arranged the timing and provision of a ride to a church on Sunday since all in the group from America chose to rest and not gather until the consecration service at Bishop Duncan William's church later in the day. Therefore, arrangements for a ride to church was 'in the hands of our Father'. The specifics are included within my book *It's A Faith Walk!*

When I entered the service, I saw men and women praising and dancing. All of the men wore long sleeved shirts and ties. They were praising 'without ceasing' in the midst of high humidity and temperature which caused me to use a fan and I was not dancing!

When I asked the pastor about the amazing level of worship and faith expressed, he provided a very simple and profound response, *They are like you. They live by faith, but, it is different for the people here because they have to pay at least $200/month in rent alone and most of the people do not earn $200/month. Their testimonies are strong for you see they have to depend upon God's provision in their life every day of their life.*

Sharing the testimonies of how our Father blesses us makes a difference!

What are your testimonies about how GOD blesses you?

Repentance for _____?

Adjustment(s) planned? _____

99

DOUBT. Psalm 73:23-26.
> **Nevertheless I am continually with You;**
> **You hold me by my right hand.**
> **24 You will guide me with Your counsel,**
> **And afterward receive me to glory.**
> **25 Whom have I in heaven but You?**
> **And there is none upon earth that I desire besides You.**
> **26 My flesh and my heart fail;**
> **But God is the strength of my heart and my portion forever.**

What do you express to the people in your life that confirms to them that our Father is the strength of your heart and portion?

Repentance for _____ ?

Adjustment(s) planned? _____

DAY FIVE

DOUBT. Psalm 74:12-17.
> **For God is my King from of old,**
> **Working salvation in the midst of the earth.**
> **13 You divided the sea by Your strength;**
> **You broke the heads of the sea serpents in the waters.**
> **14 You broke the heads of Leviathan in pieces,**
> **And gave him as food to the people inhabiting the wilderness.**
> **15 You broke open the fountain and the flood;**
> **You dried up mighty rivers.**
> **16 The day is Yours, the night also is Yours;**
> **You have prepared the light and the sun.**
> **17 You have set all the borders of the earth;**
> **You have made summer and winter.**

Above all things 'handled', our purpose and plan is 'in HIS sights' and HE awaits our agreement to proceed.

Personally, I often declare how HE brought me up and out of situations, placed my feet on a solid base and kept me from losing hope!

What has HE done for you?

What has HE brought you out of?

Who knows what HE has done for you?

Repentance for _____?

Adjustment(s) planned? _____

DAY SIX

REVERENTIAL FEAR. Psalm 76:7.
    You, Yourself, are to be feared;
    And who may stand in Your presence
    When once You are angry?

Knowing HE created all by speaking and loves unconditionally, what can you do to speak into lives and love unconditionally?

Repentance for _____?

Adjustment(s) planned? _____

DAY SEVEN

BLESSING. Numbers 6:24-26.
    *"The L*ORD *bless you and keep you;*
    *25 The L*ORD *make His face shine upon you,*
        And be gracious to you;
    *26 The L*ORD *lift up His countenance upon you,*
        And give you peace." '

Blessings received: _____

Blessings shared: _____

Declarations/Testimonies: _____

WEEK TWENTY

DAY ONE
REVERENTIAL FEAR. Psalm 76:11-12.
Make vows to the Lord your God, and pay them;
Let all who are around Him bring presents to Him who ought to be feared.
12 He shall cut off the spirit of princes;
He is awesome to the kings of the earth.

A blessing to make the vow and carry it out!

May it always be a sweet, sweet sound!

Psalm 100.
A Song of Praise for the Lord's Faithfulness to His People
<u>**A Psalm of Thanksgiving.**</u>
Make a joyful shout to the Lord, all you lands!
2 Serve the Lord with gladness;
Come before His presence with singing.
3 Know that the Lord, He is God;
It is He who has made us, and not we ourselves;
We are His people and the sheep of His pasture.
4 Enter into His gates with thanksgiving,
And into His courts with praise.
Be thankful to Him, and bless His name.
5 For the Lord is good;
His mercy is everlasting,
And His truth endures to all generations.

The gifts to HIM are our praises and worship; sweet gifts to HIM while honoring HIM for ALL HE has done and provided, plus, orchestrated for us.

Repentance for _____ ?

Adjustment(s) planned? _____

DAY TWO

<u>DOUBT</u>. **Psalm 77:10-20.**
And I said, *This is my anguish;*
But I will remember the years of the right hand of the Most High.
11 I will remember the works of the Lord;
Surely I will remember Your wonders of old.
12 I will also meditate on all Your work,
And talk of Your deeds.
13 Your way, O God, is in the sanctuary;
Who is so great a God as our God?
14 You are the God who does wonders;
You have declared Your strength among the peoples.
15 You have with Your arm redeemed Your people,
The sons of Jacob and Joseph. Selah
16 The waters saw You, O God;
The waters saw You, they were afraid;
The depths also trembled.
17 The clouds poured out water;
The skies sent out a sound;
Your arrows also flashed about.

18 The voice of Your thunder was in the whirlwind;
The lightnings lit up the world;
The earth trembled and shook.
19 Your way was in the sea,
Your path in the great waters,
And Your footsteps were not known.
20 You led Your people like a flock
By the hand of Moses and Aaron.

What has our Father done for you, for your life?

Have you told HIM?

Repentance for _____?

Adjustment(s) planned? _____

DAY THREE

UNBELIEF. Psalm 78:12-20.

> Marvelous things He did in the sight of their fathers,
> In the land of Egypt, *in* the field of Zoan.
> 13 He divided the sea and caused them to pass through;
> And He made the waters stand up like a heap.
> 14 In the daytime also He led them with the cloud,
> And all the night with a light of fire.
> 15 He split the rocks in the wilderness,
> And gave *them* drink in abundance like the depths.
> 16 He also brought streams out of the rock,
> And caused waters to run down like rivers.
> But they sinned even more against Him
> By rebelling against the Most High in the wilderness.
> 18 And they tested God in their heart
> By asking for the food of their fancy.
> 19 Yes, they spoke against God:
> They said, *Can God prepare a table in the wilderness?*
> 20 *Behold, He struck the rock,*
> *So that the waters gushed out,*
> *And the streams overflowed.*
> *Can He give bread also?*
> *Can He provide meat for His people?*

Our Father provided ALL.

CHRIST paid the price for ALL.

Even when the promised land was provided, they wanted supply to be provided. Does anything in your life appear to align with the requests of the people who personally witnessed daily provision for years?

In fact, for decades?

Repentance for _____ ?

Adjustment(s) planned? _____

DAY FOUR

UNBELIEF. Psalm 78:32.
In spite of this they still sinned,
And did not believe in His wondrous works.

What is our Father prompting you to remember in this moment?

Repentance for _____ ?

Adjustment(s) planned? _____

DAY FIVE

FEAR. Psalm 78:53 (52-54).
But He made His own people go forth like sheep,
And guided them in the wilderness like a flock;
53 And He led them on safely, so that they did not fear;
But the sea overwhelmed their enemies.
54 And He brought them to His holy border,
This mountain which His right hand had acquired.

With full guidance, knowing the enemy is overhelmed and you are safe, what will you take on today with our Father?

Repentance for _____ ?

Adjustment(s) planned? _____

DAY SIX

FEAR. Psalm 91:5 (3-7).
Surely He shall deliver you from the snare of the fowler
And from the perilous pestilence.
4 He shall cover you with His feathers,

And under His wings you shall take refuge;
His truth shall be your shield and buckler.
5 You shall not be afraid of the terror by night,
Nor of the arrow that flies by day,
6 Nor of the pestilence that walks in darkness,
Nor of the destruction that lays waste at noonday.
7 A thousand may fall at your side,
And ten thousand at your right hand;
But it shall not come near you.

Exactly as the enemy was delivered to the kings and prophets, our Father is orchestrating on your behalf. What is HE revealing to you today, in your life?

Repentance for _____?

Adjustment(s) planned? _____

DAY SEVEN

BLESSING. **Numbers 6:24-26.**
    "The LORD bless you and keep you;
    25 The LORD make His face shine upon you,
       And be gracious to you;
    26 The LORD lift up His countenance upon you,
       And give you peace." '

Blessings received: _____

Blessings shared: _____

Declarations/Testimonies: _____

WEEK TWENTY-ONE

DAY ONE

FEAR. **Psalm 94:19 (16-19).**
    Who will rise up for me against the evildoers?
    Who will stand up for me against the workers of iniquity?
    17 Unless the Lord had been my help,
    My soul would soon have settled in silence.
    18 If I say, *My foot slips,*
    Your mercy, O Lord, will hold me up.
    19 In the multitude of my anxieties within me,
    Your comforts delight my soul.

Father it is a blessing to remember each of the times YOU held me up and YOU comforted me.

Repentance for _____?

Adjustment(s) planned? _____

DAY TWO

UNBELIEF. Psalm 95:8-11.
Do not harden your hearts, as in the rebellion,
As in the day of trial in the wilderness,
9 When your fathers tested Me;
They tried Me, though they saw My work.
10 For forty years I was grieved with that generation,
And said, 'It is a people who go astray in their hearts,
And they do not know My ways.'
11 So I swore in My wrath,
'They shall not enter My rest.'

Thank you Father for the times of entering into rest with YOU. Thank you for revealing the many times YOU have been patient to show me YOUR ways and brought me through my trial in the wilderness.

Repentance for _____?

Adjustment(s) planned? _____

DAY THREE

REVERENTIAL FEAR. Psalm 96:4.
For the Lord is great and greatly to be praised;
He is to be feared above all gods.

Father I praise YOU and stand in awe of how YOU have brought me through it all.

Repentance for _____?

Adjustment(s) planned? _____

DAY FOUR

REVERENTIAL FEAR. Psalm 102:15.
So the nations shall fear the name of the Lord,
And all the kings of the earth Your glory.

Father, thank YOU for providing this time 'on earth' to share YOUR truth.

Repentance for _____?

Adjustment(s) planned? _____

DAY FIVE

DOUBT. Psalm 105:1-6.
Oh, give thanks to the Lord!
Call upon His name;
Make known His deeds among the peoples!
2 Sing to Him, sing psalms to Him;
Talk of all His wondrous works!
3 Glory in His holy name;
Let the hearts of those rejoice who seek the Lord!
4 Seek the Lord and His strength;
Seek His face evermore!
5 Remember His marvelous works which He has done,
His wonders, and the judgments of His mouth,
6 O seed of Abraham His servant,
You children of Jacob, His chosen ones!

Father thank YOU for 'being there' when I cry out to YOU. The testimony of who YOU are and ALL YOU do for me will be shared far and wide. It is amazing how YOU strengthen me when I am weak, YOU continue to amaze me when I think I am defeated and believe the judgments of man. Grateful to be chosen by YOU.

Repentance for _____?

Adjustment(s) planned? _____

DAY SIX

UNBELIEF. Psalm 106:24 (21-27).
> They forgot God their Savior,
> Who had done great things in Egypt,
> 22 Wondrous works in the land of Ham,
> Awesome things by the Red Sea.
> 23 Therefore He said that He would destroy them,
> Had not Moses His chosen one stood before Him in the breach,
> To turn away His wrath, lest He destroy them.
> 24 Then they despised the pleasant land;
> They did not believe His word,
> 25 But complained in their tents,
> And did not heed the voice of the Lord.
> 26 Therefore He raised His hand in an oath against them,
> To overthrow them in the wilderness,
> 27 To overthrow their descendants among the nations,
> And to scatter them in the lands.

Father YOU have done so many things which confirm YOU are my GOD and me and my house will ONLY serve YOU!

Repentance for _____?

Adjustment(s) planned? _____

DAY SEVEN

BLESSING. Numbers 6:24-26.
> *"The LORD bless you and keep you;*
> *25 The LORD make His face shine upon you,*
> *And be gracious to you;*
> *26 The LORD lift up His countenance upon you,*
> *And give you peace." '*

Blessings received: _____

Blessings shared:_____

Declarations/Testimonies: _____

DAY ONE

FEAR. Psalm 118:6 (2-6).
Let Israel now say,
His mercy endures forever.
3 Let the house of Aaron now say,
His mercy endures forever.
4 Let those who fear the Lord now say,
His mercy endures forever.
5 I called on the Lord in distress;
The Lord answered me and set me in a broad place.
6 The Lord is on my side;
I will not fear.
What can man do to me?

Again, in what you are facing – whatever the challenge(s) may be – the LORD is on your side!

When I was in the deep depth of the debacle regarding my corporation, the trial and the fraud and corruption within the court, 'well meaning' Christians referred to the 'pressure' as 'being the middle so refer to the middle of the bible. It was not mentioned one time, it was declared to me again & again & again:

Psalm 118:18.
> **The Lord has chastened me severely,**
> **But He has not given me over to death.**

This was supposedly an amazing declaration, a message said to be linked to global references and NASA – it sounded impressive – and it was something I was told would assist me in 'getting out of the middle of a bad situation' but, it was NOT comforting and it did not feel like it was going to assist me AT ALL. What did the 'well meaning' Christians want me to know?

Were they thinking it would be good for me to know that no matter how horrible it would be while proceeding through the morass (at points, the quick sand vs. just a muddy bog) of the debacle would be devastating but, it would not kill me?

A lesson was learned in the depth of this debacle. Never before did I entertain the option to 'end my time on earth'. In the deepest moment, I added up

109

the insurance policy and equity in assets and the amount would more than resolve all expenses so I trusted it would be a good moment in time to make the decision. Prior to this exact moment in time, I was told and I believed only people who were 'not of sound mind' would consider taking their own life.

But, GOD knew HE had a plan for me and I agreed since the age of four to do whatever HE wants me to do!

In that moment, our Father immediately prompted me to read the verse 'in context'. It is what HE has stressed to me during this devotional. Too often, a scripture is quoted 'out of context'. Through tears, I turned to the scripture to read it 'in context':

> **Psalm 118:17-19.**
> **I shall not die, but live,**
> **And declare the works of the Lord.**
> **18 The Lord has chastened me severely,**
> **But He has not given me over to death.**
> **19 Open to me the gates of righteousness;**
> **I will go through them,**
> **And I will praise the Lord.**

TEARS!

Even in these moments, tears!

In just a few moments, I found out the TRUTH.

The TRUTH 'in context' is a different story!

Then, our LORD confirmed to me: **Psalm 118:18 is NOT the middle!**

The true middle of the bible (two verses due to even number of verses):

> **Psalm 103:1-2 is the exact middle (1-5, to see the list of benefits).**
> **Bless the Lord, O my soul;**
> **And all that is within me, bless His holy name!**
> **2 Bless the Lord, O my soul,**
> **And forget not all His benefits:**
> **3 Who forgives all your iniquities,**
> **Who heals all your diseases,**
> **4 Who redeems your life from destruction,**
> **Who crowns you with loving kindness and tender mercies,**
> **5 Who satisfies your mouth with good things,**
> **So that your youth is renewed like the eagle's.**

Tearful to realize I have personally, often, repeated what I was told because I accepted it as the truth.

In the moment while inserting this information within this Devotional, tears flowed and it is all personal and this devotional is for you, for you to to express yourself to our Father in a deep, personal way. So many tears, mainly because it is personal and it was 'our moments (only me & our Father) together', but our Father prompted me to realize the scripture would be important to share because His Son was tearful, also.

The facts being shared on this day are taking up so much space for just one day, I asked for HELP! I asked if a brief confirmation is available to insert.

Our Father immediately shared the brief confirmation in scripture. HIS truth is always so precious and succinct! HE confirmed the insert by prompting me to view the scripture which is also the shortest verse in the bible:

John 11:35. Jesus wept. Wow! Simple. Succinct. More tears!

Knowing HIS mercy endures forever, how does this deepen your relationship with our Father?

Repentance for _____?

Adjustment(s) planned? _____

DAY TWO
DOUBT. Psalm 119:116.
Uphold me according to Your word, that I may live;
And do not let me be ashamed of my hope.

This is exactly the same as it was with the father of the son who was healed of seizures **(Mark 9:24)**, with the father requesting help with his unbelief. With this request, our Father has the answer also within HIS promise to us: hope and a future (not tomorrow). Will you choose to live in hope regarding your future?

Repentance for _____?

Adjustment(s) planned? _____

DAY THREE
DOUBT. Psalm 119:130.
The entrance of Your words gives light;
It gives understanding to the simple.

Yes. Father keeps it simple. HIS word lifts, encourages and provides knowledge. Will you gain understanding and proceed based upon HIS wisdom?

Repentance for _____?

Adjustment(s) planned? _____

DAY FOUR

DOUBT. Psalm 119:147.
I rise before the dawning of the morning,
And cry for help;
I hope in Your word.

What would disturb rest? The enemy.

What would provide rest? Our Father, in relationship, prayer & HIS WORD. When you seek an answer today, will you go to the WORD, enter into prayer and choose to deepen your relationship with the Father?

Repentance for _____?

Adjustment(s) planned? _____

DAY FIVE

FEAR. Psalm 119:165 (161-168).
Princes persecute me without a cause,
But my heart stands in awe of Your word.
162 I rejoice at Your word
As one who finds great treasure.
163 I hate and abhor lying,
But I love Your law.
164 Seven times a day I praise You,
Because of Your righteous judgments.
165 Great peace have those who love Your law,
And nothing causes them to stumble.
166 Lord, I hope for Your salvation,
And I do Your commandments.
167 My soul keeps Your testimonies,
And I love them exceedingly.
168 I keep Your precepts and Your testimonies,
For all my ways are before You.

Father knows everything, about everything!

Regardless, how transparent are you in your relationship with our Father?

Repentance for _____?

Adjustment(s) planned? _____

DAY SIX
REVERENTIAL FEAR. Psalm 130:4.
But there is forgiveness with You,
That You may be feared.

Seeking forgiveness, immediate repentance, is the goal.

How quickly do you seek forgiveness and repent?

Is our Father reminding you about any issues or people to forgive?

Repentance for _____?

Adjustment(s) planned? _____

DAY SEVEN
BLESSING. Numbers 6:24-26.
"The LORD bless you and keep you;
25 The LORD make His face shine upon you,
And be gracious to you;
26 The LORD lift up His countenance upon you,
And give you peace." '

Blessings received: _____

Blessings shared: _____

Declarations/Testimonies: _____

WEEK TWENTY-THREE

DAY ONE

DOUBT. Psalm 143:5.
I remember the days of old;
I meditate on all Your works;
I muse on the work of Your hands.

Reviewing ALL our Father has done for HIS people, especially for you, and remembering the blessings upon your life through the years, the decades of your amazing life, what are the works of HIS hand which you thank HIM for?

Repentance for _____?

Adjustment(s) planned? _____

DAY TWO

FEAR. Proverbs 3:24. (21-24).
My son, let them not depart from your eyes—
Keep sound wisdom and discretion;
22 So they will be life to your soul
And grace to your neck.
23 Then you will walk safely in your way,
And your foot will not stumble.
24 When you lie down, you will not be afraid;
Yes, you will lie down and your sleep will be sweet.

Blessed rest in HIM due to a relationship built during a lifetime with HIM.

Are you enjoying blessed rest with the Father?

Repentance for _____?

Adjustment(s) planned? _____

DAY THREE

FEAR. Proverbs 3:25 (25-26).
Do not be afraid of sudden terror,
Nor of trouble from the wicked when it comes;
26 For the Lord will be your confidence,
And will keep your foot from being caught.

Again, because you are HIS, you will not stumble or fall when you remain with HIM for HE shall supply your strength, your confidence and provision of ALL for HE is a 'more than enough GOD'. With this reality clearly known by you, what adventure will you embark upon with our Father today?

Repentance for _____?

Adjustment(s) planned? _____

DAY FOUR

DOUBT. Proverbs 6:23.
For the commandment is a lamp,
And the law a light;
Reproofs of instruction are the way of life,
24 To keep you from the evil woman,
From the flattering tongue of a seductress.

114

It is important the reproofs (blame or disapproval) are based on the WORD and not the influence of a seducer. The scripture is focused upon 'going forward in the world and being careful in the journey to not be flattered by a seducer, an adulterer'. Are there influences upon your life which affect your decisions or change your plans from the path our Father has laid out before you?

Repentance for _____?

Adjustment(s) planned? _____

DAY FIVE

<u>**FEAR**</u>. **Ecclesiastes 11:10 (9-10).**
<u>**Seek God in Early Life**</u>
Rejoice, O young man, in your youth,
And let your heart cheer you in the days of your youth;
Walk in the ways of your heart,
And in the sight of your eyes;
But know that for all these
God will bring you into judgment.
10 Therefore remove sorrow from your heart,
And put away evil from your flesh,
For childhood and youth are vanity.

Many references to the scripture in Proverbs to train up a child in the way they should go ... it does make the path in life easier and smoother when TRUTH is known and acted on for knowledge of the word and 'gaining understanding' results in proceeding with the Father based upon HIS wisdom. Easier with the relationship gained early in life because it is clear that HIS ways are NOT our ways!   **Isaiah 55:8-9.**

> *For My thoughts are not your thoughts,*
> *Nor are your ways My ways,* **says the Lord.**
> *9 For as the heavens are higher than the earth,*
> *So are My ways higher than your ways,*
> *And My thoughts than your thoughts.*

Will today become a special day of gaining a closer relationship with the Father and seeking a higher level of understanding to discern if you are proceeding in your life aligned with the Father to gain the Father's perspective?

Repentance for _____?

Adjustment(s) planned? _____

DAY SIX

<u>FEAR</u>. Isaiah 7:4 (1-7).
<u>Isaiah Sent to King Ahaz</u>

Now it came to pass in the days of Ahaz the son of Jotham, the son of Uzziah, king of Judah, that Rezin king of Syria and Pekah the son of Remaliah, king of Israel, went up to Jerusalem to make war against it, but could not prevail against it. 2 And it was told to the house of David, saying, *Syria's forces are deployed in Ephraim.* So his heart and the heart of his people were moved as the trees of the woods are moved with the wind.

3 Then the Lord said to Isaiah, *Go out now to meet Ahaz, you and Shear-Jashub your son, at the end of the aqueduct from the upper pool, on the highway to the Fuller's Field,* 4 *and say to him: 'Take heed, and be quiet; do not fear or be fainthearted for these two stubs of smoking firebrands, for the fierce anger of Rezin and Syria, and the son of Remaliah.* 5 *Because Syria, Ephraim, and the son of Remaliah have plotted evil against you, saying,* 6 *Let us go up against Judah and trouble it, and let us make a gap in its wall for ourselves, and set a king over them, the son of Tabel* — 7 thus says the Lord God: *It shall not stand,*
                    Nor shall it come to pass.

Orchestration by the Father is beyond human comprehension.

When our Father would speak to me about things HE was planning, it seemed like an amazing adventure 'for someone'. It took a while to realize I would be involved in the adventure, and go, do and accomplish ONLY the amazing things prepared for me by our Father before I was aware of HIS assignment. Often, I find out AFTER the assignment is complete the depth of the assignment. It took me a while to realize the truth: **Our Father trusts us to accomplish the assignment before HE asks us!**

HE has taken care of the obstacles. HE has made the crooked way straight.

Will you accept the assignment knowing the plan of the enemy to thwart your progress shall not stand, nor shall it come to pass?

Repentance for _____?

Adjustment(s) planned? _____

DAY SEVEN

BLESSING. Numbers 6:24-26.
>*"The LORD bless you and keep you;*
>25 *The LORD make His face shine upon you,*
>   *And be gracious to you;*
>26 *The LORD lift up His countenance upon you,*
>   *And give you peace." '*

Blessings received: _____

Blessings shared: _____

Declarations/Testimonies: _____

WEEK TWENTY-FOUR

DAY ONE

FEAR. Isaiah 8:12 (11-15).
Fear God, Heed His Word

For the Lord spoke thus to me with a strong hand, and instructed me that I should not walk in the way of this people, saying:

12 *Do not say, 'A conspiracy,'*

Concerning all that this people call a conspiracy,

Nor be afraid of their threats, nor be troubled.

13 *The Lord of hosts, Him you shall hallow;*

Let Him be your fear,

And let Him be your dread.

14 *He will be as a sanctuary,*

But a stone of stumbling and a rock of offense

To both the houses of Israel,

As a trap and a snare to the inhabitants of Jerusalem.

15 *And many among them shall stumble;*

They shall fall and be broken,

Be snared and taken.

The conspiracy the people speak about ... those people are the ones who shall stumble, fall and be broken, be snared and taken.

Our Father has a better plan for you!

HE is your sanctuary!

HE has a plan and it will help you avoid the traps and the snares!

When HE is your sanctuary today, what is HE revealing to you?

Repentance for _____?

Adjustment(s) planned? _____

DAY TWO

REVERENTIAL FEAR Isaiah 8:13.
The Lord of hosts, Him you shall hallow;
Let Him be your fear,
And let Him be your dread.

Amazing difference between viewing our Father from a world view or a personal relationship as our LORD!

The world definition of dread is a level of fear which is terror.

The true definition of a dread fear of our LORD is to stand in AWE of who HE is for us! Important to NOT let anything come between us to lose the relationship with HIM as our Father.

What are a few of your examples, testimonies of what has caused you to stand in AWE of HIM?

Repentance for _____?

Adjustment(s) planned? _____

DAY THREE

FEAR. Isaiah 10:24 (20-26).
The Returning Remnant of Israel
20 And it shall come to pass in that day
That the remnant of Israel,
And such as have escaped of the house of Jacob,
Will never again depend on him who defeated them,
But will depend on the Lord, the Holy One of Israel, in truth.

21 The remnant will return, the remnant of Jacob,
To the Mighty God.
22 For though your people, O Israel, be as the sand of the sea,
A remnant of them will return;
The destruction decreed shall overflow with righteousness.
23 For the Lord God of hosts
Will make a determined end
In the midst of all the land.

24 Therefore thus says the Lord God of hosts: *O My people, who dwell in Zion, do not be afraid of the Assyrian. He shall strike you with a rod and lift up his staff against you, in the manner of Egypt.* 25 *For yet a very little while and the indignation will cease, as will My anger in their destruction.* 26 And the Lord of hosts will stir up a scourge for him like the slaughter of Midian at the rock of Oreb; as His rod was on the sea, so will He lift it up in the manner of Egypt.

The Remnant is returning to our FIRST LOVE.

The Remnant is forming, across the nation and globally.

Exciting to be a participant and a witness!

Our Father is orchestrating the process of waking many up to HIS TRUTH!

What is HE revealing to you in these days?

Repentance for _____?

Adjustment(s) planned? _____

DAY FOUR

<u>FEAR</u>. Isaiah 12:2 (1-2)
<u>A Hymn of Praise</u>
And in that day you will say:
O Lord, I will praise You;
Though You were angry with me,
Your anger is turned away, and You comfort me.
2 Behold, God is my salvation,
I will trust and not be afraid;
For Yah, the Lord, is my strength and song;
He also has become my salvation.'

Cherokee Stone Artifact. Paleo Hebrew: Hallelujah = Praise be to Yah!

No bibles to turn to for the truth.

Truth was etched on stone to be available 'for all time'.

Across America, stones were etched in ancient Paleo Hebrew lettering.

The messages reveal the ancient Paleo Hebrew confirmation the truth was 'in them' when the Native American Indians abundant upon the land and sharing the truth for more than two centuries before the Pilgrims/Puritans arrived.

What were the messages? Praise be to Yah and the Ten Commandments.

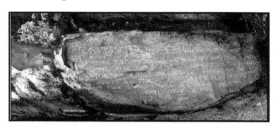

With nothing 'in print' they were willing to stand upon Praise be to Yah and the Ten Commandments. They expressed great faith. They stood firm and passed on the truth for 2300 years. With all of the resources available today, do you feel you are expressing great faith in your life?

Repentance for _____?

Adjustment(s) planned? _____

DAY FIVE

<u>**FEAR**</u>**. Isaiah 17:2 (1-3).**
<u>**Proclamation Against Syria and Israel**</u>
The burden against Damascus.
Behold, Damascus will cease from being a city,
And it will be a ruinous heap.
2 The cities of Aroer are forsaken;
They will be for flocks
Which lie down, and no one will make them afraid.
3 The fortress also will cease from Ephraim,
The kingdom from Damascus,
And the remnant of Syria;
They will be as the glory of the children of Israel,
Says the Lord of hosts.

A precious friend and deep woman of GOD, Rebecca King, shares many powerful revelations each time I share moments with her. One that I am prompted to share in this moment: On the road to Damascus journey (as Saul experienced, **Acts 9**), would your cry to our Father be: 'De mask us' (me)?

Repentance for _____?

Adjustment(s) planned? _____

DAY SIX

FEAR. Isaiah 26:3 (1-6).
A Song of Salvation
In that day this song will be sung in the land of Judah:

We have a strong city; God will appoint salvation for walls and bulwarks. 2 Open the gates, that the righteous nation which keeps the truth may enter in. 3 You will keep him in perfect peace, whose mind is stayed on You, because he trusts in You. 4 Trust in the Lord forever, for in Yah, the Lord, is everlasting strength. 5 For He brings down those who dwell on high, the lofty city; He lays it low, He lays it low to the ground, He brings it down to the dust. 6 The foot shall tread it down, the feet of the poor and the steps of the needy.

Our salvation & peace is with our Father. Is HIS peace evident in you?

Repentance for _____?

Adjustment(s) planned? _____

DAY SEVEN

BLESSING. Numbers 6:24-26.
> *"The LORD bless you and keep you;*
> *25 The LORD make His face shine upon you,*
>   *And be gracious to you;*
> *26 The LORD lift up His countenance upon you,*
>   *And give you peace." '*

Blessings received: _____

Blessings shared: _____

Declarations/Testimonies: _____

WEEK TWENTY-FIVE

DAY ONE
REVERENTIAL FEAR. Isaiah 29:23 (22-24).

Therefore thus says the LORD, who redeemed Abraham, concerning the house of Jacob:

> *Jacob shall not now be ashamed,*
> *Nor shall his face now grow pale;*
> **23** *But when he sees his children,*
> *The work of My hands, in his midst,*
> *They will hallow My name,*
> *And hallow the Holy One of Jacob,*
> *And fear the God of Israel.*
> **24** *These also who erred in spirit*
> *will come to understanding,*
> *And those who complained will learn doctrine.*

The miracle of unity in the family, immediate, extended and within the body of believers is evident when we can SEE the work of HIS hands in the lives of the people we know! Do you live expecting to see the handiwork of our Father in the lives of your children, your siblings, the ones you love?

Repentance for _____?

Adjustment(s) planned? _____

DAY TWO

<u>FEAR</u>. Isaiah 35:4 (1-4).
<u>The Future Glory of Zion</u>
The wilderness and the wasteland shall be glad for them,
And the desert shall rejoice and blossom as the rose;
2 It shall blossom abundantly and rejoice,
Even with joy and singing.
The glory of Lebanon shall be given to it,
The excellence of Carmel and Sharon.
They shall see the glory of the Lord,
The excellency of our God.
3 Strengthen the weak hands,
And make firm the feeble knees.
4 Say to those who are fearful-hearted,
Be strong, do not fear!
Behold, your God will come with vengeance,
With the recompense of God;
He will come and save you.

Ah, the glory of California and Arizona, Montana and the Dakotas. The excellence of New York and DC for they shall see the glory of the LORD!

Did I take the words right out of your mouth?

How are you declaring what is and what is to come, in your life, your family and your region, your state and your nation?

Repentance for _____?

Adjustment(s) planned? _____

DAY THREE

FEAR. Isaiah 37:6 (1-7).
Isaiah Assures Deliverance
And so it was, when King Hezekiah heard it, that he tore his clothes, covered himself with sackcloth, and went into the house of the Lord. 2 Then he sent Eliakim, who was over the household, Shebna the scribe, and the elders of the priests, covered with sackcloth, to Isaiah the prophet, the son of Amoz. 3 And they said to him, *Thus says Hezekiah: 'This day is a day of trouble and rebuke and blasphemy; for the children have come to birth, but there is no strength to bring them forth.* **4** *It may be that the Lord your God will hear the words of the Rabshakeh, whom his master the king of Assyria has sent to reproach the living God, and will rebuke the words which the Lord your God has heard. Therefore lift up your prayer for the remnant that is left.'*

5 So the servants of King Hezekiah came to Isaiah. 6 And Isaiah said to them, Thus you shall say to your master, *'Thus says the Lord: Do not be afraid of the words which you have heard, with which the servants of the king of Assyria have blasphemed Me.* **7** *Surely I will send a spirit upon him, and he shall hear a rumor and return to his own land; and I will cause him to fall by the sword in his own land.'*

When we are aligned with our Father, those who operate against with will be dealt with 'by the sword'! What is the sword in our armor? The Holy Spirit!

Therefore, when we are proceeding 'as an empty vessel' and our Father fills us with the words and guides us with the actions, we are 'in the battle' while it is truly being handled by the LORD. So, when the WORD is given direct to you from the Holy Spirit within the challenge you are facing 'in the moment', will you speak the WORD you are given?

Repentance for _____?

Adjustment(s) planned? _____

FEAR. Isaiah 40:9.
O Zion, you who bring good tidings,
Get up into the high mountain;
O Jerusalem, you who bring good tidings,
Lift up your voice with strength,
Lift it up, be not afraid;
Say to the cities of Judah, *Behold your God!*

As an ambassador, will you lift up your voice with strength and not be afraid because you represent HIM 'in the midst'?

Repentance for _____?

Adjustment(s) planned? _____

DAY FIVE

DOUBT. Isaiah 40:28-31.
Have you not known? Have you not heard?
The everlasting God, the Lord, the Creator of the ends of the earth,
Neither faints nor is weary. His understanding is unsearchable.
29 He gives power to the weak,
And to those who have no might He increases strength.
30 Even the youths shall faint and be weary,
And the young men shall utterly fall,
31 But those who wait on the Lord shall renew their strength;
They shall mount up with wings like eagles,
They shall run and not be weary, they shall walk and not faint.

A song which blessed me, repeatedly during the deep depths of the issues: ***On Eagle's Wings*** by Michael Crawford. Tears when he says ... ***HE will raise you up on Eagle's Wings ... and HE will hold you in the palm of HIS hand.*** Will you arrange time with HIM today to let HIM wrap HIS arms around you, raise you up on Eagle's Wings, and hold you in the palm of HIS hand?

Repentance for _____?

Adjustment(s) planned? _____

DAY SIX
DOUBT, also **FEAR**. Isaiah 41:10 (8-10).

But you, Israel, are My servant,
Jacob whom I have chosen, the descendants of Abraham My friend.
9 You whom I have taken from the ends of the earth,
And called from its farthest regions, and said to you, 'You are My servant,
I have chosen you and have not cast you away:
10 Fear not, for I am with you; Be not dismayed, for I am your God.
I will strengthen you, Yes, I will help you,
I will uphold you with My righteous right hand.'

Grateful HE will uphold us with HIS righteous right hand. HIS perfect religion is to see to the needs of the widows and orphans. Honored to seek them out in each region where HE places my feet. Another great Michael Crawford song that helped me focus on others vs. my issues: *Not Too Far From Here.* Whatever they need Father, may we be made aware for it is our desire to hear you say, *Well done, good and faithful servant.* Can you imagine what it will be like to see HIM, seated in the throne with CHRIST immediately to HIS right?

Repentance for _____?

Adjustment(s) planned? _____

DAY SEVEN

BLESSING. Numbers 6:24-26.
> *"The Lord bless you and keep you;*
> *25 The Lord make His face shine upon you,*
> *And be gracious to you;*
> *26 The Lord lift up His countenance upon you,*
> *And give you peace." '*

Blessings received: _____

Blessings shared: _____

Declarations/Testimonies: _____

WEEK TWENTY-SIX

DAY ONE
FEAR. Isaiah 41:13 (11-13).
Behold, all those who were incensed against you
Shall be ashamed and disgraced;

125

They shall be as nothing,
And those who strive with you shall perish.
12 You shall seek them and not find them—
Those who contended with you.
Those who war against you
Shall be as nothing,
As a nonexistent thing.
13 For I, the Lord your God, will hold your right hand,
Saying to you, 'Fear not, I will help you.'

Yes. HE will disgrace all who are angry and operating against you. In fact, they shall be as NOTHING and those who strive against you will perish!

This has happened so many times in my life. In fact, people have asked if I had anything to do with the destruction of the people who have come against me in unique and bizarre ways. NOTHING is done by me regarding the person. It can shock and surprise people when they witness the status after the months of attacks against me 'without basis or merit'.

Matthew 5:43-48.
Love Your Enemies
You have heard that it was said, 'You shall love your neighbor and hate your enemy.' 44 But I say to you, love your enemies, bless those who curse you, do good to those who hate you, and pray for those who spitefully use you and persecute you, 45 that you may be sons of your Father in heaven; for He makes His sun rise on the evil and on the good, and sends rain on the just and on the unjust. 46 For if you love those who love you, what reward have you? Do not even the tax collectors do the same? 47 And if you greet your [p]brethren only, what do you do more than others? Do not even the [q]tax collectors do so? 48 Therefore you shall be perfect, just as your Father in heaven is perfect.

PRAY FOR YOUR ENEMIES! Prayers of the righteous avail much! The war and all involved against you shall be as NOTHING, as a nonexistent thing!!! Can you imagine it?

Repentance for _____?

Adjustment(s) planned? _____

DAY TWO
FEAR. Isaiah 41:14 (14-16).
Fear not, you worm Jacob,
You men of Israel!
I will help you, **says the Lord**

And your Redeemer, the Holy One of Israel.
15 Behold I will make you into a new threshing sledge with sharp teeth;
You shall thresh the mountains and beat them small,
And make the hills like chaff.
16 You shall winnow them, the wind shall carry them away,
And the whirlwind shall scatter them;
You shall rejoice in the Lord,
And glory in the Holy One of Israel.

Father is ready, waiting to help. Will you invite HIM into the situation and let HIM help you?

Repentance for _____?

Adjustment(s) planned? _____

DAY THREE

DOUBT. Isaiah 42:3.
A bruised reed He will not break,
And smoking flax He will not quench;
He will bring forth justice for truth.

Justice is based upon truth and HE will bring forth justice for truth. What is the justice HE will bring forth on your behalf for truth?

Repentance for _____?

Adjustment(s) planned? _____

DAY FOUR

FEAR. Isaiah 43:1 (1-4).
The Redeemer of Israel
But now, thus says the Lord, who created you, O Jacob,
And He who formed you, O Israel:
Fear not, for I have redeemed you;
I have called you by your name;
You are Mine.
2 *When you pass through the waters, I will be with you;*
And through the rivers, they shall not overflow you.
When you walk through the fire, you shall not be burned,
Nor shall the flame scorch you.
3 *For I am the Lord your God,*
The Holy One of Israel, your Savior;
I gave Egypt for your ransom,
Ethiopia and Seba in your place.

4 *Since you were precious in My sight,*
You have been honored,
And I have loved you;
Therefore I will give men for you,
And people for your life.

HE has redeemed us. HE called us by name! We are HIS! Again, HE is prompting me about a special song which has blessed many fellowships: *You Know My Name* by Tasha Cobbs Leonard. HE has the plan ready for us! Wherever HE places our feet, HE will be with us for we are precious in HIS sight! What is HE saying about you?

Repentance for _____?

Adjustment(s) planned? _____

DAY FIVE

DOUBT. Isaiah 43:2.
When you pass through the waters, I will be with you;
And through the rivers, they shall not overflow you.
When you walk through the fire, you shall not be burned,
Nor shall the flame scorch you.

HE has it all planned out! HE knows the end from the beginning!

Again, another powerful song by a well know worship leader: *You Are Not Alone* by Rick Pino. The song is all about what happened when Shadrach, Meshach and Abednego were in the furnace. They were not 'alone'! There was a fourth man in the fire! The song confirms what the witnesses saw: *There's A Fourth Man In The Fire!* As Wigglesworth confirmed, when we are aligned with the word HE will position you in the right place at the right time! What is an example testimony HE arranged for you, a demonstration to witnesses?

Repentance for _____?

Adjustment(s) planned? _____

DAY SIX

FEAR. Isaiah 43:5 (5-7).
Fear not, for I am with you;
I will bring your descendants from the east,

And gather you from the west;
6 I will say to the north, 'Give them up!'
And to the south, 'Do not keep them back!'
Bring My sons from afar,
And My daughters from the ends of the earth—
7 Everyone who is called by My name,
Whom I have created for My glory;
I have formed him, yes, I have made him.

HE formed you; created you for HIS glory. HE sent you 'for such a time as this'. HE trusts you! HE called you by name, because HE has plans for you to live abundantly and prosper and to ALL who have ears to hear and eyes to see, HE will reveal the truth about who you are for HIM while you are 'on earth'. What is HE revealing to you about the plans HE formed you for while 'on earth' in these days?

Repentance for _____?

Adjustment(s) planned? _____

DAY SEVEN

BLESSING. Numbers 6:24-26.
"The LORD bless you and keep you;
25 The LORD make His face shine upon you,
*   And be gracious to you;*
26 The LORD lift up His countenance upon you,
*   And give you peace." '*

Blessings received: _____

Blessings shared:_____

Declarations/Testimonies: _____

2nd **QUARTER: What is our Father revealing to you, about you?**

_____

WEEK TWENTY-SEVEN

DAY ONE

FEAR. Isaiah 44:2 (1-5).
God's Blessing on Israel

Yet hear now, O Jacob My servant,
And Israel whom I have chosen.
2 Thus says the Lord who made you
And formed you from the womb, who will help you:
'Fear not, O Jacob My servant;
And you, Jeshurun, whom I have chosen.
3 For I will pour water on him who is thirsty,
And floods on the dry ground;
I will pour My Spirit on your descendants,
And My blessing on your offspring;
4 They will spring up among the grass
Like willows by the watercourses.'
5 One will say, 'I am the Lord's';
Another will call himself by the name of Jacob;
Another will write with his hand, 'The Lord's,'
And name himself by the name of Israel.

NOTHING was understood about the debacle my life was encased within, NOT my family or friends or professional associates I knew for many years.

Once I realized the ONLY one who understood the depth of ALL of it was our Father, I repented and sought HIS truth! HE took my hand. HE lifted me up. HE encouraged me. HE provided for me and supplied comfort in the midnight hour! IF Zach Williams would have released his songs back then: ***Fear is a Liar*** would have revealed I am NOT the only one going through the attacks by the enemy, it is happening BECAUSE I am chosen and beloved by the LORD which makes the enemy jealous! Then, after realizing the depth of the subtle yet pervasive layers of the lies resulting in 'enslavement' without our knowledge, Zach released: ***No Longer Slaves.*** When you have time to listen and view the amazing video version of both songs prepared while Zach was at Harding prison, you will be richly and mightily blessed by viewing the impact upon the hearts of the inmates! Powerful!

Will you align with our Father's plan today to lift you up and out of the situation(s) you are in as he did for me and for Zach and share your testimony which will impact lives as you continue to walk forward in faith?

Repentance for _____?

Adjustment(s) planned? _____

FEAR. Isaiah 44:8 (6-8).
<u>There Is No Other God</u>
Thus says the Lord, the King of Israel,
And his Redeemer, the Lord of hosts:
'I am the First and I am the Last;
Besides Me there is no God.
7 And who can proclaim as I do?
Then let him declare it and set it in order for Me,
Since I appointed the ancient people.
And the things that are coming and shall come,
Let them show these to them.
8 Do not fear, nor be afraid;
Have I not told you from that time, and declared it?
You are My witnesses.
Is there a God besides Me?
Indeed there is no other Rock;
I know not one.'

Realizing who we are 'in HIM' and because CHRIST 'resides in our heart', praying many are ready to hear the REAL TRUTH and awaken from the slumber the enemy has placed the people in 'on purpose'.

As in the song from King & Country: **Amen.** *Death to Life – Dark to Light*

- You are in my blood – You gave it all for me, I'll give it all for you... Amen

Idolatry Is Foolishness is the next portion of **Isaiah 44.** Powerful to review.

HE gave it ALL for you. Is there something you are holding on to or are you willing to give all to HIM?

Repentance for _____?

Adjustment(s) planned? _____

DAY THREE

DOUBT. Isaiah 46:9.
Remember the former things of old,
For I am God, and there is no other;
I am God, and there is none like Me,
10 Declaring the end from the beginning,
And from ancient times things that are not yet done,
Saying, 'My counsel shall stand,
And I will do all My pleasure,'

11 Calling a bird of prey from the east,
The man who executes My counsel, from a far country.
Indeed I have spoken it;
I will also bring it to pass.
I have purposed it;
I will also do it.

The words of our Father are ETERNAL! We forget, at times, we are ETERNAL. Our Father's word will NOT CHANGE AT ANY TIME in HIStory! Another King & Country song comes to mind: *No Turning Back.*

When all appeared to be 'a loss' so often, people close to me wondered how I could be OK with the status, how I could still enjoy life. The answer was easy: GOD, HE has brought me through ALL of it and I know what life is like when I let the enemy keep taking me lower. That is NOT going to happen any more!

As the song confirms: *I used to be ... until I got an invitation into the courts of the King.*

What will you do with your 'invitation into the courts of the King'?

Repentance for _____ ?

Adjustment(s) planned? _____

DAY FOUR

FEAR. Isaiah 51:7 (7-8).
Listen to Me, you who know righteousness,
You people in whose heart is My law:
Do not fear the reproach of men,
Nor be afraid of their insults.
8 For the moth will eat them up like a garment,
And the worm will eat them like wool;
But My righteousness will be forever,
And My salvation from generation to generation.

Again, we are ETERNAL. After all, what can mere mortals do to us?

Special gift for us to realize we KNOW righteousness.

We know GOD's law and the basis of the laws, the Ten Commandments.

Plus, we have salvation through CHRIST and HE resides in our heart.

So, how could any of the insults from people (or the demons operating within them) affect us?

Lies last for a few moments and they may cause you to feel disheartened, hurt or damaged 'temporarily' but, the TRUTH will be revealed and it is what stands for ALL TIME!

We are witnessing a major example of a leader, a deep man of GOD being insulted and attacked from every angle in these days, and the same is true for every member of his family and yet, they are remaining in TRUTH, aligned with the will of our Father to fulfill upon the RIGHTEOUS plans laid out before them 'on our behalf' because they are truly there to serve us, the people!

If people walked in discernment they would be able to easily witness and confirm in their testimonies the TRUTH regarding the 'days we are living in'!

It is endearing to realize the expression from our father about the moth and the worm. Great visuals!

Knowing HIS righteousness, plus, the promise it will be with us forever and passed on from generation to generation, what will you and our Father decide to embark upon today?

Repentance for _____?

Adjustment(s) planned? _____

DAY FIVE

UNBELIEF. Isaiah 53:1.
Who has believed our report?
And to whom has the arm of the Lord been revealed?

Seek the testimonies of the saints! It is a powerful way to become a witness to the miracles of our Father when you hear the dreams and visions, the healings and miraculous works of the hand of our LORD in their lives!

Trusting this is why our Father confirmed the perfect and undefiled religion is to see to the needs of the widows and orphans as defined in **James 1:27**, the last verse of James, *Pure and undefiled religion before God and the Father is*

133

this: to visit orphans and widows in their trouble, and to keep oneself unspotted from the world.

Tearful to hear the same confession that the believers have no idea where the orphanages are located or the condition of the widows, no matter where HE places my feet, region to region, globally. Only in America am I challenged to speak 'politically correct' and call the orphanage a 'children's home'. It is tearful because AN ORPHAN HEART is evident in believers who had two parents and yet, they feel abandoned!

Orphans clearly live with an 'orphan heart' crying out to know somebody, somewhere cares about them. They only know 'their truth': ***They were 'dropped off' and they are orphaned, seeking LOVE.***

Now, with the subsidies paid by the government, the teams working with the widows and orphans are restricted regarding what they can do even when the orphanage or the senior home for widows are church based (typically a denomination). Often I am given the name and phone number by a resident to call and pray for a team member they loved, a person fired for praying with the residents. This is even happening all across America. I've called the corporate structures over the residences for orphans and widows and they will NOT adjust to 'be there' for the widows or orphans in the deep searching of the soul they experience due to their condition.

A wonderful testimony from a church in central coast California after I shared the scripture about seeing to the needs of the widows & orphans:

1. The pastor emailed me while I was in London 30 days later to report that least 30 orphans are being placed with families in the area, families who were not aware of the location of the orphanages before I mentioned **James 1:27.**

2. The pastor and his leadership prayed about what to do on behalf of the widows in their church. GOD revealed the widows (7) were to be blessed with $3,000 each during the next Sunday service. The pastor asked for the widows to come forward and the church prayed until seven widows came forward. The widows were 'in

awe' of what our Father revealed to the leadership as they were handed $3,000 each. The widows confirmed they were always asked how much they could give from their pension and the estate of their husband.

In fact, denominations are now establishing teams of retired pastors to meet with the senior couples and widows to see if they will leave the estate to the church. Father may YOUR will be done, YOUR Kingdom come and shower truth upon us in these unique days in HIStory!

The widows I assist in various parts of the country are deeply appreciative for the help. As they age, as we all do, they are shorter and unable to reach the shelf in a store to purchase items they were able to obtain on a regular basis before. They often want a few gallons of good water to keep in stock, and they are not able to lift the gallons anymore. They still do a lot of ironing and they also need distilled water. They often need products from a drug store and it is too far for the to walk (most do not drive anymore and some never drove a car before they moved to senior housing). Some merely deserve prayer and the knowledge they are cared about and loved!

Another precious testimony of an orphan known as Lauren is provided within *For The Sake Of America.* The few moments I met with her helped her distinguish TRUTH from GOD vs the enemy. Her testimony to a local congregation the next Sunday included the fact GOD loves her so much he sent SOMEBODY to let her know she is LOVED and her life turned around; restrictions lifted, even though teachers and social workers NEVER change a record, they knew they had to do it for her ... two weeks later, because she shared the testimony with her mother and they prayed together, her mother got a job. Her mother was unemployed for a year so Lauren was 'dropped off' at the Masonic Orphanage in Macon, Georgia. She was there 18 months before I met her for a brief visit and prayer time. Within the two weeks of my visit with her, her mother had a job. Lauren's life was turning around. Plus, our Father woke a woman up at midnight who did not know my name but, heard about me and she was told by our Father to donate her car to me March, 2015, ALSO 18 months after my first trip to Georgia 'for three specific weeks'.

Knowing it is all about SOULS, what is Father prompting you to begin to do today, an action step you have not taken before?

Repentance for _____?

Adjustment(s) planned? _____

DAY SIX

FEAR. Isaiah 54:4 (4-8).
Do not fear, for you will not be ashamed;
Neither be disgraced, for you will not be put to shame;
For you will forget the shame of your youth,
And will not remember the reproach of your widowhood anymore.
5 *For your Maker is your husband,*
The Lord of hosts is His name;
And your Redeemer is the Holy One of Israel;
He is called the God of the whole earth.
6 *For the Lord has called you*
Like a woman forsaken and grieved in spirit,
Like a youthful wife when you were refused,
Says your God.
7 *For a mere moment I have forsaken you,*
But with great mercies I will gather you.
8 *With a little wrath I hid My face from you for a moment;*
But with everlasting kindness I will have mercy on you,
Says the Lord, your Redeemer.

When we are prompted to be with the orphans and widows they will forget the isolation and hold on to the prayers and words from our Heavenly Father confirming they are loved! The widows always want new music so I arrange worship music for them. They appreciate **Steven Swanson, Terry Macalmon** and the **Gaither** music CDs and channels. When I introduce them to **Josh Mills** with the song *Glory Realm*, I witness tears every time they hear the prophetic word by Ruth Heflin included within the song. Any isolation we feel, moments of isolation, it will be only moments for our Father gathers us up with HIS great mercies. In the meantime, when we proceed in love and bring joy to those who truly do feel isolated from the world, and we share a prayer with them, the encouraging words lift them up and out of their moments of loneliness.

Is our Father prompting you to see to the needs of the widows and orphans your region? Arrange a van so they can fellowship with you and fellow believers? A phone call for prayer or a prayer time with them? A trip to a store?

Repentance for _____?

Adjustment(s) planned? _____

DAY SEVEN

__BLESSING.__ **Numbers 6:24-26.**
> *"The LORD bless you and keep you;*
> 25 *The LORD make His face shine upon you,*
>   *And be gracious to you;*
> 26 *The LORD lift up His countenance upon you,*
>   *And give you peace." '*

Blessings received: _____

Blessings shared: _____

Declarations/Testimonies: _____

WEEK TWENTY-EIGHT

DAY ONE

__FEAR.__ **Isaiah 54:14 (11-15).**
O you afflicted one,
Tossed with tempest, and not comforted,
Behold, I will lay your stones with colorful gems,
And lay your foundations with sapphires.
12 I will make your pinnacles of rubies,
Your gates of crystal,
And all your walls of precious stones.
13 All your children shall be taught by the Lord,
And great shall be the peace of your children.
14 In righteousness you shall be established;
You shall be far from oppression, for you shall not fear;
And from terror, for it shall not come near you.
15 Indeed they shall surely assemble, but not because of Me.
Whoever assembles against you shall fall for your sake.

We are HIS beloved, is HE yours?

Repentance for _____?

Adjustment(s) planned? _____

DAY TWO

<u>REVERENTIAL FEAR</u>. Isaiah 59:19.
So shall they fear
The name of the Lord from the west,
And His glory from the rising of the sun;
When the enemy comes in like a flood,
The Spirit of the Lord will lift up a standard against him.

Remaining in thanksgiving!

When the lies start to swirl, I stop all action and THANK our FATHER for EVERY THING. I keep the list going until HIS peace returns!

No matter WHAT the situation looks like, doing all to remain in praise and thanksgiving, retaining peace.

A dear friend and woman of GOD, Rebecca King, shared a very deep message regarding 'living in eternal time' where no traumas exist. She offered the option to pray over the injury, any symptoms based upon the trauma, declaring the symptoms were NOT meant for us and thank our Father for full healing. Amazing results for me, with a water pocket on my knee due to being a passenger in an auto accident years before! An injury which resulted in the feeling of two red hot swords inserting in that spot EACH TIME I was walking into a meeting, climbing the steps to a church a descending the steps into a conference room to speak as a representative for our Father. Coincidence? I think not! Regardless, the injury of many years was healed in the moment!

It was so clear to me when she explained: *Have you noticed when you fall or you are in a car accident, everything starts moving 'in slow motion'? This is due to the enemy 'squeezing' the trauma into eternal time.*

What is GOD prompting you to pray about in this moment due to symptoms of a trauma which was NOT meant for you?

Repentance for _____?

Adjustment(s) planned? _____

<u>UNBELIEF</u>. **Isaiah 65:2 (1-5).**
<u>**The Righteousness of God's Judgment**</u>
I was sought by those who did not ask for Me;
I was found by those who did not seek Me.
I said, 'Here I am, here I am,'
To a nation that was not called by My name.
2 I have stretched out My hands all day long to a rebellious people,
Who walk in a way that is not good,
According to their own thoughts;
3 A people who provoke Me to anger continually to My face;
Who sacrifice in gardens,
And burn incense on altars of brick;
4 Who sit among the graves,
And spend the night in the tombs;
Who eat swine's flesh,
And the broth of abominable things is in their vessels;
5 Who say, 'Keep to yourself,
Do not come near me,
For I am holier than you!'
These are smoke in My nostrils,
A fire that burns all the day.

Evil rituals are all around us, in every nation of the world.

Their calendar days of specific evil rituals have never changed.

We are not 'as aware' in these days because we have established a very comfortable life and we consider our lives as civilized and orderly and evil rituals as just 'something from ancient days'.

Often, the 'ancient days theory' becomes an excuse since many dismiss the idea due to the fact the gospel has gone to the entire world, and there are reports that all nations have received the gospel. These facts are true.

However, evil rituals, the enemy's plans to capture as many souls as possible has never changed since ancient days! The blood based rituals, the annual Satanic calendar identifying dates of human sacrifice, of dismembering and killing to have the blood and then, to do rituals with the blood and body parts. Nothing about the evil rituals has changed since ancient times.

Due to claiming your salvation, our Father rejoices in the truth that you choose to be in the fellowship, the Family of GOD!

Knowing this, what is our Father prompting you to remember and release to him today? Are there any action steps you can take based on the knowledge you have so you can walk in your purpose and plan for your life while 'on earth'?

Repentance for _____?

Adjustment(s) planned? _____

DAY FOUR

REVERENTIAL FEAR. Isaiah 66:2.
For all those things My hand has made,
And all those things exist,
Says the Lord.
But on this one will I look:
On him who is poor and of a contrite spirit,
And who trembles at My word.

Our life, our soul, knowing CHRIST resides in our heart is what is important to our Father. What is HE confirming to you, about you, today?

Repentance for _____?

Adjustment(s) planned? _____

DAY FIVE

FEAR. Jeremiah 1:8 (4-8).
The Prophet Is Called
Then the word of the Lord came to me, saying:
5 Before I formed you in the womb I knew you;
Before you were born I sanctified you;
I ordained you a prophet to the nations.
6 Then said I:
Ah, Lord God!
Behold, I cannot speak, for I am a youth.
7 But the Lord said to me:
Do not say, 'I am a youth,'

For you shall go to all to whom I send you,
And whatever I command you, you shall speak.
8 *Do not be afraid of their faces,*
For I am with you to deliver you, **says the Lord.**

The church is formed with the apostles and prophets and CHRIST as the Chief Cornerstone, with the pastors, teachers and evangelists.

Before we were born we were connected with our Father. HE knew us and sanctified us and prepared us for the purpose and plan HE prepared for us. From day one HE is with us. HE will deliver us from whatever traps are set up to affect us and attempt us to enter into fear, doubt or unbelief.

Will you seek the plans our Father has for you since HE formed you in the womb?

Repentance for _____?

Adjustment(s) planned? _____

DAY SIX

REVERENTIAL FEAR. Jeremiah 5:22-24.
'Do you not fear Me?' **says the Lord.**
'Will you not tremble at My presence,
Who have placed the sand as the bound of the sea,
By a perpetual decree, that it cannot pass beyond it?
And though its waves toss to and fro,
Yet they cannot prevail;
Though they roar, yet they cannot pass over it.
23 *But this people has a defiant and rebellious heart;*
They have revolted and departed.
24 *They do not say in their heart,*
Let us now fear the Lord our God,
Who gives rain, both the former and the latter, in its season.
He reserves for us the appointed weeks of the harvest.

Everything is 'in position' exactly as our Father placed it according to HIS purpose, 'to be, in the exact position at the exact time'. HE confirms, again, HE's got this! HE is the ONLY one who knows the end from the beginning: *... the rain, both former and the latter, in its season. He reserves for us the appointed weeks of the harvest.* What is HE revealing about your season & harvest?

Repentance for _____?

Adjustment(s) planned? _____

DAY SEVEN

BLESSING. Numbers 6:24-26.
> *"The LORD bless you and keep you;*
> *25 The LORD make His face shine upon you,*
> *And be gracious to you;*
> *26 The LORD lift up His countenance upon you,*
> *And give you peace." '*

Blessings received: _____

Blessings shared:_____

Declarations/Testimonies: _____

DAY ONE

UNBELIEF. Jeremiah 7:26.
Yet they did not obey Me or incline their ear, but stiffened their neck. They did worse than their fathers.

Believers did not listen to the many prophets our Father sent.

Will you discern the truth from a prophet and know GOD sent them and expand the truth in the region so many hear the truth from the LORD?

Or, will you 'become a stiff neck, a disobedient person' affecting this generation in ways which cause them to turn away from the LORD?

Repentance for _____?

Adjustment(s) planned? _____

DAY TWO

FEAR. Jeremiah 10:5 (1-5).
Idols and the True God
Hear the word which the Lord speaks to you, O house of Israel.
2 Thus says the Lord:
Do not learn the way of the Gentiles;
Do not be dismayed at the signs of heaven,
For the Gentiles are dismayed at them.
3 For the customs of the peoples are futile;
For one cuts a tree from the forest,
The work of the hands of the workman, with the ax.
4 They decorate it with silver and gold;
They fasten it with nails and hammers
So that it will not topple.
5 They are upright, like a palm tree,
And they cannot speak;
They must be carried,
Because they cannot go by themselves.
Do not be afraid of them,
For they cannot do evil,
Nor can they do any good.

The Gentiles followed the pagan calendar and rituals.

This scripture includes the pagan rituals at Christmas.

Father desires for us to know HIM, HIS ways, HIS feasts and festivals.

The Gentiles did NOT operate in power and authority of the LORD.

Our Father hopes we will learn HIS truth so we WILL operate in HIS power and authority. What is the truth our Father is revealing to you, about your life?

Repentance for _____?

Adjustment(s) planned? _____

DAY THREE

REVERENTIAL FEAR. Jeremiah 10:7.
Who would not fear You, O King of the nations?
For this is Your rightful due.
For among all the wise men of the nations,
And in all their kingdoms,
There is none like You.

A reminder of the blessing for us to be HIS, to stand in awe of who HE is, experiencing life knowing HE protects us at all times because HE loves us and divinely protects all who live in reverential fear of our Father.

HE is over ALL people, all nations, all kingdoms, including us. As a joint her with Christ, what is HE revealing to you about your specific life plan?

Repentance for _____?

Adjustment(s) planned? _____

DAY FOUR

FEAR. Jeremiah 17:8 (5-8).
Thus says the Lord:
Cursed is the man who trusts in man
And makes flesh his strength,
Whose heart departs from the Lord.
6 For he shall be like a shrub in the desert,
And shall not see when good comes,
But shall inhabit the parched places in the wilderness,
In a salt land which is not inhabited.
7 Blessed is the man who trusts in the Lord,

And whose hope is the Lord.
8 For he shall be like a tree planted by the waters,
Which spreads out its roots by the river,
And will not fear when heat comes;
But its leaf will be green,
And will not be anxious in the year of drought,
Nor will cease from yielding fruit.

It was immediately easy to visualize the cursed, dry and salty person!

Then, to realize it was the result of departing from the LORD!

Then, to be prompted by our Father to remember, to realize all of the provision 'just for me' which is evident to all in my life, even during the lean years, the deep years of drought.

Plus, to know I was never 'without HIM' or 'without an option' or 'without supplies'. For people who knew I was 'without a solid residence' for more than a decade, and yet our Father still provided to the point they became jealous merely by seeing the blessings, the evidence of the LORDs hand in my life.

Those who became jealous thought and shared their options that I should take a different path because it appeared nothing was going to work out for me!

They did not know how I prayed due to what I was dealing with or how I was learning from our Father day by day since they only had (and they were only interested in) a world view of dismissing the faith walk. Some even trusted 'everything came easy to me' and others had to be 'making it work out for me' because they were 'stiff necked'. They turned away from the LORD and stated HE did not provide for them so they ONLY accepted a 'world success plan'. They were unable to accept how Father provided for me, arranged & provided global travel and provisions for me which would cost far more than I could afford.

No matter what people may say about you, about your life, they do not know what our Father knows about you or what HE is doing with you and for you! Another song comes to mind: *God Only Knows* by King and Country, a song which quickly rose to the top of the charts long before they turned it into a duet with Dolly Parton.

When the people in the world speak against you, will you still testify?

Maybe after you hear the song *Testify* by Social Misfits, featuring Crowder?

Repentance for _____?

Adjustment(s) planned? _____

DAY FIVE

<u>FEAR</u>. **Jeremiah 30:10 (5-11).**
For thus says the Lord:
'We have heard a voice of trembling,
Of fear, and not of peace.
6 Ask now, and see,
Whether a man is ever in labor with child?
So why do I see every man with his hands on his loins
Like a woman in labor,
And all faces turned pale?
7 Alas! For that day is great,
So that none is like it;
And it is the time of Jacob's trouble,
But he shall be saved out of it.
8 'For it shall come to pass in that day,'
Says the Lord of hosts,
'That I will break his yoke from your neck,
And will burst your bonds;
Foreigners shall no more enslave them.
9 But they shall serve the Lord their God,
And David their king,
Whom I will raise up for them.
10 'Therefore do not fear, O My servant Jacob,' says the Lord,
'Nor be dismayed, O Israel;
For behold, I will save you from afar,
And your seed from the land of their captivity.
Jacob shall return, have rest and be quiet,
And no one shall make him afraid.
11 For I am with you,' says the Lord, 'to save you;
Though I make a full end of all nations where I have scattered you,
Yet I will not make a complete end of you.
But I will correct you in justice,
And will not let you go altogether unpunished.'

HIS plan for us is good. His justice is righteous. HE is always with us.

Nations come and go but, we will be with HIM for all eternity.

Some prayer partners came into my life and I thanked our Father for the lifetime prayer warriors! Within two years, through various circumstances, they all transitioned to heaven! There were moments when I sought the truth to hear our Father confirm to me that I was NOT left behind!

A precious song was shared in an email the night before lunch and a movie plans with a special, local prayer warrior: **Be Blessed** by Bishop Paul Morton. My prayer warrior friend did not show up for lunch, I called and left a message, and again when I arrived at the theater since she was not there, either. After the movie, her husband answered her phone and stated she was in heaven ...

Is HE revealing anything which requires correction, anything blocking the blessings? The precious message in the song: *I'll pray for you, you pray for me, and let's watch GOD change things!*

HIS plan for us is good. His justice is righteous. HE is always with us.

Nations come and go but, we will be with HIM for all eternity.

Repentance for _____?

Adjustment(s) planned? _____

DAY SIX

REVERENTIAL FEAR. Jeremiah 32:40-41 (36-41).
Now therefore, thus says the Lord, the God of Israel, concerning this city of which you say, 'It shall be delivered into the hand of the king of Babylon by the sword, by the famine, and by the pestilence: 37 Behold, I will gather them out of all countries where I have driven them in My anger, in My fury, and in great wrath; I will bring them back to this place, and I will cause them to dwell safely. 38 They shall be My people, and I will be their God; 39 then I will give them one heart and one way, that they may fear Me forever, for the good of them and their children after them. 40 And I will make an everlasting covenant with them, that I will not turn away from doing them good; but I will put My fear in their hearts so that they will not depart from Me. 41 Yes, I will rejoice over them to do them good, and I will assuredly plant them in this land, with all My heart and with all My soul.'

We will be HIS people. HE will be our GOD.

HE will unite us and future generations for HE has a covenant with us!

What HE does for us causes us to stand in awe of HIM!

Therefore, we will NOT depart from HIM!

Based upon all He has done and continues to do for you because He loves you, what is He prompting you to do to express His love to other people?

Repentance for _____?

Adjustment(s) planned? _____

DAY SEVEN

BLESSING. **Numbers 6:24-26.**
"The Lord bless you and keep you;
25 The Lord make His face shine upon you,
And be gracious to you;
26 The Lord lift up His countenance upon you,
And give you peace." '

Blessings received: _____

Blessings shared: _____

Declarations/Testimonies: _____

DAY ONE

REVERENTIAL FEAR. Jeremiah 33:9 (4-9).

For thus says the Lord, the God of Israel, concerning the houses of this city and the houses of the kings of Judah, which have been pulled down to fortify against the siege mounds and the sword: 5 'They come to fight with the Chaldeans, but only to fill their places with the dead bodies of men whom I will slay in My anger and My fury, all for whose wickedness I have hidden My face from this city.

6 Behold, I will bring it health and healing; I will heal them and reveal to them the abundance of peace and truth. 7 And I will cause the captives of Judah and the captives of Israel to return, and will rebuild those places as at the first. 8 I will cleanse them from all their iniquity by which they have sinned against Me, and I will pardon all their iniquities by which they have sinned and by which they have transgressed against Me. 9 Then it shall be to Me a name of joy, a praise, and an honor before all nations of the earth, who shall hear all the good that I do to them; they shall fear and tremble for all the goodness and all the prosperity that I provide for it.'

In the world, do you hear the LORD being honored?

Do you hear words of blessings shared one to another?

Do you participate in, witness and testify illnesses or healings?

Do you honor the LORD, share HIS word and blessings as HE directs?

Repentance for _____?

Adjustment(s) planned? _____

DAY TWO

FEAR. Jeremiah 40:9 (7-10).

And when all the captains of the armies who were in the fields, they and their men, heard that the king of Babylon had made Gedaliah the son of Ahikam governor in the land, and had committed to him men, women, children, and the poorest of the land who had not been carried away captive to Babylon, 8 then they came to Gedaliah at Mizpah—Ishmael the son of Nethaniah, Johanan and Jonathan the sons of Kareah, Seraiah the son of Tanhumeth, the sons of Ephai the Netophathite, and Jezaniah the son of a Maachathite, they and their men. 9 And Gedaliah the son of Ahikam, the son of Shaphan, took an oath before them and their men, saying, *Do not be afraid to serve the Chaldeans. Dwell in the land and serve the king of Babylon, and it shall be well with you. 10 As for me, I will indeed dwell at*

Mizpah and serve the Chaldeans who come to us. But you, gather wine and summer fruit and oil, put them in your vessels, and dwell in your cities that you have taken.

If you were directed to pack a few things and go to a location He needs you to be 'for now', would you be OK going to a location where our Father places your feet?

Repentance for _____?

Adjustment(s) planned? _____

DAY THREE

<u>FEAR</u>. **Jeremiah 42:11 (7-12).**
And it happened after ten days that the word of the Lord came to Jeremiah. 8 Then he called Johanan the son of Kareah, all the captains of the forces which were with him, and all the people from the least even to the greatest, 9 and said to them, *Thus says the Lord, the God of Israel, to whom you sent me to present your petition before Him:* **10** *'If you will still remain in this land, then I will build you and not pull you down, and I will plant you and not pluck you up. For I relent concerning the disaster that I have brought upon you.* **11** *Do not be afraid of the king of Babylon, of whom you are afraid; do not be afraid of him,'* **says the Lord,** *'for I am with you, to save you and deliver you from his hand.* **12** *And I will show you mercy, that he may have mercy on you and cause you to return to your own land.'*

Wherever HE places your feet, HE will provide for you and strengthen you while HE shows you HIS mercy.

When I received a word from a prophet that my life would be as Jacob while climbing up the ladder but for every step up, I would go back two steps.

What? I can learn, comprehend and understand so USE ME LORD!

Within days, HE sent a prophet to me to confirm each time I go up a step and go back two I am to envision a special slingshot action because our Father is preparing to catapult me. Wow! A completely different perspective.

When you go to our Father about the messages you receive, whether they appear to be an encouragement or a correction, will you be OK going back a couple of steps so HE can catapult you into the land and plan HE has prepared for you to arrive at the perfect time?

150

Repentance for _____?

Adjustment(s) planned? _____

DAY FOUR

<u>FEAR</u>. **Jeremiah 46:27 (25-27).**
The Lord of hosts, the God of Israel, says: *Behold, I will bring punishment on Amon of No, and Pharaoh and Egypt, with their gods and their kings—Pharaoh and those who trust in him.* **26** *And I will deliver them into the hand of those who seek their lives, into the hand of Nebuchadnezzar king of Babylon and the hand of his servants. Afterward it shall be inhabited as in the days of old,* **says the Lord.**
<u>God Will Preserve Israel</u>

27 *But do not fear, O My servant Jacob,*
And do not be dismayed, O Israel!
For behold, I will save you from afar,
And your offspring from the land of their captivity;
Jacob shall return, have rest and be at ease;
No one shall make him afraid.

Father has a plan.

Others will be dealt with, while HIS plan for HIS people will proceed, guiding them toward their inheritance, their land and their rest in HIM!

Will you 'be at ease' knowing HE's got this, HE's got you and HE's making a way for you, so all may be well with your soul?

Repentance for _____?

Adjustment(s) planned? _____

DAY FIVE

<u>FEAR</u>. **Jeremiah 46:28.**
Do not fear, O Jacob My servant, **says the Lord,**
For I am with you;
For I will make a complete end of all the nations
To which I have driven you,
But I will not make a complete end of you.
I will rightly correct you,
For I will not leave you wholly unpunished.

Again, no reason to worry, HE's got it all handled! HE will correct as needed. What correction is HE prompting you to think about working out with HIS help?

151

Repentance for _____?

Adjustment(s) planned? _____

DAY SIX

<u>FEAR</u>. **Jeremiah 51:46 (45-48).**
My people, go out of the midst of her!
And let everyone deliver himself from the fierce anger of the Lord.
46 *And lest your heart faint,*
And you fear for the rumor that will be heard in the land
(A rumor will come one year,
And after that, in another year
A rumor will come,
And violence in the land,
Ruler against ruler),
47 *Therefore behold, the days are coming*
That I will bring judgment on the carved images of Babylon;
Her whole land shall be ashamed,
And all her slain shall fall in her midst.
48 *Then the heavens and the earth and all that is in them*
Shall sing joyously over Babylon;
For the plunderers shall come to her from the north, **says the Lord.**

Father will deal with Babylon! Knowing HE will deal with those controlling you, your life, finances, business, family, what will change in your life?

Repentance for _____?

Adjustment(s) planned? _____

DAY SEVEN

<u>BLESSING.</u> **Numbers 6:24-26.**
> *"The LORD bless you and keep you;*
> **25** *The LORD make His face shine upon you,*
> *And be gracious to you;*
> **26** *The LORD lift up His countenance upon you,*
> *And give you peace." '*

Blessings received: _____

Blessings shared: _____

Declarations/Testimonies: _____

DAY ONE

FEAR. Lamentations 3:57 (55-60).
I called on Your name, O Lord,
From the lowest pit.
56 You have heard my voice:
Do not hide Your ear
From my sighing, from my cry for help.
57 You drew near on the day I called on You,
And said, *Do not fear!*
58 O Lord, You have pleaded the case for my soul;
You have redeemed my life.
59 O Lord, You have seen how I am wronged;
Judge my case.
60 You have seen all their vengeance,
All their schemes against me.

Easier for us, now, since CHRIST has freed us from the pit and the Holy Spirit is easily available because our Father has provided the Holy Spirit to us. Our Father & CHRIST plead our case and CHRIST has redeemed our life. Father's judgment is the ONLY concern! So, again, what can mortals do to you?

Repentance for _____?

Adjustment(s) planned? _____

DAY TWO

FEAR. Ezekiel 3:9 (1-9).
The Responsibility of the Prophet
Moreover He said to me, *Son of man, eat what you find; eat this scroll, and go, speak to the house of Israel.* 2 So I opened my mouth, and He caused me to eat that scroll.

3 And He said to me, *Son of man, feed your belly, and fill your stomach with this scroll that I give you.* So I ate, and it was in my mouth like honey in sweetness.

4 Then He said to me: *Son of man, go to the house of Israel and speak with My words to them.* 5 *For you are not sent to a people of unfamiliar speech and of hard language, but to the house of Israel,* 6 *not to many people of unfamiliar speech and of hard language, whose words you cannot understand. Surely, had I sent you to them, they would have listened to you.* 7 *But the house of Israel will not listen to you, because they will not listen to*

153

Me; for all the house of Israel are impudent and hard-hearted. **8** *Behold, I have made your face strong against their faces, and your forehead strong against their foreheads.* **9** *Like adamant stone, harder than flint, I have made your forehead; do not be afraid of them, nor be dismayed at their looks, though they are a rebellious house.*

Every instruction for the assignment is provided when we agree to the assignment and continue to walk forward in faith. It all resembles the fact 'you have to put your foot in the sea before the water is lifted up to let you walk on the soil'. The strengthening process described for the forehead resembles the old adage to let it pass 'like water off a duck's back'. This is what it is to travel in ministry with our Father. If the words of the people can deter or stop you, the assignment is at risk. Our Father has the entire orchestration planned out in advance. The question is, will you hear HIS voice and align with His plan?

Repentance for _____?

Adjustment(s) planned? _____

DAY THREE

DOUBT. Ezekiel 34:16.
I will seek what was lost and bring back what was driven away, bind up the broken and strengthen what was sick; but I will destroy the fat and the strong, and feed them in judgment.

Yikes! On the surface, it appears I need to buy a treadmill and get on for it for an hour, often! However, what our Father is referring to is sidelining HIS plan. When we become comfortable with 'how it is around here' we slow down, we become busy in our personal plans and the assignment stalls. Each attempt to have us 'stall out' during the plan is another option to 'be strengthened'. Are you willing to be strengthened and continue to walk forward in faith?

Repentance for _____?

Adjustment(s) planned? _____

DAY FOUR
FEAR. Daniel 10:12 (10-14).
Prophecies Concerning Persia and Greece

Suddenly, a hand touched me, which made me tremble on my knees and on the palms of my hands. 11 And he said to me, *O Daniel, man greatly beloved, understand the words that I speak to you, and stand upright, for I have now been sent to you.* While he was speaking this word to me, I stood trembling.

12 Then he said to me, *Do not fear, Daniel, for from the first day that you set your heart to understand, and to humble yourself before your God, your words were heard; and I have come because of your words. 13 But the prince of the kingdom of Persia withstood me twenty-one days; and behold, Michael, one of the chief princes, came to help me, for I had been left alone there with the kings of Persia. 14 Now I have come to make you understand what will happen to your people in the latter days, for the vision refers to many days yet to come.*

Amazing. After walking forward for many months, it was so amazing to hear the endearments, to hear that I am comprehending, understanding what is going on and what needs to happen next. It's as though a partner is walking through each step with me and HE speaks to me over my right shoulder, always over my right shoulder. The endearments confirm how much our Father appreciates the fact we will say, *Yes LORD, you can send me.*

What assignment is our Father is revealing to you? Will you agree to go?

Repentance for _____?

Adjustment(s) planned? _____

DAY FIVE

FEAR. Daniel 10:19 (15-19).

When he had spoken such words to me, I turned my face toward the ground and became speechless. 16 And suddenly, one having the likeness of the sons of men touched my lips; then I opened my mouth and spoke, saying to him who stood before me, *My lord, because of the vision my sorrows have overwhelmed me, and I have retained no strength. 17 For how can this servant of my lord talk with you, my lord? As for me, no strength remains in me now, nor is any breath left in me.*

18 Then again, the one having the likeness of a man touched me and strengthened me. 19 And he said, *O man greatly beloved, fear not! Peace be to you; be strong, yes, be strong!*

We are to greet each other, *Peace be with you.*

You are the beloved of the LORD, as Daniel.

Is His PEACE evident in you as it was in Daniel?

Repentance for _____?

Adjustment(s) planned? _____

DAY SIX

FEAR. Joel 2:21-22 (18-24; immediately after The Call to Repentance).
The Land Refreshed
Then the Lord will be zealous for His land,
And pity His people.
19 The Lord will answer and say to His people,
Behold, I will send you grain and new wine and oil,
And you will be satisfied by them;
I will no longer make you a reproach among the nations.
20 *But I will remove far from you the northern army,*
And will drive him away into a barren and desolate land,
With his face toward the eastern sea
And his back toward the western sea;
His stench will come up,
And his foul odor will rise,
Because he has done monstrous things.
21 Fear not, O land;
Be glad and rejoice,
For the Lord has done marvelous things!
22 Do not be afraid, you beasts of the field;
For the open pastures are springing up,
And the tree bears its fruit;
The fig tree and the vine yield their strength.
23 Be glad then, you children of Zion,
And rejoice in the Lord your God;
For He has given you the former rain faithfully,
And He will cause the rain to come down for you—
The former rain,
And the latter rain in the first month.
24 The threshing floors shall be full of wheat,
And the vats shall overflow with new wine and oil.

All blessings are repeatedly being prepared for us. There was a pattern with our Father prompting me to repeat the same verse to many people, to pastors, to business leaders, to specific people in the prayer lines: *Eye has not seen, nor ear heard, nor have entered into the heart of man the things which God has prepared* (in store) *for those who love* (have revered) *Him.* What is our Father revealing to you about the things HE has prepared for you?

156

Repentance for _____?

Adjustment(s) planned? _____

DAY SEVEN

BLESSING. Numbers 6:24-26.
> *"The Lord bless you and keep you;*
> 25 *The Lord make His face shine upon you,*
> *And be gracious to you;*
> 26 *The Lord lift up His countenance upon you,*
> *And give you peace." '*

Blessings received: _____

Blessings shared: _____

Declarations/Testimonies: _____

WEEK THIRTY-TWO

DAY ONE

REVERENTIAL FEAR. Amos 3:8.
> *A lion has roared!*
> *Who will not fear?*
> *The Lord God has spoken!*
> *Who can but prophesy?*

When our Father speaks, when CHRIST defends us, it is a powerful sight to observe the roar of the LION on our behalf. HE prepares the way and speaks on our behalf before we arrive. HE sets the atmosphere for HIS words to be shared to the multitude. After HE does all of this, will you share HIS words of prophesy with the people HE places in your path today?

Repentance for _____?

Adjustment(s) planned? _____

DAY TWO
REVERENTIAL FEAR. Jonah 1:16.

Then the men feared the Lord exceedingly, and offered a sacrifice to the Lord and took vows.

When we get it. When we deeply grasp, to our core and in our heart where CHRIST resides, that our Father is handling ALL details, orchestrating beyond our comprehension, on our behalf because HE loves us unconditionally. When we begin to grab on to the magnitude of how BIG HE is and how much BIGGER HIS plans are than we can possibly understand in human terms before HE walks forward with us, we will stand in complete awe of HIS MAJESTY. Again, there is a song I leave on replay while preparing for meetings, services and time of prayer to let go of my opinions and thoughts and lean on the majesty of our LORD: *Majesty* by Ron Kenoly. He has many great songs. This one is just one favorite. Do you see Father as your Majesty on the throne of heaven when you cry out to him?

Repentance for _____?

Adjustment(s) planned? _____

DAY THREE
REVERENTIAL FEAR. Habakkuk 3:2.
O Lord, I have heard Your speech and was afraid;
Lord, revive Your work in the midst of the years!
In the midst of the years make it known;
In wrath remember mercy.

Grateful for HIS mercy! Which experiences come to mind when you think about the times in your life when HE granted HIS mercy on you?

Repentance for _____?

Adjustment(s) planned? _____

DAY FOUR
FEAR. Zephaniah 3:16 (14-17; after wickedness of Jerusalem & Faithful Remnant identified)
Joy in God's Faithfulness
Sing, O daughter of Zion!
Shout, O Israel!
Be glad and rejoice with all your heart,

O daughter of Jerusalem!
15 The Lord has taken away your judgments,
He has cast out your enemy.
The King of Israel, the Lord, is in your midst;
You shall see disaster no more.
16 In that day it shall be said to Jerusalem:
Do not fear;
Zion, let not your hands be weak.
17 *The Lord your God in your midst,*
The Mighty One, will save;
He will rejoice over you with gladness,
He will quiet you with His love,
He will rejoice over you with singing.

A moment to dance like David danced when the Ark was moved to Jerusalem. After the wickedness was revealed in Jerusalem and faithful remnant was identified, it was clearly a time for joy and rejoicing to change the atmosphere, the environment. What will it take for your atmosphere, your environment to be filled with praise and joy, rejoicing and dancing?

Repentance for _____?

Adjustment(s) planned? _____

DAY FIVE

FEAR. Haggai 2:5 (1-5).
The Coming Glory of God's House
In the seventh month, on the twenty-first of the month, the word of the Lord came by Haggai the prophet, saying: 2 *Speak now to Zerubbabel the son of Shealtiel, governor of Judah, and to Joshua the son of Jehozadak, the high priest, and to the remnant of the people, saying: 3 'Who is left among you who saw this temple in its former glory? And how do you see it now? In comparison with it, is this not in your eyes as nothing? 4 Yet now be strong, Zerubbabel,' says the Lord; 'and be strong, Joshua, son of Jehozadak, the high priest; and be strong, all you people of the land,' says the Lord, 'and work; for I am with you,' says the Lord of hosts. 5 'According to the word that I covenanted with you when you came out of Egypt, so My Spirit remains among you; do not fear!'*

Be strong, be of good courage and know the Father is with you from the time of the worst moments to these moments. We can do ALL our Father is asking of us for the return of former glory to our life, our family, our fellowship,

159

our region, our government, our nation. Are you in covenant with our Father so the Spirit will remain with you?

Repentance for _____?

Adjustment(s) planned? _____

DAY SIX

<u>FEAR</u>. **Zechariah 8:13 (9-13).**
Thus says the Lord of hosts:
'Let your hands be strong,
You who have been hearing in these days
These words by the mouth of the prophets,
Who spoke in the day the foundation was laid
For the house of the Lord of hosts,
That the temple might be built.
10 For before these days
There were no wages for man nor any hire for beast;
There was no peace from the enemy for whoever went out or came in;
For I set all men, everyone, against his neighbor.
11 But now I will not treat the remnant of this people as in the former days,' says the Lord of hosts.
12 'For the seed shall be prosperous,
The vine shall give its fruit,
The ground shall give her increase,
And the heavens shall give their dew—
I will cause the remnant of this people
To possess all these.
13 And it shall come to pass
That just as you were a curse among the nations,
O house of Judah and house of Israel,
So I will save you, and you shall be a blessing.
Do not fear,
Let your hands be strong.'

Yes, when hands are strong we can 'get to work' when we align with our Father and allow HIM to guide us in our life while transitioning from being cursed to being blessed and to become a blessing. It was naive of me to think, at the time, that because I was traveling with the LORD I was automatically a blessing. It was a shock to realize how far off I was from the truth. Now, it is comical to think about how much training I needed to learn HIS ways! What is the task set before you which will help transition your life to become a blessing?

Repentance for _____?

Adjustment(s) planned? _____

DAY SEVEN

BLESSING. Numbers 6:24-26.
"The LORD bless you and keep you;
25 The LORD make His face shine upon you,
And be gracious to you;
26 The LORD lift up His countenance upon you,
And give you peace." '

Blessings received: _____

Blessings shared:_____

Declarations/Testimonies: _____

WEEK THIRTY-THREE

DAY ONE

FEAR. Zechariah 8:15 (14-17).
For thus says the Lord of hosts:
'Just as I determined to punish you
When your fathers provoked Me to wrath,'
Says the Lord of hosts,
'And I would not relent,
15 So again in these days
I am determined to do good
To Jerusalem and to the house of Judah.
Do not fear.
16 These are the things you shall do:
Speak each man the truth to his neighbor;
Give judgment in your gates for truth, justice, and peace;
17 Let none of you think evil in your heart against your neighbor;
And do not love a false oath.
For all these are things that I hate,'
Says the Lord.

Compromising, aligning with and taking an oath 'to a group, a society, especially a secret society' separates us from our Father. Should we choose to proceed with a plan to invite others into the society, the world plan, away from our Father and HIS kingdom, it would be something that would provoke the anger of our Father. Truth is provided often throughout the scriptures. ONLY items 'held secret' by our Father are the good things HE has 'in store' for us! CHRIST did NOT speak 'in secret'. Everything HE spoke was the same with the multitude or with the disciples. It is what is often 'at the root' of conflicts. Who do we serve?

I Kings 18:20-21.

<u>Elijah's Mount Carmel Victory</u>

So Ahab sent for all the children of Israel, and gathered the prophets together on Mount Carmel. 21 And Elijah came to all the people, and said, *How long will you falter between two opinions? If the Lord is God, follow Him; but if Baal, follow him.* **But the people answered him not a word.**

This is exactly what our Father revealed to me after a speaking engagement. Tearful, as the only person sitting at a table in the restaurant of the resort, asking our Father how it can be a simple message everyone can understand and then choose. He prompted me to pick up the salt shaker in my right hand and the pepper shaker in my left. Then, HE asked me if I thought I represented the salt of the earth. Of course, I said *Yes.* HE confirmed when we are aligned with HIM, doing as HE asks and saying what HE wants us to say, we are in HIS kingdom, and everything else is NOT.

Wow! So succinct and simple! Frozen in time. No idea how long I sat and held the two shakers in my hands!

Joshua 24:14-15. Covenant.
Now therefore, fear the Lord, serve Him in sincerity and in truth, and put away the gods which your fathers served on the other side of the River and in Egypt. Serve the Lord! 15 And if it seems evil to you to serve the Lord, choose for yourselves this day whom you will serve, whether the gods which your fathers served that were on the other side of the River, or the gods of the Amorites, in whose land you dwell. But as for me and my house, we will serve the Lord.

Are you in covenant?

What are you being prompted to remember, a name or a word shared, 'a message in secret' which you did not want any other people to know?

Repentance for _____?

Adjustment(s) planned? _____

DAY TWO

<u>REVERENTIAL FEAR</u>. Malachi 1:14.
But cursed be the deceiver
Who has in his flock a male,
And takes a vow,
But sacrifices to the Lord what is blemished—
For I am a great King,
Says the Lord of hosts,
And My name is to be feared among the nations (people).

Father knows ALL, hears ALL, sees ALL. HE knows when we have been bad or good; sorry, I had to insert that one due to the level of lies shared in TV, ads, films, deceiving people by telling them Santa knows who has been good or bad, checks his list twice so believe in HIM for HE will bring you what you want. It is a 'tale' which is a lie used to cause believers to depart from the truth, from the only LORD to believe in who has good planned for us and loves us unconditionally. December 25 is NOT the birth date of Christ. He was born and believers followed the Hebrew calendar which is NOT structured with the same feasts and festivals on the same date every year. The Christmas Day 'since 312 - 325 AD' is a pagan celebration to the sun gods & all about nature, the tree, wreath, etc. Father's plan is to not cut down a tree or ornament it; **Jeremiah 10.** All of the sun gods were born on December 25 except Dionysus so they moved his birthday to December 25. Perhaps it was due to his focus being the vineyards? In any case, ALL are DEAD and yet, people still choose to worship a list of DEAD gods, even when they know there is ONLY one living LORD!

There are many other examples of lies used to deceive generations but, I will just share one simple deceitful nursery rhyme to help you begin your journey with our Father to hear direct from him what the enemy has done through people who serve the other gods. They are 'positioned' to share the lies in music, books, films, etc. The nursery rhyme which is 'at the root' of the change in our education system is repeated to children, generation to generation. The words are repeated and repeated per line. I've shortened it to the basics:

Mary Had A Little Lamb

Mary had a little lamb, its (HIS) fleece was white as snow
And everywhere that Mary went, the lamb was sure to go
He followed her to school one day, which was against the rule
It made the children laugh and play to see a lamb at school
And so the teacher turned him out, but still he lingered near
And waited patiently, til Mary did appear

Against the rule for the LAMB of GOD to be at the school,because the influence of the LAMB of GOD brought joy to the children. So, the teach sent the LAMB of GOD out of the school. However, the LAMB of GOD lingered near, available to ALL, while waiting patiently for Mary and the children to leave the school, laugh and play at the end of the day since HE never leaves or forsakes us, HE waits on us, patiently with unconditional love no matter what influences us during the day.

What is our Father revealing to you about HIS closeness to you due to the influences affecting you?

Repentance for _____?

Adjustment(s) planned? _____

DAY THREE

REVERENTIAL FEAR. Malachi 2:5 (1-6).
Corrupt Priests
And now, O priests, this commandment is for you.
2 If you will not hear,
And if you will not take it to heart,
To give glory to My name,
Says the Lord of hosts,
I will send a curse upon you,
And I will curse your blessings.
Yes, I have cursed them already,
Because you do not take it to heart.
3 Behold, I will rebuke your descendants
And spread refuse on your faces,
The refuse of your solemn feasts;
And one will take you away with it.
4 Then you shall know that I have sent this commandment to you,

164

That My covenant with Levi may continue,
Says the Lord of hosts.
5 *My covenant was with him, one of life and peace,*
And I gave them to him that he might fear Me;
So he feared Me
And was reverent before My name.
6 *The law of truth was in his mouth,*
And injustice was not found on his lips.
He walked with Me in peace and equity,
And turned many away from iniquity.

A clear message!

Often, I am asked why it sounds like I live by the 'old law' when that is the 'old covenant'. When I said, *'It is our covenant'*, they said, **Christ formed a 'new covenant',** and they used the example, **We do not have to Honor the Sabbath and Keep it Holy.** Shocked! *Are we really supposed to pick and choose which commandments we will follow?*

Even people who profess to 'be in ministry' say the old testament is just really good history and CHRIST said LOVE is the commandment HE gave us so that is our 'new covenant'.

Shocking to hear from believers, especially anyone in ministry since everything in the WORD relates to TODAY. There are really, really good examples of what TO DO and what we are NOT TO DO! Words of comfort when nothing in the world supports being comforted!

Finally, since I was asked so often, I took the question to the LORD.

When I remind them about what CHRIST actually said **if we would keep HIS commandments**, knowing CHRIST and the LORD are one, as confirmed in **John 14:15-18.**

Jesus Promises Another Helper
If you love Me, keep My commandments.
16 *And I will pray the Father, and He will give you another Helper, that He may abide with you forever—* **17** *the Spirit of truth, whom the world cannot receive, because it neither sees Him nor knows Him; but you know Him, for He dwells with you and will be in you.* **18** *I will not leave you orphans; I will come to you.*

What is your covenant with the Father?

Are you hearing HIS voice, the voice of the comforter direct from our Father and HIS SON, our CHRIST?

Repentance for _____?

Adjustment(s) planned? _____

DAY FOUR

<u>FEAR</u>. Malachi 3:5 (1-5).
<u>The Coming Messenger</u>
Behold, I send My messenger,
And he will prepare the way before Me.
And the Lord, whom you seek,
Will suddenly come to His temple,
Even the Messenger of the covenant,
In whom you delight.
Behold, He is coming,
Says the Lord of hosts.
2 But who can endure the day of His coming?
And who can stand when He appears?
For He is like a refiner's fire
And like launderers' soap.
3 He will sit as a refiner and a purifier of silver;
He will purify the sons of Levi,
And purge them as gold and silver,
That they may offer to the Lord
An offering in righteousness.
4 Then the offering of Judah and Jerusalem
Will be pleasant to the Lord,
As in the days of old,
As in former years.
5 And I will come near you for judgment;
I will be a swift witness
Against sorcerers,
Against adulterers,
Against perjurers,
Against those who exploit wage earners and widows and orphans,
And against those who turn away an alien—
Because they do not fear Me,
Says the Lord of hosts.

Prompted to remember the first time I heard the procedure of a silversmith:

1. heating the silver until it is so hot ALL of the 'dross' (the waste, scum, worthless portion, junk, rubbish, all of the 'foreign matter' is removed from it,
2. precision in forming it into a 'work of art' which will be useful and valued,

3. polishing it to perfection, until the silversmith can see his image on it!

When our Father who formed you in HIS image in the womb looks on you, does HE still see HIS image on you?

Repentance for _____?

Adjustment(s) planned? _____

DAY FIVE

FEAR. Matthew 1:20 (18-21).
Christ Born of Mary
Now the birth of Jesus Christ was as follows: *After His mother Mary was betrothed to Joseph, before they came together, she was found with child of the Holy Spirit.*
19 Then Joseph her husband, being a just man, and not wanting to make her a public example, was minded to put her away secretly. 20 But while he thought about these things, behold, an angel of the Lord appeared to him in a dream, saying, *Joseph, son of David, do not be afraid to take to you Mary your wife, for that which is conceived in her is of the Holy Spirit.* **21** *And she will bring forth a Son, and you shall call His name Jesus, for He will save His people from their sins.*

Easy to think of the 'images' of Mary & Joseph and think it was so amazing for them and how special they were 'amongst men'. However, Mary had to face family and lifetime friends in the synagogue while they did not have a way to comprehend what was happening. Joseph was older and his acceptance was key to protecting Mary. Even though siblings KNEW the miracles, they did NOT believe who CHRIST was until HE resurrected.

The 'resurrection reality status' was brought to my attention when I went to our Father because even though my father knew who I was (not originally but, after witnessing my life for a couple of decades: *Always loved you but, never understood you. Now that I see how you handle situations ... I understand you as deeply as I love you.* My siblings have a hard time 'figuring out my life' and then, when miracles take place and Father provides and arranges 'beyond comprehension' for me, they see it – it does not make sense to them 'in world plan terms' – so they have a really hard time believing what our Father does for me in my life. When our Father reminded me that the siblings of CHRIST had the same problem, not realizing who Christ was for our Father until HE resurrected. Tearful, but it helped me put ALL of the 'concern about what they think' behind me and go forward!

Are you willing to put all thoughts about what your family and others think about you when you are 'on assignment, proceeding by the direct guidance of our Father' in your daily life?

Repentance for _____?

Adjustment(s) planned? _____

DAY SIX

FEAR. Matthew 6:25-34 (22-34).
The Lamp of the Body
The lamp of the body is the eye. If therefore your eye is good, your whole body will be full of light. 23 But if your eye is bad, your whole body will be full of darkness. If therefore the light that is in you is darkness, how great is that darkness!

You Cannot Serve God and Riches
24 No one can serve two masters; for either he will hate the one and love the other, or else he will be loyal to the one and despise the other. You cannot serve God and mammon.

Do Not Worry
25 Therefore I say to you, do not worry about your life, what you will eat or what you will drink; nor about your body, what you will put on. Is not life more than food and the body more than clothing? 26 Look at the birds of the air, for they neither sow nor reap nor gather into barns; yet your heavenly Father feeds them. Are you not of more value than they? 27 Which of you by worrying can add one cubit to his stature?

28 So why do you worry about clothing? Consider the lilies of the field, how they grow: they neither toil nor spin; 29 and yet I say to you that even Solomon in all his glory was not arrayed like one of these. 30 Now if God so clothes the grass of the field, which today is, and tomorrow is thrown into the oven, will He not much more clothe you, O you of little faith?

31 Therefore do not worry, saying, 'What shall we eat?' or 'What shall we drink?' or 'What shall we wear?' 32 For after all these things the Gentiles seek. For your heavenly Father knows that you need all these things. 33 But seek first the kingdom of God and His righteousness, and all these things shall be added to you. 34 Therefore do not worry about tomorrow, for tomorrow will worry about its own things. Sufficient for the day is its own trouble.

Is the light, CHRIST, evident within you or darkness? Due to 'no worry about tomorrow', what will you 'take on' with our Father today?

Repentance for _____?

Adjustment(s) planned? _____

DAY SEVEN

BLESSING. Numbers 6:24-26.
> *"The LORD bless you and keep you;*
> *25 The LORD make His face shine upon you,*
> *And be gracious to you;*
> *26 The LORD lift up His countenance upon you,*
> *And give you peace." '*

Blessings received: _____

Blessings shared: _____

Declarations/Testimonies: _____

WEEK THIRTY-FOUR

DAY ONE

REVERENTIAL FEAR. Matthew 9:8.
Jesus Forgives and Heals a Paralytic
So He got into a boat, crossed over, and came to His own city.

2 Then behold, they brought to Him a paralytic lying on a bed. When Jesus saw their faith, He said to the paralytic, *Son, be of good cheer; your sins are forgiven you.* 3 And at once some of the scribes said within themselves, *This Man blasphemes!*

4 But Jesus, knowing their thoughts, said, *Why do you think evil in your hearts? 5 For which is easier, to say, 'Your sins are forgiven you,' or to say, 'Arise and walk'? 6 But that you may know that the Son of Man has power on earth to forgive sins*—then He said to the paralytic, *Arise, take up your bed, and go to your house.* 7 And he arose and departed to his house.

8 Now when the multitudes saw *it,* they marveled and glorified God, who had given such power to men.

When the miracles of the LORD were evident all around me, and the testimonies of ALL our Father was doing through me, I actually received

169

ominous warnings to STOP – until I received at least eight years of training by a leader in the body of Christ who was a leader for at least thirteen years! It was hard to NOT laugh, to remain 'in love' while explaining there is NOTHING man can do to train me to travel without an extra coin or tunic and know that all will be handled and I will return home safe when the assignment is complete.

When I was asked to become a 'team of three' to commission the mega church pastors to become apostles, without hesitation I immediately declined. The two men who were going to 'travel and do this with me said it was going to be easy money because the mega churches would be tithing to us and we would split it three ways'.

Still shocked about the errors in the concept and execution problems within their plan while I was being told I was 'without extra income due to my denial of opportunities'! Again, without hesitation, it was easy to respond, *No way can I commission an apostle and send them to other nations 'on assignment' and arrange their travel, the introductions ... only the LORD.* Tears while they were confirming they were going to be encouraging and supportive but, not launching them to other nations. All I can say is, *Father forgive us for what we have done to make up our own structure within the body, as though it is the structure of your church for much of what we have done is NOT!*

When miracles are being performed and direct messages from our Father are delivered while you are 'on assignment, as an Ambassador' and yet, the truth is NOT understood, and witnesses choose to gather together and speak against you and what you are doing and saying, will you remain in truth and stand up for the truth, or will you fold and operate in a plan not aligned with our Father or be stopped and NOT continue with the plan laid out before you?

Has someone said something to you which has stopped or restrained you?

Repentance for _____?

Adjustment(s) planned? _____

DAY TWO

FEAR. Matthew 10:19 (16-20).
Persecutions Are Coming

Behold, I send you out as sheep in the midst of wolves. Therefore be wise as serpents and harmless as doves. 17 But beware of men, for they will deliver you up to councils and scourge you in their synagogues. 18 You will be brought before governors and kings for My sake, as a testimony to them and to the Gentiles. 19 But when they deliver you up, do not worry about how or what you should speak. For it will be given to you in that hour what you should speak; 20 for it is not you who speak, but the Spirit of your Father who speaks in you.

One of my funniest experiences of being an 'empty vessel' happened during my last hours of being with the government leaders in The Kingdom of Tonga. The Minister of Finance, Tasi, told the 30 department heads that I would be coaching each of them and providing a scripture before departing to the airport.

A bit of panic due to the fact my luggage was already at the airport and all I had was a small tablet, a pen and a bottle of water. Then, our Father calmed me when HE told me that HE is with me, and HE is walking with me exactly as HE did with each of the people in the bible, and they delivered HIS words exactly as I will deliver them because HE will provide the scripture message for each one.

When I met with them, I made a note about each message delivered by our Father. When I arrived at the airport, I obtained my personal items for the flight, including my bible, and our Father prompted me to EACH scripture for EACH message HE delivered through me for the sake of the leaders of the government!

Will you become an empty vessel, so you can deliver the exact message the person in your path today needs for the sake of their soul?

Repentance for _____?

Adjustment(s) planned? _____

DAY THREE

FEAR. Matthew 10:26 (21-26).
Now brother will deliver up brother to death, and a father his child; and children will rise up against parents and cause them to be put to death. 22 And you will be hated by all for My name's sake. But he who endures to the end will be saved. 23 When they persecute you in this city, flee to another. For assuredly, I say to you, you will not have gone through the cities of Israel before the Son of Man comes.

24 A disciple is not above his teacher, nor a servant above his master. 25 It is enough for a disciple that he be like his teacher, and a servant like his master. If they have called the master of the house Beelzebub, how much more will they call those of his household! 26 Therefore do not fear them. For there is nothing covered that will not be revealed, and hidden that will not be known.

Patience, waiting for the truth to become KNOWN to those who would deliver you up to death (words to damage your name or result in physical death) is a gift which has required our FATHER's love while walking through this life!

Because a court situation was the root of a big shift in my life, our Father protected me as Esther and HE sent me to help others know about the battle as Deborah but, it shocked me to my core when people started telling me, *You have the patience of Job.* I did not think I was being patient. Clearly, I had a lot to learn due to the depth of the debacle which was impacting every aspect of my life. However, our Father prompted me to immediately begin studying the book of Job. Tears through each chapter. By the time I got to Chapter 19, I had to take a break. I was blaming GOD for my status, for everything the men in the world were doing to me. I trusted I was not being protected!

Grateful we serve a Father who loves us unconditionally!

HE still comforted me when I was ready to 'end my life'.

HE consoled me when I was 'losing hope' due to trusting I had become a magnet for EVERY well-meaning Christian who wanted to tell me ONE MORE REASON why my life was a complete disaster and I was NOT aligned with GOD! Then, finally, I reached **Job 38.**

The Lord Reveals His Omnipotence to Job
Then the Lord answered Job out of the whirlwind, and said:
2 Who *is* this who darkens counsel
By words without knowledge?
3 Now prepare yourself like a man;
I will question you, and you shall answer Me.

In the whirlwind, HE spoke. HE shared HIS wisdom and plan which far exceeds what I know about ANY subjects HE covered in each line of Job 38!

We know words but, we lack knowledge. Yikes! **Hosea 4:6. My people are destroyed for the lack of knowledge.**

In that moment, I wanted the destruction of my life and my faith to end!

Instead of relishing in truth with our Father, HE told me I did not comprehend the truth about **the lack of knowledge** while HE prompted me to read the verse in context: **Hosea 4:6-8.**

Now let no man contend, or rebuke another;
For your people are like those who contend with the priest.
5 Therefore you shall stumble in the day;
The prophet also shall stumble with you in the night;
And I will destroy your mother.
6 My people are destroyed for lack of knowledge.
Because you have rejected knowledge,
I also will reject you from being priest for Me;
Because you have forgotten the law of your God,
I also will forget your children.

Finally, realized the battle, as it was with Job, was NOT about me, it's about the souls, about the generations! There was NOTHING I could do to change the world view about me but, that is not the focus. The LORD will deal with the details when we continue on the path with HIM.

ALL that matters is what our Father has planned for us, to prosper us!

Father's plans are BIGGER than you imagine, so with this knowledge 'in mind', knowing that NONE are above us but GOD, what are you hearing & doing with GOD for the sake of souls & future generations?

Repentance for _____?

Adjustment(s) planned? _____

DAY FOUR

FEAR. Matthew 10:28 (27-28).
Jesus Teaches the Fear of God
Whatever I tell you in the dark, speak in the light; and what you hear in the ear, preach on the housetops. 28 And do not fear those who kill the body but cannot kill the soul. But rather fear Him who is able to destroy both soul and body in hell. 29 Are not two sparrows sold for a copper coin? And not one of them falls to the ground apart from your Father's will. 30 But the very hairs of your head are all numbered. 31 Do not fear therefore; you are of more value than many sparrows.

And our Father provides ALL for the sparrows, and for us! Realizing truth, I was thinking 'I got this' – 'I am seeking knowledge' – 'All is well'. However, speaking in the light when even the leadership in the church would not listen was tough. I remember the tough comments because they felt like a sword through the heart! One example: *I have 40 years of Christian education, you can't tell me anything.* Then, Father held me and told me the message was not delivered 'to me', it was delivered 'to HIM', because I represent HIM. Plus, HE told me I am not responsible.

Shocked. NOT RESPONSIBLE? HE sent me to the people. HE had a message for me to deliver to them, and HIS message was not being received. Then, HE reminded me of the message HE shared years before, *If it takes 1000 people to open a heart to CHRIST for salvation, I may be 575 or 999 and not witness the moment the heart accepts CHRIST but, the fact the heart was touched is what is important to our Father.*

What are you willing to speak to impact a life, without knowing the results?

Repentance for _____?

Adjustment(s) planned? _____

DAY FIVE

FEAR. Matthew 10:31 (29-31).
Are not two sparrows sold for a copper coin? And not one of them falls to the ground apart from your Father's will. 30 But the very hairs of your head are all numbered. 31 Do not fear therefore; you are of more value than many sparrows.

What is our Father reminding you about you, about your value to HIM?

Repentance for _____?

Adjustment(s) planned? _____

DAY SIX

DOUBT. Matthew 11:4-6.
Jesus answered and said to them, *Go and tell John the things which you hear and see: 5 The blind see and the lame walk; the lepers are cleansed and the deaf hear; the dead are raised up and the poor have the gospel preached to them. 6 And blessed is he who is not offended because of Me.*

Challenged in prison, after he lept in the womb when Mary entered, after baptizing CHRIST & the LORD confirming, John is questioning, doubting he knows the truth. Then, John was beheaded. Are you questioning the TRUTH?

Repentance for _____?

Adjustment(s) planned? _____

DAY SEVEN

<u>**BLESSING.**</u> **Numbers 6:24-26.**
> *"The LORD bless you and keep you;*
> *25 The LORD make His face shine upon you,*
> *And be gracious to you;*
> *26 The LORD lift up His countenance upon you,*
> *And give you peace." '*

Blessings received: _____

Blessings shared: _____

Declarations/Testimonies: _____

WEEK THIRTY-FIVE

DAY ONE

<u>**UNBELIEF.**</u> **Matthew 12:22-24.**
<u>**A House Divided Cannot Stand**</u>
Then one was brought to Him (CHRIST) who was demon-possessed, blind and mute; and He healed him, so that the blind and mute man both spoke and saw. 23 And all the multitudes were amazed and said, *Could this be the Son of David?*
24 Now when the Pharisees heard it they said, *This fellow does not cast out demons except by Beelzebub, the ruler of the demons.*

Knowing they said it to CHRIST is upsetting and knowing they do not accept CHRIST is in you can also be upsetting. Have you been told by 'well meaning Christians' that you are NOT hearing from the Father, you do NOT represent HIM? Did it stop you from fulfilling on the purpose and plan laid out before you, a plan which leads you to your destiny?

Repentance for _____?

Adjustment(s) planned? _____

DAY TWO

UNBELIEF. Matthew 12:38-39 (38-42).
The Scribes and Pharisees Ask for a Sign
Then some of the scribes and Pharisees answered, saying, *Teacher, we want to see a sign from You.*

39 But He answered and said to them, A*n evil and adulterous generation seeks after a sign, and no sign will be given to it except the sign of the prophet Jonah. 40 For as Jonah was three days and three nights in the belly of the great fish, so will the Son of Man be three days and three nights in the heart of the earth. 41 The men of Nineveh will rise up in the judgment with this generation and condemn it, because they repented at the preaching of Jonah; and indeed a greater than Jonah is here. 42 The queen of the South will rise up in the judgment with this generation and condemn it, for she came from the ends of the earth to hear the wisdom of Solomon; and indeed a greater than Solomon is here.*

A special reminder of 'who they were to CHRIST' is in the wording of a phrase shared by a dear friend, Rebecca King regarding **Pharisees & Sadducees;** They were NOT fair you see and that was so sad you see (Phar I/u see and that was so Sadd u s(c)ee). They were highly regarded religious leaders.

In your life are you focused on the perfect religion, seeing to the needs of the widows and orphans, or are you being religious toward others before gaining knowledge and wisdom from the Father?

Repentance for _____?

Adjustment(s) planned? _____

DAY THREE

UNBELIEF. Matthew 13:54-58.
When He had come to His own country, He taught them in their synagogue, so that they were astonished and said, *Where did this Man get this wisdom and these mighty works? 55 Is this not the carpenter's son? Is not His mother called Mary? And His brothers James, Joses, Simon, and Judas? 56 And His sisters, are they not all with us? Where then did this Man get all these things?* **57 So they were offended at Him.**

But Jesus said to them, *A prophet is not without honor except in his own country and in his own house.* **58 Now He did not do many mighty works there because of their unbelief.**

You will be challenged by the highly religious. Even Elijah came from a place that does not have it's own dot on the map. No matter where you came from or what you think you can accomplish, through our Father ALL things are possible and we are not 'on earth' to become someone who 'performs mighty works' for the people. We are here to be an example, to disciple and direct people to the Father. Is your life an example, a demonstration of HIS love for the people, doing what you are prompted to do by our Father and saying what you hear HIM saying to and through you?

Repentance for _____ ?

Adjustment(s) planned? _____

DAY FOUR

FEAR. **Matthew 14:27 (25-33).**
Now in the fourth watch of the night Jesus went to them, walking on the sea. 26 And when the disciples saw Him walking on the sea, they were troubled, saying, *It is a ghost!* And they cried out for fear. 27 But immediately Jesus spoke to them, saying, *Be of good cheer! It is I; do not be afraid.* 28 And Peter answered Him and said, *Lord, if it is You, command me to come to You on the water.*

29 So He said, *Come.* And when Peter had come down out of the boat, he walked on the water to go to Jesus. 30 But when he saw that the wind was boisterous, he was afraid; and beginning to sink he cried out, saying, *Lord, save me!* 31 And immediately Jesus stretched out His hand and caught him, and said to him, *O you of little faith, why did you doubt?* 32 And when they got into the boat, the wind ceased. 33 Then those who were in the boat came and worshiped Him, saying, *Truly You are the Son of God.*

Prompted to think about what I was declaring during the moments when I heard the song, *Even If You Don't* by Mercy Me, for the very first time. Without hesitation, I was saying, *HE does take care of us ... HE does supply for us ...* when our Father wrapped me in HIS arms and whispered, *There are times when it is not part of MY plan because it will not provide MY Best (HIS Best!), for MY people.* In a moment, it all came back into perspective. HE loves us no matter when the problem is resolved. We want to see answers to prayers, quick results. Our Father always wants us to receive HIS Best!

Timing within HIS plan is the key, and we do NOT know HIS timing!

During the depth of the legal battle, the corporation debacle, it was not easy to see what our Father was doing. At a conference, our Father sent a woman who was not received as a prophet for 12 years in her church but, she felt she had to grab the microphone and deliver a prophetic message. It was for me! It resulted in the name of the ministry being confirmed again and again during the next few months. Bottom line: It was a message about letting CHRIST forgive those who came against me as deeply as HE has forgiven me. Yikes! Ouch!

How quickly do you forgive as deeply as you are forgiven?

Who are you when it appears the answers to your specific prayers are not realized, yet, as you hoped?

Repentance for _____?

Adjustment(s) planned? _____

DAY FIVE

<u>**UNBELIEF.**</u> **Matthew 16:4 (1-4).**
<u>**The Pharisees and Sadducees Seek a Sign**</u>
Then the Pharisees and Sadducees came, and testing Him asked that He would show them a sign from heaven. 2 He answered and said to them, *When it is evening you say, 'It will be fair weather, for the sky is red'; 3 and in the morning, 'It will be foul weather today, for the sky is red and threatening.' Hypocrites! You know how to discern the face of the sky, but you cannot discern the signs of the times.*

4 A wicked and adulterous generation seeks after a sign, and no sign shall be given to it except the sign of the prophet Jonah. **And He left them and departed.**

Are you willing to continue on your faith walk being a demonstration and a voice guided by our Father whether signs and miracles are evident while you are 'in their midst' or not?

Repentance for _____?

Adjustment(s) planned? _____

DAY SIX

<u>**DOUBT.**</u> **Matthew 16:9.**
Do you not yet understand, or remember the five loaves of the five thousand and how many baskets you took up?

Truth is truth. It is NOT a requirement to turn water into wine or feed 5000 with what appeared to be provision a small lunch for only a few.

It is NOT a requirement to 'perform' miracles each time the believers gather. However, gatherings have often become as much about pleasing the people and acknowledging them instead of honoring our Father, speak about ALL of the blessings HE has provided and share the testimonies of the TRUTH far & wide. What are your testimonies regarding who our LORD is in your life?

Repentance for _____?

Adjustment(s) planned? _____

DAY SEVEN

BLESSING. Numbers 6:24-26.
> *"The LORD bless you and keep you;*
> *25 The LORD make His face shine upon you,*
> *And be gracious to you;*
> *26 The LORD lift up His countenance upon you,*
> *And give you peace." '*

Blessings received: _____

Blessings shared: _____

Declarations/Testimonies: _____

WEEK THIRTY-SIX

DAY ONE

UNBELIEF. Matthew 21:32.
Jesus said to them, *Assuredly, I say to you that tax collectors and harlots enter the kingdom of God before you.*
32 For John came to you in the way of righteousness, and you did not believe him; but tax collectors and harlots believed him; and when you saw it, you did not afterward relent and believe him.

When our Father reveals truth to you, do you resist or receive it?

When HE sends what HE knows you need in your life, do you receive it?

Repentance for _____?

Adjustment(s) planned? _____

DAY TWO

<u>FEAR</u>. Matthew 28:5 (1-8).
<u>He Is Risen</u>
Now after the Sabbath, as the first day of the week began to dawn, Mary Magdalene and the other Mary came to see the tomb. 2 And behold, there was a great earthquake; for an angel of the Lord descended from heaven, and came and rolled back the stone from the door, and sat on it. 3 His countenance was like lightning, and his clothing as white as snow. 4 And the guards shook for fear of him, and became like dead men.

5 But the angel answered and said to the women, *Do not be afraid, for I know that you seek Jesus who was crucified. 6 He is not here; for He is risen, as He said. Come, see the place where the Lord lay. 7 And go quickly and tell His disciples that He is risen from the dead, and indeed He is going before you into Galilee; there you will see Him. Behold, I have told you.*

8 So they went out quickly from the tomb with fear and great joy, and ran to bring His disciples word.

Amazing, miraculous moment in time. Would you question it, or rejoice?

Repentance for _____?

Adjustment(s) planned? _____

DAY THREE

<u>FEAR</u>. Matthew 28:10 (9-10).
<u>The Women Worship the Risen Lord</u>
And as they went to tell His disciples, behold, Jesus met them, saying, *Rejoice!* So they came and held Him by the feet and worshiped Him. 10 Then Jesus said to them, *Do not be afraid. Go and tell My brethren to go to Galilee, and there they will see Me.*

Often, especially during times of worship with fellow believers, I focus on inviting CHRIST into the midst of the fellowship. It is the same when I speak because HE can do more for the people in 45 seconds than I can do in 45 minutes! Are you inviting and rejoicing with the Father & CHRIST in your life?

Repentance for _____?

Adjustment(s) planned? _____

DAY FOUR

REVERENTIAL FEAR. Mark 2:12.
Immediately he arose, took up the bed, and went out in the presence of them all, so that all were amazed and glorified God, saying, *We never saw anything like this!*

When our Father speaks and operates through us, the people experience HIS demonstration of truth and when HE receives the credit, since it is NOT in 'our power' when we represent HIM, the people are amazed and they will unite 'in HIS glory'. **John 17:22.** Jesus gave us the glory while HE was here so that we would unite together as one, as HE and the Father are one. To be it and see it, we are to represent HIM: **John 3:30.** *He must increase, but I must decrease.* By becoming an Ambassador of the Kingdom, are you witnessing the impact of the TRUTH in the lives of the people in your family, your region?

Repentance for _____?

Adjustment(s) planned? _____

DAY FIVE

UNBELIEF. Mark 3:22.
And the scribes who came down from Jerusalem said, *He has Beelzebub,* **and,** *By the ruler of the demons He casts out demons.* **23 So He called them to Himself and said to them in parables:** *How can Satan cast out Satan?* **24** *If a kingdom is divided against itself, that kingdom cannot stand.* **25** *And if a house is divided against itself, that house cannot stand.*

So many amazing, miraculous things happen around me. Typically, two groups are represented, those who have become witnesses and they 'expect the miraculous', and those who are skeptical who wonder if it is the only living LORD or Satan. Easy to answer, ONLY the LORD would send me to a nation where HE needs me to speak a word or be a demonstration of HIS truth to change a nation, orchestrate all details, flights, housing and handling all needs when they are needed, and bring me home with significant testimonies and arrange for opportunities to share the testimonies of HIS blessings, grace and mercy. What will you say when the multitude asks you who you represent?

Repentance for _____?

Adjustment(s) planned? _____

DAY SIX

<u>FEAR</u>. Mark 5:36 (35-43).

While He was still speaking, some came from the ruler of the synagogue's house who said, *Your daughter is dead. Why trouble the Teacher any further?*

36 As soon as Jesus heard the word that was spoken, He said to the ruler of the synagogue, *Do not be afraid; only believe.* 37 And He permitted no one to follow Him except Peter, James, and John the brother of James. 38 Then He came to the house of the ruler of the synagogue, and saw a tumult and those who wept and wailed loudly. 39 When He came in, He said to them, *Why make this commotion and weep? The child is not dead, but sleeping.*

40 And they ridiculed Him. But when He had put them all outside, He took the father and the mother of the child, and those who were with Him, and entered where the child was lying. 41 Then He took the child by the hand, and said to her, *Talitha, cumi,* which is translated, *Little girl, I say to you, arise.* 42 Immediately the girl arose and walked, for she was twelve years of age. And they were overcome with great amazement. 43 But He commanded them strictly that no one should know it, and said that something should be given her to eat.

Jesus was not there to be 'known for the result'. The testimony was for the family to share far and wide. HE was not to be disturbed by those who did NOT believe! Then, HE provided the clear message: *Do Not Be Afraid, only BELIEVE.* Will you shift focus to the specific issue 'at hand' and believe?

Repentance for _____?

Adjustment(s) planned? _____

DAY SEVEN

<u>BLESSING.</u> Numbers 6:24-26.
> *"The LORD bless you and keep you;*
> *25 The LORD make His face shine upon you,*

182

And be gracious to you;
26 The LORD lift up His countenance upon you,
And give you peace." '

Blessings received: _____

Blessings shared: _____

Declarations/Testimonies: _____

WEEK THIRTY-SEVEN

DAY ONE

UNBELIEF. Mark 6:1-6.
Then He went out from there and came to His own country, and His disciples followed Him. 2 And when the Sabbath had come, He began to teach in the synagogue. And many hearing Him were astonished, saying, *Where did this Man get these things? And what wisdom is this which is given to Him, that such mighty works are performed by His hands!* **3** *Is this not the carpenter, the Son of Mary, and brother of James, Joses, Judas, and Simon? And are not His sisters here with us?* **So they were offended at Him.**

4 But Jesus said to them, *A prophet is not without honor except in his own country, among his own relatives, and in his own house.* **5 Now He could do no mighty work there, except that He laid His hands on a few sick people and healed them. 6 And He marveled because of their unbelief. Then He went about the villages in a circuit, teaching.**

If they reject you for doing and saying what our Father is asking you to do, exactly as they did CHRIST, you are in great company! CHRIST confirmed that HE only did what HE saw the Father do and say what HE heard the Father say. So, the question is, will you purpose to follow the example of CHRIST and only do do what Father is asking you to do and say what HE is prompting you to say?

Repentance for _____?

Adjustment(s) planned? _____

DAY TWO

FEAR. Mark 6:50 (45-52).
Jesus Walks on the Sea

Immediately He made His disciples get into the boat and go before Him to the other side, to Bethsaida, while He sent the multitude away. 46 And when He had sent them away, He departed to the mountain to pray. 47 Now when evening came, the boat was in the middle of the sea; and He was alone on the land. 48 Then He saw them straining at rowing, for the wind was against them. Now about the fourth watch of the night He came to them, walking on the sea, and would have passed them by. 49 And when they saw Him walking on the sea, they supposed it was a ghost, and cried out; 50 for they all saw Him and were troubled. But immediately He talked with them and said to them, *Be of good cheer! It is I; do not be afraid.* 51 Then He went up into the boat to them, and the wind ceased. And they were greatly amazed in themselves beyond measure, and marveled. 52 For they had not understood about the loaves, because their heart was hardened.

Father knows and CHRIST knows when we need assistance. Knowing this is true, will you invite them into your situation or keep waiting for them to intervene?

Repentance for _____?

Adjustment(s) planned? _____

DAY THREE

UNBELIEF. Mark 8:12.
But He sighed deeply in His spirit, and said, *Why does this generation seek a sign? Assuredly, I say to you, no sign shall be given to this generation.*

The Pharisees, the highly religious ones, are the ones who want to be 'shown a sign by CHRIST, yet again'. As soon as HE showed them who HE was, they spoke and operated against him. *Father, forgive us whenever we appear to you as the Pharisees and Sadducees operated with CHRIST.* What is our Father prompting you to remember, especially about your actions and communications with people within the fellowship and those involved in ministry? Any judgments made which can be turned over to Father now?

Repentance for _____?

Adjustment(s) planned? _____

DAY FOUR

FEAR. Mark 13:11 (5-13).

184

And Jesus, answering them, began to say: *Take heed that no one deceives you. 6 For many will come in My name, saying, 'I am He,' and will deceive many. 7 But when you hear of wars and rumors of wars, do not be troubled; for such things must happen, but the end is not yet. 8 For nation will rise against nation, and kingdom against kingdom. And there will be earthquakes in various places, and there will be famines and troubles. These are the beginnings of sorrows.*

9 But watch out for yourselves, for they will deliver you up to councils, and you will be beaten in the synagogues. You will be brought before rulers and kings for My sake, for a testimony to them. 10 And the gospel must first be preached to all the nations. 11 But when they arrest you and deliver you up, do not worry beforehand, or premeditate what you will speak. But whatever is given you in that hour, speak that; for it is not you who speak, but the Holy Spirit. 12 Now brother will betray brother to death, and a father his child; and children will rise up against parents and cause them to be put to death. 13 And you will be hated by all for My name's sake. But he who endures to the end shall be saved.

Do the words used by others to judge you, to restrict you, to try and change your mind or control you resemble words you have used to judge others? Has the enemy been able to use you to cause division? Have you judged people within the body of believers while not judging the people in the world? While you review to see if there is a pattern in 'where you find fault', do you see an opportunity to disciple, to speak into the lives of those involved so they can hear and see the truth and unite in truth?

Repentance for _____?

Adjustment(s) planned? _____

DAY FIVE

FEAR. Luke 1:13 (5-17).
John's Birth Announced to Zacharias

There was in the days of Herod, the king of Judea, a certain priest named Zacharias, of the division of Abijah. His wife was of the daughters of Aaron, and her name was Elizabeth. 6 And they were both righteous before God, walking in all the commandments and ordinances of the Lord blameless. 7 But they had no child, because Elizabeth was barren, and they were both well advanced in years.

185

8 So it was, that while he was serving as priest before God in the order of his division, **9** according to the custom of the priesthood, his lot fell to burn incense when he went into the temple of the Lord. **10** And the whole multitude of the people was praying outside at the hour of incense. **11** Then an angel of the Lord appeared to him, standing on the right side of the altar of incense. **12** And when Zacharias saw him, he was troubled, and fear fell upon him.

13 But the angel said to him, *Do not be afraid, Zacharias, for your prayer is heard; and your wife Elizabeth will bear you a son, and you shall call his name John. **14** And you will have joy and gladness, and many will rejoice at his birth. **15** For he will be great in the sight of the Lord, and shall drink neither wine nor strong drink. He will also be filled with the Holy Spirit, even from his mother's womb. **16** And he will turn many of the children of Israel to the Lord their God. **17** He will also go before Him in the spirit and power of Elijah, 'to turn the hearts of the fathers to the children,' and the disobedient to the wisdom of the just, to make ready a people prepared for the Lord.*

When the LORD sends a message, it is often 'beyond human comprehension'! ONLY those who have ears to hear and eyes to see will RECEIVE the message.

Often asked, *How do you know the voice prompting you is the LORD?*

The only thing our LORD holds in secret, is the good He has for us! The enemy would NOT be interested in my ability to drive hundreds of miles on an 'empty' tank! The enemy would not retain & sustain me and keep the gas tank full for days, driving hundreds of miles from San Diego to Central Coast; attend many meetings and make connections before my next trip while our Father is orchestrating with a husband and wife to attend a church for their first time and hand me an envelope to pay for the rental car and gas that a leader in the body was going to arrange many days prior!

Facts with two amazing revelations within 24 hours: When I was departing a one-week conference in Northern California by invitation of a leader in the body of CHRIST, a conference where he was a speaker, I went to the hotel to drive him to the airport. It was the moment in time where he was going to provide a blessing of 'more than enough' to pay for the rental car and gas. When I arrived, I was informed he checked out two hours prior to my arrival due to scheduling an earlier flight. What?

Father heard a lot from me, and I mean a lot without even taking a breath, all about how Christians are to be truthful and the man is a leader who had my contact information so he is not operating in integrity. The entire trip was planned because he wanted to talk to me and GOD confirmed the blessing would be an amount far exceeding my costs. The conference was north of Santa Rosa and I drove from San Diego. No gas and no way to buy gas. Not happy!

I was still upset when I began driving south on the 5 Freeway. Not realizing how many miles I had driven, I was already half way back to San Diego when the Holy Spirit prompted me to exit the freeway. He instructed to park the car in a parking lot of a tall business building with cars and people everywhere.

In fact, I was still so upset, our Father had to draw my attention to the fact that I did not even notice that this trip would already require two gas stops at this point and my gas gauge was still on full and had not even moved off of full, yet.

The Father gave me a vision and word that was so vivid and yet, HE wanted me to write it down so I would share it word for word with the man who did not provide the blessing. Why? Father knew the words would have even more significance to the man because he served in Special Forces during the Vietnam War:

Not enough of my men are preparing and putting on their steel toed boots to march with Me, so I am having to call forth my women, even my widows and my orphans, to prepare my Army to march with Me before the SONrise.

This message was received & delivered immediately on my return to San Diego. It deeply blessed the man who was prompted by our Father to provide the blessing. No action was taken on HIS part, even though our Father shared a vision with him about me being the mouse to the elephant at the same time our Father was revealing the amazing status of the body of CHRIST not being prepared, yet. He confirmed that he was content with gnawing at the ankle of the elephant, but I was not. I was screaming and biting hard but, the elephant would not move. So I ran up and started screaming and swinging on the tail but, the elephant would not move. So, I ran to the left ear and started biting the ear and shouting, *Move!* Then, I ran to the right ear, biting and shouting until the elephant finally MOVED! Then, GOD confirmed to him that the elephant is the church, the body of CHRIST with his position at the ankle, still.

The gas tank remained full for days. Result? Hundreds witnessed it!

In the midst of a potential disaster of any magnitude in your life, what has our Father said to you, revealed to you and orchestrated for you, on your behalf?

Repentance for _____?

Adjustment(s) planned? _____

DAY SIX

FEAR. Luke 1:30 (26-33).
Christ's Birth Announced to Mary

Now in the sixth month the angel Gabriel was sent by God to a city of Galilee named Nazareth, 27 to a virgin betrothed to a man whose name was Joseph, of the house of David. The virgin's name was Mary. 28 And having come in, the angel said to her, *Rejoice, highly favored one, the Lord is with you; blessed are you among women!*

29 But when she saw him, she was troubled at his saying, and considered what manner of greeting this was. 30 Then the angel said to her, *Do not be afraid, Mary, for you have found favor with God. 31 And behold, you will conceive in your womb and bring forth a Son, and shall call His name Jesus. 32 He will be great, and will be called the Son of the Highest; and the Lord God will give Him the throne of His father David. 33 And He will reign over the house of Jacob forever, and of His kingdom there will be no end.*

The assignment Mary agreed to resulted in a change in time, for all time. All time was re-calculated to align with life 'Before Christ' (BC) and 'Anno Domini' (AD) which means 'in the year of our LORD'. Only in recent years have the legal documents stopped expressing the date of the document as being 'decreed and declared' to the courts 'in the year of our LORD'.

We are each part of the master plan our Father is orchestrating for us and future generations. What is our Father revealing to you, a step you can take with the amazing skills, talents and abilities HE has instilled within you?

Repentance for _____?

Adjustment(s) planned? _____

DAY SEVEN

BLESSING. Numbers 6:24-26.
> *"The LORD bless you and keep you;*
> *25 The LORD make His face shine upon you,*
>   *And be gracious to you;*
> *26 The LORD lift up His countenance upon you,*
>   *And give you peace."* '

Blessings received: _____

Blessings shared:_____

Declarations/Testimonies: _____

WEEK THIRTY-EIGHT

DAY ONE

FEAR. Luke 2:10 (8-14).
<u>Glory in the Highest</u>
Now there were in the same country shepherds living out in the fields, keeping watch over their flock by night. 9 And behold, an angel of the Lord stood before them, and the glory of the Lord shone around them, and they were greatly afraid. 10 Then the angel said to them, *Do not be afraid, for behold, I bring you good tidings of great joy which will be to all people.* **11** *For there is born to you this day in the city of David a Savior, who is Christ the Lord.* **12** *And this will be the sign to you: You will find a Babe wrapped in swaddling cloths, lying in a manger.*

13 And suddenly there was with the angel a multitude of the heavenly host praising God and saying:
14 *Glory to God in the highest,*
    And on earth peace, goodwill toward men!

Majestic moments in all of history.

However, when our Father announces to us through the Holy Spirit or an angel that amazing events will take place, what is your response?

Do you dismiss it and ignore it or do you seek the wisdom to comprehend your part in the majestic plan being revealed to you?

Repentance for _____?

Adjustment(s) planned? _____

DAY TWO

<u>UNBELIEF.</u> Luke 4:14-30.

Then Jesus returned in the power of the Spirit to Galilee, and news of Him went out through all the surrounding region. 15 And He taught in their synagogues, being glorified by all.

Jesus Rejected at Nazareth

16 So He came to Nazareth, where He had been brought up. And as His custom was, He went into the synagogue on the Sabbath day, and stood up to read. 17 And He was handed the book of the prophet Isaiah. And when He had opened the book, He found the place where it was written:

18 *The Spirit of the Lord is upon Me,*
Because He has anointed Me
To preach the gospel to the poor;
He has sent Me to heal the brokenhearted,
To proclaim liberty to the captives
And recovery of sight to the blind,
To set at liberty those who are oppressed;
19 *To proclaim the acceptable year of the Lord.*

20 Then He closed the book, and gave it back to the attendant and sat down. And the eyes of all who were in the synagogue were fixed on Him. 21 And He began to say to them, *Today this Scripture is fulfilled in your hearing.* 22 So all bore witness to Him, and marveled at the gracious words which proceeded out of His mouth. And they said, *Is this not Joseph's son?*

23 He said to them, *You will surely say this proverb to Me, 'Physician, heal yourself! Whatever we have heard done in Capernaum, do also here in Your country.'* 24 Then He said, *Assuredly, I say to you, no prophet is accepted in his own country. 25 But I tell you truly, many widows were in Israel in the days of Elijah, when the heaven was shut up three years and six months, and there was a great famine throughout all the land; 26 but to none of them was Elijah sent except to Zarephath, in the region of Sidon, to a woman who was a widow. 27 And many lepers were in Israel in the time of Elisha the prophet, and none of them was cleansed except Naaman the Syrian.*

28 So all those in the synagogue, when they heard these things, were filled with wrath, 29 and rose up and thrust Him out of the city; and they led Him to the brow of the hill on which their city was built, that they might throw Him down over the cliff. 30 Then passing through the midst of them, He went His way.

CHRIST spoke and then confirmed, the scripture is fullfilled in your hearing. As with the Father, when HE spoke 'into existence'. It seemed so 'far fetched' that they immediately questioned his 'earthly lineage'. After all, he's just the son of a carpenter!

When you express the word of the LORD, do the people 'get in action' or do they begin questioning your background?

CHRIST continued to share wisdom with them. When the region experienced drought and famine, Elijah was prompted to assist a specific widow which became a testimony for the entire region, and Elisha was prompted to assist one of the lepers. However, the 'religious' among them felt ALL should be assisted and healed instead of an example.

Father provides the truth, the example, and trusts we will take action and assist the widows and stand firm with those experiencing a dis-ease in their life.

Whether you have been trained to say, ***GOD will handle it, fix it, heal them*** or not, as of this moment in time what is HE prompting you to realize about you and what you can do for the widow(s), orphan(s) and those experiencing a dis-ease?

Repentance for _____?

Adjustment(s) planned? _____

DAY THREE

FEAR. Luke 5:10 (1-11).
Four Fishermen Called as Disciples
So it was, as the multitude pressed about Him to hear the word of God, that He stood by the Lake of Gennesaret, 2 and saw two boats standing by the lake; but the fishermen had gone from them and were washing their nets. 3 Then He got into one of the boats, which was Simon's, and asked him to put out a little from the land. And He sat down and taught the multitudes from the boat.

4 When He had stopped speaking, He said to Simon, *Launch out into the deep and let down your nets for a catch.*

5 But Simon answered and said to Him, *Master, we have toiled all night and caught nothing; nevertheless at Your word I will let down the net.* 6 And when they had done this, they caught a great number of fish, and their net

was breaking. 7 So they signaled to their partners in the other boat to come and help them. And they came and filled both the boats, so that they began to sink. 8 When Simon Peter saw it, he fell down at Jesus' knees, saying, *Depart from me, for I am a sinful man, O Lord!*

9 For he and all who were with him were astonished at the catch of fish which they had taken; 10 and so also were James and John, the sons of Zebedee, who were partners with Simon. And Jesus said to Simon, *Do not be afraid. From now on you will catch men.* 11 So when they had brought their boats to land, they forsook all and followed Him.

They remained 'at sea' and 'toiled all night' and 'caught nothing'.

Have you ever experienced a similar result? Focusing on a project, a problem, hour after hour, without a result?

Location. Timing. Being in the right place at the right time.

Repentance for _____?

Adjustment(s) planned? _____

DAY FOUR

<u>REVERENTIAL FEAR</u>. Luke 5:26 (20-26).
<u>Jesus Forgives and Heals a Paralytic</u>
When He (CHRIST) saw their faith, He said to him, *Man, your sins are forgiven you.* 21 And the scribes and the Pharisees began to reason, saying, *Who is this who speaks blasphemies? Who can forgive sins but God alone?*

22 But when Jesus perceived their thoughts, He answered and said to them, *Why are you reasoning in your hearts? 23 Which is easier, to say, 'Your sins are forgiven you,' or to say, 'Rise up and walk'? 24 But that you may know that the Son of Man has power on earth to forgive sins*—He said to the man who was paralyzed, I *say to you, arise, take up your bed, and go to your house.*

25 Immediately he rose up before them, took up what he had been lying on, and departed to his own house, glorifying God.

26 And they were all amazed, and they glorified God and were filled with fear, saying, *We have seen strange things today!*

Powerful summary in a very short, succinct delivery of the two options which provide the same result: ***Healed in Jesus' name!***

During a meeting in Macon, Georgia, a man was sitting on the floor in the back of the room 'whittling' a piece of wood into a walking stick. His knife slipped and cut his hand. The bleeding was significant while nobody in the room was close and observing what was happening with him. Within moments, however, a five year old girl who was seated near the front got up and walked to the back of the room. She approached the man, touched his hand and said, *Be healed in Jesus' name.*

After the meeting, the man offered his testimony.

His injury was healed without a scar so, nobody wanted to believe it.

However, the five year old girl spoke up. She pointed to the truth because there was blood on the man's shirt, on the wood and on the hand of the five year old girl. Then, the people who were dismissing the truth stood in awe!

Are you willing to forgive the sins or proclaim healing when prompted?

Will you share the testimony of healing far and wide?

Repentance for _____?

Adjustment(s) planned? _____

DAY FIVE

FEAR. Luke 8:50 (49-56).

While He was still speaking, someone came from the ruler of the synagogue's house, saying to him, *Your daughter is dead. Do not trouble the Teacher.*

50 But when Jesus heard it, He answered him, saying, *Do not be afraid; only believe, and she will be made well.*

51 When He came into the house, He permitted no one to go in except Peter, James, and John, and the father and mother of the girl.

52 Now all wept and mourned for her; but He said, *Do not weep; she is not dead, but sleeping.*

53 And they ridiculed Him, knowing that she was dead.

54 But He put them all outside, took her by the hand and called, saying, *Little girl, arise.* 55 Then her spirit returned, and she arose immediately. And He commanded that she be given something to eat. 56 And her parents were astonished, but He charged them to tell no one what had happened.

Again, the dismissing of the opportunity to speak truth and believe.

Then, CHRIST specifically told them to NOT be afraid, ONLY BELIEVE.

Then, he ONLY entered with specific disciples who BELIEVE in healing to enter with him, along with the parents of the girl.

Repentance for _____?

Adjustment(s) planned? _____

DAY SIX

<u>**UNBELIEF.** Luke 11:14-15.</u>
<u>**A HOUSE DIVIDED CANNOT STAND.**</u>
And He was casting out a demon, and it was mute. So it was, when the demon had gone out, that the mute spoke; and the multitudes marveled. 15 But some of them said, *He casts out demons by Beelzebub, the ruler of the demons.*

Imagine being in a room with Jesus and hearing someone speak about representing the Beelzebub. Some scriptures separate the name to Baal or Bell Zebub. The spelling is not significant since the truth is, there are ONLY two kingdoms. Whether a mute or an epileptic experiencing seizures, Jesus proved we must believe!

Mark 9:23-24.
Jesus said to him, *If you can believe, all things are possible to him who believes.* **24 Immediately the father of the child cried out and said with tears,** *Lord, I believe; help my unbelief!*

25 When Jesus saw that the people came running together, He rebuked the unclean spirit, saying to it, *Deaf and dumb spirit, I command you, come out of him and enter him no more!* **26 Then the spirit cried out, convulsed him greatly, and came out of him. And he became as one dead, so that many said,** *He is dead.* **27 But Jesus took him by the hand and lifted him up, and he arose.**

28 And when He had come into the house, His disciples asked Him privately, *Why could we not cast it out?*

29 So He said to them, *This kind can come out by nothing but prayer and fasting.*

Are you willing to believe, commanding the deaf and dumb spirit be removed from your heart and mind?

Repentance for _____?

Adjustment(s) planned? _____

DAY SEVEN

<u>**BLESSING.**</u> Numbers 6:24-26.
"The Lᴏʀᴅ bless you and keep you;
25 The Lᴏʀᴅ make His face shine upon you,

And be gracious to you;
26 The LORD lift up His countenance upon you,
And give you peace." '

Blessings received: _____

Blessings shared:_____

Declarations/Testimonies: _____

WEEK THIRTY-NINE

DAY ONE

UNBELIEF. Luke 11:16.
Others, testing Him, sought from Him a sign from heaven. 17 But He, knowing their thoughts, said to them: *Every kingdom divided against itself is brought to desolation, and a house divided against a house falls. 18 If Satan also is divided against himself, how will his kingdom stand? Because you say I cast out demons by Beelzebub. 19 And if I cast out demons by Beelzebub, by whom do your sons cast them out? Therefore they will be your judges. 20 But if I cast out demons with the finger of God, surely the kingdom of God has come upon you. 21 When a strong man, fully armed, guards his own palace, his goods are in peace. 22 But when a stronger than he comes upon him and overcomes him, he takes from him all his armor in which he trusted, and divides his spoils. 23 He who is not with Me is against Me, and he who does not gather with Me scatters.*

Seeking the signs is NOT the focus. To align with the Father and CHRIST is the foundation. Without knowledge, without discernment going forward in life, instead of building on a firm foundation on the TRUTH we live a life of 'guessing'.

This day, who do you and your house choose to serve?

Repentance for _____?

Adjustment(s) planned? _____

DAY TWO

UNBELIEF. Luke 11:29 (29-30).
SEEKING A SIGN.

195

And while the crowds were thickly gathered together, He began to say, *This is an evil generation. It seeks a sign, and no sign will be given to it except the sign of Jonah the prophet.* **30** *For as Jonah became a sign to the Ninevites, so also the Son of Man will be to this generation.*

Our Father orchestrated for Jonah and ALL came to the truth in Nineveh. The status did not remain. Nahum was sent to 'see about Nineveh' 100 years later and he found that it had declined because it returned to violence, idolatry, and arrogance.

Now, TRUTH was 'with the people' with CHRIST walking among the people 'on earth'; the truth 'in human form' was the sign for the generation and all generations to come.

Knowing CHRIST is at the right hand, speaking for us on our behalf, and our Father's hand is upon us and HE is orchestrating for us as HE did for Jonah, we have the truth, the reason to believe.

Will you believe, no matter what challenges you during the day?

Repentance for _____?

Adjustment(s) planned? _____

DAY THREE

FEAR. Luke 12:4 (1-5).
<u>Beware of Hypocrisy</u>
In the meantime, when an innumerable multitude of people had gathered together, so that they trampled one another, He began to say to His disciples first of all, *Beware of the leaven of the Pharisees, which is hypocrisy.* **2** *For there is nothing covered that will not be revealed, nor hidden that will not be known.* **3** *Therefore whatever you have spoken in the dark will be heard in the light, and what you have spoken in the ear in inner rooms will be proclaimed on the housetops.*
<u>Jesus Teaches the Fear of God</u>
4 *And I say to you, My friends, do not be afraid of those who kill the body, and after that have no more that they can do.* **5** *But I will show you whom you should fear: Fear Him who, after He has killed, has power to cast into hell; yes, I say to you, fear Him!*

Repentance for _____?

Adjustment(s) planned? _____

DAY FOUR

REVERENTIAL FEAR. Luke 12:4-5.
JESUS TEACHES THE FEAR OF GOD
And I say to you, My friends, do not be afraid of those who kill the body, and after that have no more that they can do. 5 But I will show you whom you should fear: Fear Him who, after He has killed, has power to cast into hell; yes, I say to you, fear Him!

Again, the choice is the same: *Choose this day who you will serve?*

Repentance for _____?

Adjustment(s) planned? _____

DAY FIVE

FEAR. Luke 12:7 (6-7).
Are not five sparrows sold for two copper coins? And not one of them is forgotten before God. 7 But the very hairs of your head are all numbered. Do not fear therefore; you are of more value than many sparrows.

Value of you is beyond all. Our Father arranged everything for you and continues to orchestrate for you, for HE formed you, sent you for these days with a purpose and plan and HE retains and sustains you to fulfill your destiny.

What is HE revealing to you about you which lifts you up and encourages you toward HIS promise of hope and a future?

Repentance for _____?

Adjustment(s) planned? _____

DAY SIX

FEAR. Luke 12:11 (8-11).
Confess Christ Before Men
Also I say to you, whoever confesses Me before men, him the Son of Man also will confess before the angels of God. 9 But he who denies Me before men will be denied before the angels of God.

10 And anyone who speaks a word against the Son of Man, it will be forgiven him; but to him who blasphemes against the Holy Spirit, it will not be forgiven.

197

11 *Now when they bring you to the synagogues and magistrates and authorities, do not worry about how or what you should answer, or what you should say.* **12** *For the Holy Spirit will teach you in that very hour what you ought to say.*

A huge lesson learned. Any time I go 'with a personal plan, a message, an agenda' it is NOT going to impact the lives of the people as much as proceeding as an empty vessel and allowing the Holy Spirit to 'bring to mind' and speak the truth direct from our Father and CHRIST. Proof is provided to me, often! When people send comments about radio or TV interviews, I have to go back and listen to the interview because the Holy Spirit provided a message which is something I need to hear, also!

When I shared a statement *All I have to do is show up* with my host family in London, the statement became my introduction by my host! A well known speaker was scheduled for an important leadership meeting at their church but, his flight was canceled. Therefore, I became the speaker without notice because I 'showed up'.

Many months later, the pastor insisted I had to have a copy of the tape.

A couple of years later, I was driving to Los Angeles for a very important meeting. Our Father did not give me a word about the meeting, yet, and I was not ready to deliver a message. In the midst of my 'chat with Father', HE offered for me to pull over and pull the audio tape out of the glove compartment and insert it in the player. I attempted to let our Father know I did not have an audio tape in the glove compartment but, HE insisted I did. So, I pulled over on the Freeway and opened the glove compartment, found an audio tape on top of the documents and inserted it ... the message of my voice long ago was the word I needed to hear before the meeting! Grateful HE is in charge and orchestrates the details. Standing firm with you while you hear HIS message for you!

Will you become an empty vessel and allow the Holy Spirit to speak through you, for your sake and for the sake of the souls who cross your path?

Repentance for _____?

Adjustment(s) planned? _____

BLESSING. **Numbers 6:24-26.**
> *"The LORD bless you and keep you;*
> **25** *The LORD make His face shine upon you,*
>   *And be gracious to you;*
> **26** *The LORD lift up His countenance upon you,*
>   *And give you peace." '*

Blessings received: _____

Blessings shared:_____

Declarations/Testimonies: _____

3rd QUARTER: What is our Father revealing to you, about you?

_____

WEEK FORTY

DAY ONE

FEAR. **Luke 12:32 (32-34).**
Do not fear, little flock, for it is your Father's good pleasure to give you the kingdom. **33** *Sell what you have and give alms; provide yourselves money bags which do not grow old, a treasure in the heavens that does not fail, where no thief approaches nor moth destroys.* **34** *For where your treasure is, there your heart will be also.*

The truth is, the promise is the rainbow and the treasure is you! Everything you do for other people, especially the widows and the orphans, to love the people and share from what you are and what you have.

A special church our Father arranged for me to visit each time I returned from an international trip 'for a weekend' captured HIS truth: They were unaware of the fact their region had an orphanage; families began submitting for foster care to adoption! A list of needs of the widows and then, others in the church was made. Plus, a list of all who could contribute their time and services, mechanics to dentists, to housekeepers, etc., etc. The two lists were a MATCH!

Our Father seeded the fellowship with the sources and resources so ALL would be blessed and NONE would leave in lack!

This is the plan. When we proceed to bless one another within a cycle of blessings, the testimonies spread in the region. The fellowship grows when they see Christians 'in action' with one another because they see us as the real ambassadors of Christ in the community. I can honestly confirm, when you give away the 'stuff', the wisdom and resources to those 'in need' our Father fills us again! It was NOT all about money. It was all about the animals, grains and needs to bless the fellowship and IF the tithe was 'too heavy' to bring, it was OK to sell the tithe in the marketplace and bring the money to the fellowship.

What is our Father revealing to you about your part of the plan, the person, the family, an orphan or a widow you are able to bless from what you have and what you can do to bless them?

Repentance for _____?

Adjustment(s) planned? _____

DAY TWO

DOUBT. Luke 22:19.
And He took bread, gave thanks and broke it, and gave it to them, saying, *This is My body which is given for you; do this in remembrance of Me.*

We hear the words repeated about the body and the blood. It becomes routine. Importance is 'in preparation', described prior to the 'communion words':

Luke 22:14-16. Jesus Institutes the Lord's Supper
When the hour had come, He sat down, and the twelve apostles with Him. 15 Then He said to them, *With fervent desire I have desired to eat this Passover with you before I suffer; 16 for I say to you, I will no longer eat of it until it is fulfilled in the kingdom of God.*

What we are hearing 'in the preparation' is as significant as the 'communion words' we hear regarding the bread and the wine.

Reference to the Passover, sacrificing the lamb, putting the blood of the lamb on the doorpost with the blood protecting us and our family. CHRIST was becoming the sacrificed lamb for the evil to 'pass over and not affect us'!

The doubt is eliminated in the understanding (gaining knowledge) of the preparation for communion 'as the reminder' of who we are, who HE is for us and that HIS blood is what protects us and heals us; the cleansing power of the blood!

Realizing the depth of the sacrifice, the truth about the blood, deepens the interest in celebrating the feast of Passover.

Wherever I have been at the time of Passover, several people want to know the truth and help prepare the feast and participate in the honoring of the message and partaking of the specific representations. The children appreciate learning the truth and they have taken on the 'reading of the message' in celebrations of the feast. The Passover plate and the meal which follows are still be held years after I was 'in the midst with them during Passover'.

If you want the information and prayers of blessing, submit an email or the contact form on the web site and we will send the information. The plate shown is a plastic version which I have obtained from a local grocery store. It is not a requirement to serve the Passover on a specific plate. The position of the representative items on a plate is what matters. The bread used is the same Challah bread or Sabbath bread which is also available at some grocery stores. It is often used on Friday evening for the 'family gathering' for the evening meal. The testimonies are shared while 'breaking bread' together and the Sabbath is honored and 'kept holy' with another gathering together on Saturday evening to share testimonies of what Father has revealed during the Sabbath.

While you pray about the 'preparing', about the 'protection and healing, cleansing power of the blood' and the honoring of the feasts and festivals, you will notice the re-alignment of our life, our family, and the family of believers, to the truth, the amazing plan our Father has 'laid out before us'.

What is our Father revealing to you as you pray about these facts, the truth about HIS plan for us, so evil will Passover us?

Repentance for _____?

Adjustment(s) planned? _____

DAY THREE

UNBELIEF. John 1:11.
He came to His own, and His own did not receive Him.

After ALL our CHRIST, our Savior and our Redeemer did for them and for us, and yet, they did not receive HIM, why would we expect it to be any different or easier for the world to receive us?

Repentance for _____?

Adjustment(s) planned? _____

DAY FOUR

UNBELIEF. John 3:11-12.
Most assuredly, I say to you, We speak what We know and testify what We have seen, and you do not receive Our witness. 12 If I have told you earthly things and you do not believe, how will you believe if I tell you heavenly things?

202

Truth!

When you 'hear truth', does it resonate with you?

When you 'share truth', does it resonate with the people in our life? In your family? In your home?

Have we spent too much time only speaking of things other people 'easily accept'?

How can we share the mighty, miraculous testimonies of our awesome LORD when people are not able to comprehend the truth about what is happening 'in the natural', 'in human time and comprehension'?

Repentance for _____?

Adjustment(s) planned? _____

DAY FIVE

UNBELIEF. John 4:48.
Then Jesus said to him, *Unless you people see signs and wonders, you will by no means believe.*

So true. Even the disciple, Thomas, known as 'doubting Thomas' because he had to be a witness to what happened 'on the cross'. CHRIST knew how much the truth would mean to those who have NOT seen, and yet, they believe!

Do you believe? Do the people in your home and in your life know you believe?

Repentance for _____?

Adjustment(s) planned? _____

DAY SIX

UNBELIEF. John 5:37-38.
And the Father Himself, who sent Me, has testified of Me. You have neither heard His voice at any time, nor seen His form. 38 But you do not have His word abiding in you, because whom He sent, Him you do not believe.

Amazing to hear how people think they know exactly how the LORD operates! Some 'well meaning' people say, *If GOD was going to do it, it would have happened by now!* When they think they know the 'timing of GOD', they forget that ETERNAL is NOT 'limited' by time as we know it 'on earth'.

The toughest verse to accept, the verse repeated to me so often I asked GOD if HE could please remove 'a day is as a thousand years' verse from the scriptures! Trusting there are days when I do bring a smile to HIS face, because HE let me 'sit with it' for a long, long, time before HE confirmed to me, exactly as HE has confirmed with the fear, doubt and unbelief scriptures, *view it 'in context':*

II Peter 3:8-9.
But, beloved, do not forget this one thing, that with the Lord one day is as a thousand years, and a thousand years as one day. 9 The Lord is not slack concerning His promise, as some count slackness, but is longsuffering toward us, not willing that any should perish but that all should come to repentance.

Father wanted me to be restored by repentance!

Not once did I hear 'the rest of the story'.

HE wants us close. HE wants us whole. HE wants us to be restored to full power and authority so HE can send us to do what needs us to be done and for us to be strengthened to say what is to be said!

There is no way to figure out the LORD. He is ahead of us, above us, beyond us, and altogether miraculous in the creation of all, including each of us!

Are you willing to 'remain available' for the most amazing journey of a lifetime, aligning with our Father and moving forward on the path HE has laid out before you?

Repentance for _____ ?

Adjustment(s) planned? _____

DAY SEVEN

BLESSING. Numbers 6:24-26.
"The LORD bless you and keep you;
25 The LORD make His face shine upon you,

204

And be gracious to you;
26 The LORD lift up His countenance upon you,
And give you peace." '

Blessings received: _____

Blessings shared: _____

Declarations/Testimonies: _____

WEEK FORTY-ONE

DAY ONE

<u>UNBELIEF.</u> John 5:46-47 (41-47).
I do not receive honor from men. 42 But I know you, that you do not have the love of God in you. 43 I have come in My Father's name, and you do not receive Me; if another comes in his own name, him you will receive. 44 How can you believe, who receive honor from one another, and do not seek the honor that comes from the only God? 45 Do not think that I shall accuse you to the Father; there is one who accuses you—Moses, in whom you trust. 46 For if you believed Moses, you would believe Me; for he wrote about Me. 47 But if you do not believe his writings, how will you believe My words?

Skeptics will always exist. Father and CHRIST know our heart, our thoughts. Nothing is hidden. As Thomas ('doubting Thomas') questioned the truth while in the presence of Jesus, while being discipled directly by Jesus, walking 'with Jesus and knowing him and knowing the truth by witnessing the truth' and he doubted the truth by hearing the disciples speak truth to him.

Seeing and Believing
Now Thomas, called the Twin, one of the twelve, was not with them when Jesus came. 25 The other disciples therefore said to him, *We have seen the Lord.*
So he said to them, *Unless I see in His hands the print of the nails, and put my finger into the print of the nails, and put my hand into His side, I will not believe.*
26 And after eight days His disciples were again inside, and Thomas with them. Jesus came, the doors being shut, and stood in the midst, and said, *Peace to you!* 27 Then He said to Thomas, *Reach your finger here, and look at My hands; and reach your hand here, and put it into My side. Do not be unbelieving, but believing.*

28 And Thomas answered and said to Him, *My Lord and my God!*

29 Jesus said to him, *Thomas, because you have seen Me, you have believed. Blessed are those who have not seen and yet have believed.*

Knowing truth removes 'guessing, accepting rumors and gossip'.

Discernment confirms truth and identifies lies, guesses, rumors and gossip.

We did not walk with CHRIST, see him 'in the natural, on earth' but, we are the beloved of the LORD, we believe!

It is ONLY the truth which sets us free!

Father we thank you for TRUTH, for the WORD speaking TRUTH, for the Holy Spirit revealing the TRUTH to us from YOU & YOUR SON. Grateful!

What are you prompted to remember, facts shared with you which were the truth but, the lies, guesses, rumors and gossip from others kept you from hearing and acting on the truth?

Repentance for _____?

Adjustment(s) planned? _____

DAY TWO

FEAR. John 6:20 John 6:20 (15-21).
Jesus Walks on the Sea
Therefore when Jesus perceived that they were about to come and take Him by force to make Him king, He departed again to the mountain by Himself alone.
16 Now when evening came, His disciples went down to the sea, 17 got into the boat, and went over the sea toward Capernaum. And it was already dark, and Jesus had not come to them. 18 Then the sea arose because a great wind was blowing. 19 So when they had rowed about three or four miles, they saw Jesus walking on the sea and drawing near the boat; and they were afraid. 20 But He said to them, *It is I; do not be afraid.* 21 Then they willingly received Him into the boat, and immediately the boat was at the land where they were going.

Once CHRIST joined them, IMMEDIATELY the boat was at the destination. When we invite our Father and CHRIST into our situation(s), repenting for all that is in the 'in between', the crooked is made straight. Which situation(s) in your life transitioned from overwhelming to peaceful resolution are you being prompted to remember?

Repentance for _____?

Adjustment(s) planned? _____

DAY THREE

UNBELIEF. John 6:36.
But I said to you that you have seen Me and yet do not believe.

The question is simple: Do you believe?

Repentance for _____?

Adjustment(s) planned? _____

DAY FOUR

UNBELIEF. John 7:5.
For even His brothers did not believe in Him.

Father prompted me to realize the brothers of CHRIST did not believe HIM until AFTER the crucifixion! My upsets about not being understood or believed when our Father gave me the exact word to deliver to people whether in my immediate family, especially my siblings, or other people, stopped in that exact moment. Repentance and unforgiveness was quickly dealt with and many times since that day.

A good reminder that CHRIST shared the truth: ***Only did what HE saw HIS Father do and said what HE heard HIS Father say!*** **John 5:19; 12:49.**

Are you willing to believe and share the truth even if NOBODY believes what you are saying or doing?

Repentance for _____?

Adjustment(s) planned? _____

DAY FIVE

UNBELIEF. John 8:45.
But because I tell the truth, you do not believe Me.

It is still the same today. Trusting you have experienced times when it seemed nobody believed you or what you were going through. Gossip, rumors and lies are believed and shared without questioning or researching. They easily become what is 'believed' because it is repeated, often. When deep truth is shared, it is harder to believe if it does not 'resonate'. Often, when people do not have discernment or seek wisdom from our Father, the deep wisdom shared does appear 'foreign' to them. Do you believe what is in the 'atmosphere' as the truth or do you seek truth direct from our Father?

Repentance for _____?

Adjustment(s) planned? _____

DAY SIX

UNBELIEF. John 9:18.
But the Jews did not believe concerning him, that he had been blind and received his sight, until they called the parents of him who had received his sight.

What did they not believe? The miracle of healing the blind man.

Why did they continue to question the healing until they spoke to the parents of the man? The son was born blind. Cleary, he was healed!

What was the 'additional problem'? The man was healed on Sabbath!

Why was this a significant problem for the Pharisees? Work! In the time of Moses, a man was put to death for picking up sticks on the Sabbath.

When everything appears to be against you, against the truth, will you stand firm in the truth until the truth is received and accepted?

Repentance for _____?

Adjustment(s) planned? _____

DAY SEVEN

BLESSING. Numbers 6:24-26.
"The Lord bless you and keep you;
25 The Lord make His face shine upon you,
And be gracious to you;
26 The Lord lift up His countenance upon you,
And give you peace." '

Blessings received: _____

Blessings shared:_____

Declarations/Testimonies: _____

WEEK FORTY-TWO

DAY ONE

UNBELIEF. John 10:24-26.
Then the Jews surrounded Him and said to Him, *How long do You keep us in doubt? If You are the Christ, tell us plainly.*
25 Jesus answered them, *I told you, and you do not believe. The works that I do in My Father's name, they bear witness of Me.* **26 But you do not believe, because you are not of My sheep, as I said to you.**

Doubt and unbelief is not always resolved by 'repeating truth'. Tough to watch great presentations to believers and yet, lives are not changed. When people hear truth, witness the truth in the life of another person or due to a miracle, lives are changed. When our Father spoke, what was not in existence came into existence. When CHRIST spoke, people chose to be available to hear HIS words. Men followed HIM and became 'fishers of men'. Since Father is available to us through the Holy Spirit, as is CHRIST and CHRIST resides in our heart. We proceed to conform to the heart and mind of CHRIST desiring more of CHRIST and less of us, daily. **John 13:35,** do we express our love for one another? Do people recognize us as believers, as followers of CHRIST, as representatives, ambassadors of Christ because they witness us living and loving as Christians?

Repentance for _____?

Adjustment(s) planned? _____

DAY TWO

UNBELIEF. John 10:37-38.

209

If I do not do the works of My Father, do not believe Me; **38** *but if I do, though you do not believe Me, believe the works, that you may know and believe that the Father is in Me, and I in Him.*

Father prompted me to share a similar word, often: *It does not matter that you remember my name. What does matter is that GOD sent a woman your way, and since that day your life will never be the same.*

While I was in Australia, I was invited to preach in a Four Square Church housed within the Aboriginal Cultural Center.

Pastor Rex Morgan, the son and daughter-in-law(love) of my host family & Erica (8). Erica heard from GOD. HE told Erica that HE sent me to Australia for her. She only wanted to know, *When GOD sends you, what type of plane does GOD use?*

It is NOT about me 'being in the midst', it is about what GOD reveals to the people 'because I showed up to represent HIM'. When our Father places you 'in the midst' and provides a word for a person, or for the fellowship, do you represent HIM? Do you witness lives changing?

Repentance for _____ ?

Adjustment(s) planned? _____

UNBELIEF. John 10:31-33. <u>Renewed Efforts to Stone Jesus</u>
Then the Jews took up stones again to stone Him. 32 Jesus answered them, *Many good works I have shown you from My Father. For which of those works do you stone Me?*
33 The Jews answered Him, saying, *For a good work we do not stone You, but for blasphemy, and because You, being a Man, make Yourself God.*

They stoned Stephen and Paul. Stephen witnessed an open heaven, described it to the men stoning him since he saw CHRIST at the right hand of the Father but, they did not look or choose to believe. Paul was left outside the city for dead.

When I shared with our Father how disbelief was more evident than faith so I did not think I delivered the message to the fellowship; before I realized I was in the midst of complaining to our Father, HE asked, *Did they stone you to death?* It took a moment to take that in but, I answered truthfully, *Of course not.* Without hesitation HE said, *If they would have ... I would have transported you to another city to preach as I did for Paul.* Without taking a moment to think it through, I continued to complain about how much they loved me last week but, this week was so different. HE said, *That is what it was like for my SON.* Then he asked, *Are they cutting down a tree and forming it into a cross?* Feeling a bit silly when I said, *Of course not.* Without 'known obstacles' HE prompted me to carry on, keep going forward. No matter what it looks like to 'other people', will you carry on, keep going until the message is delivered or the assignment in the region completed?

Repentance for _____?

Adjustment(s) planned? _____

UNBELIEF. John 12:37-38.
<u>Who Has Believed Our Report</u>?
But although He had done so many signs before them, they did not believe in Him, 38 that the word of Isaiah the prophet might be fulfilled, which he spoke:
Lord, who has believed our report?
And to whom has the arm of the Lord been revealed?

In other words, WHERE ARE THE BELIEVERS? ARE THEY HIDING?

When we know the truth, after we witness the miracle, what stops us from shouting the truth from our rooftops? What restricts us? Other people? Non-believers or believers? Or, it is us?

Repentance for _____?

Adjustment(s) planned? _____

DAY FIVE

FEAR. John 12:15 (12-15). <u>The Triumphal Entry</u>
The next day a great multitude that had come to the feast, when they heard that Jesus was coming to Jerusalem, 13 took branches of palm trees and went out to meet Him, and cried out: *Hosanna! 'Blessed is He who comes in the name of the Lord!' The King of Israel!*

14 Then Jesus, when He had found a young donkey, sat on it; as it is written: 15 *Fear not, daughter of Zion; Behold, your King is coming, Sitting on a donkey's colt.*

John 14:27 (25-28). <u>The Gift of His Peace</u>
These things I have spoken to you while being present with you. 26 But the Helper, the Holy Spirit, whom the Father will send in My name, He will teach you all things, and bring to your remembrance all things that I said to you. 27 Peace I leave with you, My peace I give to you; not as the world gives do I give to you. Let not your heart be troubled, neither let it be afraid. 28 You have heard Me say to you, 'I am going away and coming back to you.' If you loved Me, you would rejoice because I said, 'I am going to the Father,' for My Father is greater than I.

John 16:33 (25-33). <u>Jesus Christ Has Overcome the World</u>
These things I have spoken to you in figurative language; but the time is coming when I will no longer speak to you in figurative language, but I will tell you plainly about the Father. 26 In that day you will ask in My name, and I do not say to you that I shall pray the Father for you; 27 for the Father Himself loves you, because you have loved Me, and have believed that I came forth from God. 28 I came forth from the Father and have come into the world. Again, I leave the world and go to the Father.

29 His disciples said to Him, See, now You are speaking plainly, and using no figure of speech! *30* Now we are sure that You know all things, and have no need that anyone should question You. By this we believe that You came forth from God.

31 Jesus answered them, Do you now believe? *32* Indeed the hour is coming, yes, has now come, that you will be scattered, each to his own, and will leave Me alone. And yet I am not alone, because the Father is with Me. *33 These things I have spoken to you, that in Me you may have peace. In the world you will have tribulation; but be of good cheer, I have overcome the world.*

HE accomplished ALL. HE came, brought peace and overcame the world.

How does your legacy of bringing peace and overcoming the world align with the plan for your life while 'on earth'?

Repentance for _____?

Adjustment(s) planned? _____

DAY SIX

DOUBT. John 20:27.
Then He said to Thomas, *Reach your finger here, and look at My hands; and reach your hand here, and put it into My side. Do not be unbelieving, but believing.*

When we are a witness to the truth, do we testify that we believe?

Repentance for _____?

Adjustment(s) planned? _____

DAY SEVEN

BLESSING. Numbers 6:24-26.
   "The LORD bless you and keep you;
   25 The LORD make His face shine upon you,
      And be gracious to you;
   26 The LORD lift up His countenance upon you,
      And give you peace." '

Blessings received: _____

Blessings shared: _____

Declarations/Testimonies: _____

WEEK FORTY-THREE

DAY ONE

DOUBT. John 20:30-31.

213

And truly Jesus did many other signs in the presence of His disciples, which are not written in this book; 31 but these are written that you may believe that Jesus is the Christ, the Son of God, and that believing you may have life in His name.

Often, I remind myself who I am in CHRIST so I will be 'ready' when HE wants me to deliver a message to believers or non-believers. It is NOT a plan to 'enter into a conversation' without the Holy Spirit. As the famous quote for an ad states (about a credit card), *Never leave home without HIM!*

Do you enter into each day, believing who you truly do represent and making sure HE is 'with you'?

Repentance for _____ ?

Adjustment(s) planned? _____

DAY TWO

<u>**UNBELIEF.**</u> Luke 22:67 (66-69).
<u>**Jesus Faces the Sanhedrin**</u>
As soon as it was day, the elders of the people, both chief priests and scribes, came together and led Him into their council, saying, 67 If You are the Christ, tell us.
But He said to them, *If I tell you, you will by no means believe. 68 And if I also ask you, you will by no means answer Me or let Me go. 69 Hereafter the Son of Man will sit on the right hand of the power of God.*

When we are being challenged, HE will answer for us. HE knows their thoughts and HE answered before they even asked or knew what to ask. Does HE become your spokesperson when you are in the midst of a challenge?

Repentance for _____ ?

Adjustment(s) planned? _____

DAY THREE

<u>**UNBELIEF.**</u> Acts 7:21.
But when he was set out, Pharaoh's daughter took him away and brought him up as her own son.

All babies were being killed, again. However, it was a powerful decision for the mother of Moses to send him in a basket on the Nile River. His destiny was known by our Father since HE knows the end from the beginning. Moses was going to be discovered and adopted. Whether you were raised by your family or you were adopted, are you willing to lead fellow believers to the truth?

Repentance for _____?

Adjustment(s) planned? _____

DAY FOUR

REVERENTIAL FEAR. Acts 9:31.
The Church Prospers
Then the churches throughout all Judea, Galilee, and Samaria had peace and were edified. And walking in the fear of the Lord and in the comfort of the Holy Spirit, they were multiplied.
The ultimate location: Walking in the fear of the LORD and in the comfort

of the Holy Spirit ... multiplication, aka, the fellowship will grow.

The enemy wants you to be isolated, believing what you have to say does not have value. When our Father is walking with you and CHRIST resides in your heart and the Holy Spirit is prompting you to speak a word to bless the people in your path today, will you speak?

Repentance for _____?

Adjustment(s) planned? _____

DAY FIVE

UNBELIEF. Acts 13:50 (44-52).
On the next Sabbath almost the whole city came together to hear the word of God. 45 But when the Jews saw the multitudes, they were filled with envy; and contradicting and blaspheming, they opposed the things spoken by Paul. 46 Then Paul and Barnabas grew bold and said, *It was necessary that the word of God should be spoken to you first; but since you reject it, and judge yourselves unworthy of everlasting life, behold, we turn to the Gentiles. 47 For so the Lord has commanded us:*

'I have set you as a light to the Gentiles,
That you should be for salvation to the ends of the earth.'

48 Now when the Gentiles heard this, they were glad and glorified the word of the Lord. And as many as had been appointed to eternal life believed.

49 And the word of the Lord was being spread throughout all the region. 50 But the Jews stirred up the devout and prominent women and the chief men of the city, raised up persecution against Paul and Barnabas, and expelled them from their region. 51 But they shook off the dust from their feet against them, and came to Iconium. 52 And the disciples were filled with joy and with the Holy Spirit.

Remembering the moments when I was informed a well known missionary and ministry leader declared he wanted to be the first (and, the only?) Gentile to be buried in a Jewish cemetery in Israel. It was a confusing declaration since we are 'no longer Gentiles'. We are not to do as the Gentiles do, once we know the truth and claim our salvation and live our life, working out our salvation daily!

Are you feeling like 'a light to the Gentiles' or would you prefer to return to 'live the life of a Gentile'?

Repentance for _____ ?

Adjustment(s) planned? _____

DAY SIX

UNBELIEF. Acts 14:2 (1-3).
Now it happened in Iconium that they went together to the synagogue of the Jews, and so spoke that a great multitude both of the Jews and of the Greeks believed. 2 But the unbelieving Jews stirred up the Gentiles and poisoned their minds against the brethren. 3 Therefore they stayed there a long time, speaking boldly in the Lord, who was bearing witness to the word of His grace, granting signs and wonders to be done by their hands.

The apostles (Paul and Barnabas) traveled region to region, sent to speak to the Gentiles in each region. Now, they reached Iconium. Taking sides was obvious and it is still evident to this day.

Regardless, the apostles spoke the truth, boldly.

After everything, when it reached the point where the apostles were informed they were going to be stoned, they moved on to another region.

The pattern repeated and repeated city to city, throughout the region.

Due to 'no threats of stoning', what is restricting you from speaking boldly?

Repentance for _____?

Adjustment(s) planned? _____

DAY SEVEN

<u>BLESSING.</u> Numbers 6:24-26.
> *"The LORD bless you and keep you;*
> 25 *The LORD make His face shine upon you,*
>   *And be gracious to you;*
> 26 *The LORD lift up His countenance upon you,*
>   *And give you peace." '*

Blessings received: _____

Blessings shared: _____

Declarations/Testimonies: _____

WEEK FORTY-FOUR

DAY ONE

<u>UNBELIEF.</u> Acts 17:13 (10-15).
<u>Ministering at Berea</u>
Then the brethren immediately sent Paul and Silas away by night to Berea. When they arrived, they went into the synagogue of the Jews. 11 These were more fair-minded than those in Thessalonica, in that they received the word with all readiness, and searched the Scriptures daily to find out whether these things were so. 12 Therefore many of them believed, and also not a few of the Greeks, prominent women as well as men. 13 But when the Jews from Thessalonica learned that the word of God was preached by Paul at Berea, they came there also and stirred up the crowds. 14 Then immediately the brethren sent Paul away, to go to the sea; but both Silas and Timothy remained there. 15 So those who conducted Paul brought him to Athens; and receiving a command for Silas and Timothy to come to him with all speed, they departed.

Those who chose to 'stir up' and 'question man vs. our Father' will appear within any gathering at any time. Often they are the 'religious ones' in the gathering, as the Pharisees & Sadducees repeatedly challenged Jesus believing HE could NOT be the Messiah, the CHRIST. The truth 'about religion' is that it ONLY refers to 'seeing to the needs of the widows and orphans'. **James 1:26-27.**

> *If anyone among you thinks he is religious, and does not bridle his tongue but deceives his own heart, this one's religion is useless. 27 Pure and undefiled religion before God and the Father is this: to visit orphans and widows in their trouble, and to keep oneself unspotted from the world.*

Often the term 'religious' is used while it is not in reference to the biblical confirmation of religion which is 'seeing to the needs of the widows and orphans'. What is Father revealing to you about your involvement with the widows and orphans? What is HE prompting you to know about your location, is it 'changing', is it 'for now', or is it your location 'from now on'?

Repentance for _____?

Adjustment(s) planned? _____

DAY TWO

<u>FEAR</u>. **Acts 18:9 (9-11).**
Now the Lord spoke to Paul in the night by a vision, *Do not be afraid, but speak, and do not keep silent;* **10** *for I am with you, and no one will attack you to hurt you; for I have many people in this city.* **11 And he continued there a year and six months, teaching the word of God among them.**

Antioch became a location for Paul to remain 'for a time'. After being prompted to move city to city in a few days or weeks, our Father orchestrated for the truth to be shared in the region of Antioch for 18 months.

Are you being prompted to remain in your area for an extended period of time? Is the truth expanding in your area? Are lives changing?

Repentance for _____?

Adjustment(s) planned? _____

DAY THREE

<u>UNBELIEF</u>. **Acts 19:9.**

218

Paul at Ephesus

And it happened, while Apollos was at Corinth, that Paul, having passed through the upper regions, came to Ephesus. And finding some disciples 2 he said to them, *Did you receive the Holy Spirit when you believed?*

So they said to him, *We have not so much as heard whether there is a Holy Spirit.*

3 And he said to them, *Into what then were you baptized?*

So they said, *Into John's baptism.*

4 Then Paul said, *John indeed baptized with a baptism of repentance, saying to the people that they should believe on Him who would come after him, that is, on Christ Jesus.*

5 When they heard this, they were baptized in the name of the Lord Jesus. 6 And when Paul had laid hands on them, the Holy Spirit came upon them, and they spoke with tongues and prophesied. 7 Now the men were about twelve in all.

8 And he went into the synagogue and spoke boldly for three months, reasoning and persuading concerning the things of the kingdom of God. 9 But when some were hardened and did not believe, but spoke evil of the Way before the multitude, he departed from them and withdrew the disciples, reasoning daily in the school of Tyrannus. 10 And this continued for two years, so that all who dwelt in Asia heard the word of the Lord Jesus, both Jews and Greeks.

Baptism of repentance along with the power of the Holy Spirit is only available after the resurrection of CHRIST because HE confirmed the Holy Spirit would come and be the comforter. The WAY was preached with twelve disciples joining Paul. As they traveled, they did not remain with those who were 'hardened' and spoke evil. They continued to speak TRUTH, the WAY, to all who had ears to hear and eyes to see.

The people were saved but, they did not have the Holy Spirit. Have you received the Holy Spirit?

When people were not receiving the message our Father prompted me to deliver, a message from the Holy Spirit, I used to keep doing and saying all I could to 'convince them'. Since they were believers, I trusted they were saved and heard the Father's voice through the Holy Spirit. Our Father politely informed me that I was not responsible if they received the message, I was only responsible to deliver the message. It was difficult at first to just move on, especially since our Father placed it on my heart to care about the souls of the people whether they were believers or not when I was prompted to share truth with them.

In the toughest moment, while tears flowed, our Father showed me a vision of a hand grenade in my hand; pin pulled and I opened my hand and released the hand grenade, while HE confirmed: *The message was delivered and it was not my responsibility to be sure the person* (**or people**) *took action or not. It was only my responsibility to deliver the message.*

When I was in central Georgia for two nights, I was praying about packing everything and leaving Georgia at the moment when I was invited by my hostess to 'help decorate the location for a six-year old birthday party'.

A man started asking questions to get to know me, since I was not from the area or known by the guests. When everyone walked outside for a group picture, I did not go with them. The man stopped and entered into a 'conversation with GOD'. It was evident due to his hand motions and conversation taking place without another person around.

Within moments, he returned and asked me where I was from. When I said, **San Diego,** he said, *That's what GOD said.* Then, his right hand formed exactly as my hand formed to hold the hand grenade during the vision while he told me about a prophecy from the Brownsville Revival prophet: *The move of GOD is going into Georgia. GOD is preparing someone in San Diego and you will know them when you meet them because they would have set off fires throughout Georgia.* In that moment, he opened his palm exactly as the hand grenade was released from my palm in the vision, and I was in nearly every section of Georgia before this moment in time.

The prophet told the leaders to gather in Albany so he moved from Atlanta to Albany.

The associate pastor in Brownsville also moved to Albany and established a church.

When the leaders became discouraged, the Brownsville Revival prophet returned and told them, *Do not become discouraged. GOD is preparing the person …*

Twenty-five years later, GOD sent me to Albany for a birthday party the night before I was leaving Georgia.

This night was three years after finding out Graham Cooke was sent from England to Macon, Georgia during his first assignment to America (22 years before I was sent to Macon) to provide a message for unity. Graham confirmed unity is critical and it does not require removing denominational structures but, it is important to unite the believers within five to ten years.

Tears flowed.

The orchestration of more than two decades by our Father did not result in people being ready to unite as believers in the TRUTH, yet. Even though it did not happen during the two decades before I arrived, it is still the desire of our Father that we unite together as believers and share our testimonies.

Are you being prompted to share your faith and unite together with other believers in your region, regardless of their denominational beliefs?

Repentance for _____?

Adjustment(s) planned? _____

DAY FOUR

FEAR. Acts 20:10 (7-10).
Ministering at Troas
Now on the first day of the week, when the disciples came together to break bread, Paul, ready to depart the next day, spoke to them and continued his message until midnight. 8 There were many lamps in the upper room where they were gathered together. 9 And in a window sat a certain young man named Eutychus, who was sinking into a deep sleep. He was overcome by sleep; and as Paul continued speaking, he fell down from the third story and was taken up dead. 10 But Paul went down, fell on him, and embracing him said, *Do not trouble yourselves, for his life is in him.*

Do you believe what the crowd believes, or the TRUTH and only TRUTH?

Repentance for _____?

Adjustment(s) planned? _____

DAY FIVE

FEAR. Acts 27:24 (20-24).

Now when neither sun nor stars appeared for many days, and no small tempest beat on us, all hope that we would be saved was finally given up.

21 But after long abstinence from food, then Paul stood in the midst of them and said, *Men, you should have listened to me, and not have sailed from Crete and incurred this disaster and loss.* 22 *And now I urge you to take heart, for there will be no loss of life among you, but only of the ship.* 23 *For there stood by me this night an angel of the God to whom I belong and whom I serve,* 24 *saying, 'Do not be afraid, Paul; you must be brought before Caesar; and indeed God has granted you all those who sail with you.'*

Is our Father prompting you to remember an experience, a situation you entered into before seeking HIM about it?

Repentance for _____?

Adjustment(s) planned? _____

DAY SIX

UNBELIEF. Acts 28:24 (23-24).

So when they (some of the people in Rome) *had appointed him* (Paul) *a day, many came to him at his lodging, to whom he explained and solemnly testified of the kingdom of God, persuading them concerning Jesus from both the Law of Moses and the Prophets, from morning till evening.* 24 *And some were persuaded by the things which were spoken, and some disbelieved.*

In any gathering, some will seek confirmation from our Father and some will rely on their own intellect. Since our focus is the 'souls', is our Father bringing to mind a time when you thought it was more important to 'be right' or 'religious' in a gathering than to seek HIS truth and love all who have gathered?

Repentance for _____?

Adjustment(s) planned? _____

DAY SEVEN

BLESSING. Numbers 6:24-26.
> *"The LORD bless you and keep you;*
> 25 *The LORD make His face shine upon you,*
>   *And be gracious to you;*
> 26 *The LORD lift up His countenance upon you,*
>   *And give you peace." '*

Blessings received: _____

Blessings shared: _____

Declarations/Testimonies: _____

WEEK FORTY-FIVE

DAY ONE

UNBELIEF. Romans 1:18-19.
God's Wrath on Unrighteousness
For the wrath of God is revealed from heaven against all ungodliness and unrighteousness of men, who suppress the truth in unrighteousness, 19 because what may be known of God is manifest in them, for God has shown it to them.

Is righteousness and truth evident, manifest in you, to people in your life?

Repentance for _____?

Adjustment(s) planned? _____

DAY TWO

UNBELIEF. Romans 4:20-21.
He did not waver at the promise of God through unbelief, but was strengthened in faith, giving glory to God, 21 and being fully convinced that what He had promised He was also able to perform.

Abraham did not enter into unbelief when the promise of a son, at nearly 100 years old, was granted. Abraham did not waiver, he believed: *A promise granted by faith, through grace.*

When you receive a message from GOD, do you believe or waiver?

Repentance for _____?

Adjustment(s) planned? _____

DAY THREE

FEAR. Romans 5:1 (1-5).
Faith Triumphs in Trouble
Therefore, having been justified by faith, we have peace with God through our Lord Jesus Christ, 2 through whom also we have access by faith into this grace in which we stand, and rejoice in hope of the glory of God. 3 And not only that, but we also glory in tribulations, knowing that

tribulation produces perseverance; 4 and perseverance, character; and character, hope. 5 Now hope does not disappoint, because the love of God has been poured out in our hearts by the Holy Spirit who was given to us.

The promise is: hope and a future.

The 'learning phase' is rejoicing in hope of the glory of GOD and retaining hope and glory in the midst of problems, knowing that what we are experiencing will produce perseverance; perseverance, character; character, hope.

Our Comforter, the Holy Spirit will remain with us and our Father & CHRIST will guide us.

Knowing the promise and the process are you willing to remain aligned with our Father, standing on the promise of hope and a future?

Repentance for _____?

Adjustment(s) planned? _____

DAY FOUR
UNBELIEF. Romans 10:14-15.
How then shall they call on Him in whom they have not believed? And how shall they believe in Him of whom they have not heard? And how shall they hear without a preacher? 15 And how shall they preach unless they are sent? As it is written:
How beautiful are the feet of those who preach the gospel of peace,
Who bring glad tidings of good things!

In a town just west of Minneapolis, a woman was immediately prompted by our Father to pray with a specific teller the moment she entered the bank.

The teller was so deeply touched, she shared the testimony far and wide.

Within days, people were praying specifically for neighbors and customers in the businesses and the love of GOD spread throughout the town and surrounding community.

Do you follow through in the moment when GOD prompts you to pray for someone or to give them a specific word?

Repentance for _____?

Adjustment(s) planned? _____

DAY FIVE
UNBELIEF. Romans 10:16.

224

But they have not all obeyed the gospel. For Isaiah says, *Lord, who has believed our report?*

Are you being prompted to share TRUTH with someone, whether believer or non-believer?

Repentance for _____?

Adjustment(s) planned? _____

DAY SIX

DOUBT. Romans 14:1-4.
The Law of Liberty

Receive one who is weak in the faith, but not to disputes over doubtful things. 2 For one believes he may eat all things, but he who is weak eats only vegetables. 3 Let not him who eats despise him who does not eat, and let not him who does not eat judge him who eats; for God has received him. 4 Who are you to judge another's servant? To his own master he stands or falls. Indeed, he will be made to stand, for God is able to make him stand.

Whoever is in your path today, will you love them for exactly who they are?

Repentance for _____?

Adjustment(s) planned? _____

DAY SEVEN

BLESSING. Numbers 6:24-26.
   "The Lord bless you and keep you;
   25 The Lord make His face shine upon you,
      And be gracious to you;
   26 The Lord lift up His countenance upon you,
      And give you peace." '

Blessings received: _____

Blessings shared: _____

Declarations/Testimonies: _____

WEEK FORTY-SIX

DAY ONE

DOUBT. Romans 15:1.
Bearing Others' Burdens

We then who are strong ought to bear with the scruples of the weak, and not to please ourselves.

With ALL Father has provided, is HE revealing ways to bless others?

Repentance for _____?

Adjustment(s) planned? _____

DAY TWO

DOUBT. Romans 15:4.
For whatever things were written before were written for our learning, that we through the patience and comfort of the Scriptures might have hope.

Knowing our Father will never leave or forsake you, and hearing the testimonies of the saints being delivered from battles, family issues, attacks of the enemy, are you strengthened in faith?

Repentance for _____?

Adjustment(s) planned? _____

DAY THREE

DOUBT. I Corinthians 10:11.
Now all these things happened to them as examples, and they were written for our admonition, upon whom the ends of the ages have come.

The WORD is available to be referred to 'in the moment' and the examples are provided to lift you up, encourage you and reveal the depth of unconditional love our Father has for you.

Knowing HIS truth, is there something HE is prompting you to do?

Repentance for _____?

Adjustment(s) planned? _____

DAY FOUR
DOUBT. I Corinthians 11:25 (23-25).

Institution of the Lord's Supper

For I received from the Lord that which I also delivered to you: that the Lord Jesus on the same night in which He was betrayed took bread; and when He had given thanks, He broke *it* and said, *Take, eat; this is My body which is broken for you; do this in remembrance of Me.* 25 In the same manner *He* also *took* the cup after supper, saying, *This cup is the new covenant in My blood. This do, as often as you drink it, in remembrance of Me.*

Repentance for _____?

Adjustment(s) planned? _____

DAY FIVE

__UNBELIEF.__ I Corinthians 14:22-24.

Therefore tongues are for a sign, not to those who believe but to unbelievers; but prophesying is not for unbelievers but for those who believe. 23 Therefore if the whole church comes together in one place, and all speak with tongues, and there come in those who are uninformed or unbelievers, will they not say that you are out of your mind? 24 But if all prophesy, and an unbeliever or an uninformed person comes in, he is convinced by all, he is convicted by all.

Unity. Gaining understanding and knowledge, becoming the fellowship of believers. When non-believers enter into a believing fellowship, hearts are convicted. What is your role in assisting the uniting of believers in the fellowship and receiving non-believers in love?

Repentance for _____?

Adjustment(s) planned? _____

DAY SIX

__DOUBT.__ Ephesians 4:14 (11-16).

And He Himself gave some to be apostles, some prophets, some evangelists, and some pastors and teachers, 12 for the equipping of the saints for the work of ministry, for the edifying of the body of Christ, 13 till we all come to the unity of the faith and of the knowledge of the Son of God, to a perfect man, to the measure of the stature of the fullness of Christ;

14 that we should no longer be children, tossed to and fro and carried about with every wind of doctrine, by the trickery of men, in the cunning

craftiness of deceitful plotting, 15 but, speaking the truth in love, may grow up in all things into Him who is the head—Christ— 16 from whom the whole body, joined and knit together by what every joint supplies, according to the effective working by which every part does its share, causes growth of the body for the edifying of itself in love.

Are you aware of who you are, what your position is within the body and how to express your faith and the love of our Father?

Repentance for _____?

Adjustment(s) planned? _____

DAY SEVEN

BLESSING. Numbers 6:24-26.
> *"The LORD bless you and keep you;*
> *25 The LORD make His face shine upon you,*
>   *And be gracious to you;*
> *26 The LORD lift up His countenance upon you,*
>   *And give you peace." '*

Blessings received: _____

Blessings shared:_____

Declarations/Testimonies: _____

WEEK FORTY-SEVEN

DAY ONE

FEAR. Philippians 4:6 (1-7).
Be Anxious for Nothing; Think These Thoughts
Therefore, my beloved and longed-for brethren, my joy and crown, so stand fast in the Lord, beloved.
Be United, Joyful, and in Prayer
2 I implore Euodia and I implore Syntyche to be of the same mind in the Lord. 3 And I urge you also, true companion, help these women who labored with me in the gospel, with Clement also, and the rest of my fellow workers, whose names are in the Book of Life.
4 Rejoice in the Lord always. Again I will say, rejoice!
5 Let your gentleness be known to all men. The Lord is at hand.

6 Be anxious for nothing, but in everything by prayer and supplication, with thanksgiving, let your requests be made known to God; 7 and the peace of God, which surpasses all understanding, will guard your hearts and minds through Christ Jesus.

Again, we are reminded to use discernment to know who we are keeping company with and even to recognize who is in the Book of Life, and how to come along side them and help them. Are you leading by example in your home, church, etc., by being anxious for nothing and letting GOD's peace which surpasses all understanding rule your heart?

Repentance for _____?

Adjustment(s) planned? _____

DAY TWO

UNBELIEF. II Thessalonians 2:12 (5-12).

Do you not remember that when I was still with you I told you these things? 6 And now you know what is restraining, that he may be revealed in his own time. 7 For the mystery of lawlessness is already at work; only He who now restrains will do so until He is taken out of the way. 8 And then the lawless one will be revealed, whom the Lord will consume with the breath of His mouth and destroy with the brightness of His coming. 9 The coming of the lawless one is according to the working of Satan, with all power, signs, and lying wonders, 10 and with all unrighteous deception among those who perish, because they did not receive the love of the truth, that they might be saved. 11 And for this reason God will send them strong delusion, that they should believe the lie, 12 that they all may be condemned who did not believe the truth but had pleasure in unrighteousness.

Knowing what our Father is prompting us to do or say is key because when we 'invite HIM into the situation' by accepting the assignment, we are protected!

Once we go forth to do and say what is asked of us, the assignment is complete. Then, our Father will handle anything else that needs to be handled because HE is 'in the midst'!

A powerful confirmation was provided to me when I was 'invited to be on the platform' the next morning after delivering a specific message to a prophet (also a pastor) in Phoenix, Arizona. Personally, I did not know the prophet's name before a pastor called me and shared the name and phone number along with a request to pray for the prophet. After a time of prayer, I was prompted to call the prophet. He was in tears. He was a prophet for more than 50 years and he was in a deep, dark time in his life, crying out to our Father and not hearing a word. Immediately after he asked GOD to have someone who does not know him call him with a word. He was so touched by the word, he asked me to visit with him the next day, for Sabbath. It was an amazing time with scribes seated around us and writing every word shared. The prophet was so deeply touched, he asked me to be on the platform with him the next morning. While I was deep in prayer, our Father confirmed I needed to pack and check out of the hotel because HE had another assignment for me. I was confused for a moment, but HE provided clarity: *He was your assignment. You are not his assignment.*

Before sunrise, I was packed and on my way to the next assignment location. Unaware of anything beyond the location, trusting without knowing what our Father was orchestrating HIS plan and purpose would be fulfilled. Each time, I stand in awe!

Are you receiving confirmation from our Father that you are still at a location where the assignment is 'on-going', or was the assignment fulfilled long ago and GOD is waiting for you to proceed on the next assignment?

Repentance for _____?

Adjustment(s) planned? _____

DAY THREE

UNBELIEF. II Thessalonians 3:2 (1-2).
Pray for Us
Finally, brethren, pray for us, that the word of the Lord may run swiftly and be glorified, just as it is with you, 2 and that we may be delivered from unreasonable and wicked men; for not all have faith.

Interesting timing of this scripture after the message yesterday. During the time with the prophet and the scribes, one of the scribes said **(as in Acts 9:25 and II Corinthians 11:33)**, *Whenever you need someone to be there when they lower you in a basket through the window, you can trust I will be there*

230

for you. I was honored to hear his interest in helping me. However, the truth is our Father does NOT send us 'on assignment' or 'into a situation' where we would not be able to handle what takes place while we are 'in the midst'. If we enter 'without HIM' or 'without prayer' or 'in our own power', we would be 'on our own' but, when we represent HIM in doing and saying what HE asks us to do and say 'in the moment' because we entered as an empty vessel and yielded the results to HIM, we proceed with HIS divine protection.

Knowing 'not all have faith' where you are being sent, will you surrender all and represent HIM?

Repentance for _____?

Adjustment(s) planned? _____

DAY FOUR

UNBELIEF. I Timothy 1:13 (12-13).
Glory to God for His Grace
And I thank Christ Jesus our Lord who has enabled me, because He counted me faithful, putting me into the ministry, 13 although I was formerly a blasphemer, a persecutor, and an insolent man; but I obtained mercy because I did it ignorantly in unbelief.

Yes. HE lifted us up and out of 'stuff'. When HE said I was to title the ministry HIS Best!, He sent confirmations in unique ways and yet, the most amazing confirmation was a word from a woman who had not shared a word for 12 years. She knew it was an urgent message, so she grabbed the microphone and shared the depth of legal debacle I was experiencing. She said our Father lined up all of the men and starting from the left, I was to forgive each one and then move on to the next one. Then, because I was focused on the men, I did not realize Jesus walked into the courtroom. Excited because now Jesus will handle the long line of men but, he asks one question: *Will you let ME forgive them as much as I have forgiven you?* Before I could think about forgiveness, I wanted Jesus to know how much and for how long … but, Father stopped me and tears flowed while I said, *Yes.*

The ministry name is the result of our Father responding again and again for me to give ALL people HIS Best!

Repentance for _____?

Adjustment(s) planned? _____

DAY FIVE

REVERENTIAL FEAR. I Timothy 1:17.
Now to the King eternal, immortal, invisible, to God who alone is wise, be honor and glory forever and ever. Amen.

True. All honor to HIM. No matter what, no matter when, no matter who, will you give all honor to HIM?

Repentance for _____?

Adjustment(s) planned? _____

DAY SIX

REVERENTIAL FEAR. I Timothy 6:16 (12-16).
Fight the good fight of faith, lay hold on eternal life, to which you were also called and have confessed the good confession in the presence of many witnesses. 13 I urge you in the sight of God who gives life to all things, and before Christ Jesus who witnessed the good confession before Pontius Pilate, 14 that you keep this commandment without spot, blameless until our Lord Jesus Christ's appearing, 15 which He will manifest in His own time, He who is the blessed and only Potentate, the King of kings and Lord of lords, 16 who alone has immortality, dwelling in unapproachable light, whom no man has seen or can see, to whom be honor and everlasting power. Amen.

Fighting infers conflict and struggle. It's not always going to be easy to have faith. There will be times you will have to fight how you feel to engage your faith. But, it's so worth it! Will you keep up the good fight of faith, giving all to honor HIM?

Repentance for _____?

Adjustment(s) planned? _____

DAY SEVEN

BLESSING. Numbers 6:24-26.

*"The L*ORD* bless you and keep you;*
*25 The L*ORD* make His face shine upon you,*
And be gracious to you;
*26 The L*ORD* lift up His countenance upon you,*
And give you peace." '

Blessings received: _____

Blessings shared: _____

Declarations/Testimonies: _____

WEEK FORTY-EIGHT

DAY ONE

<u>DOUBT</u>. I Timothy 6:20-21.
<u>Guard the Faith</u>
Timothy! Guard what was committed to your trust, avoiding the profane and idle babblings and contradictions of what is falsely called knowledge— 21 by professing it some have strayed concerning the faith.
Grace be with you. Amen.

Father will help you guard your faith.

HE is your rear-guard. HE supports every step of the purpose and plan HE has orchestrated for you! When aligned with HIM, you can SOAR.

What is restraining you from soaring?

Repentance for _____**?**

Adjustment(s) planned? _____

DAY TWO

<u>DOUBT</u>. II Timothy 2:16.
But shun profane and idle babblings, for they will increase to more ungodliness.

Since ALL said and done is either blessing or cursing, do you speak truth in a conversation and then depart from the conversation if it curses instead of blesses?

233

Repentance for _____?

Adjustment(s) planned? _____

DAY THREE

__DOUBT__. II Timothy 3:14-17.

But you must continue in the things which you have learned and been assured of, knowing from whom you have learned them, 15 and that from childhood you have known the Holy Scriptures, which are able to make you wise for salvation through faith which is in Christ Jesus.

16 All Scripture is given by inspiration of God, and is profitable for doctrine, for reproof, for correction, for instruction in righteousness, 17 that the man of God may be complete, thoroughly equipped for every good work.

Knowing how important you are to the overall plan of the Father while you are 'on earth', are you willing to complete an assignment knowing you are thoroughly equipped to proceed?

Repentance for _____?

Adjustment(s) planned? _____

DAY FOUR

__UNBELIEF__. Titus 1:15 (10-16).
__The Elders' Task__

For there are many insubordinate, both idle talkers and deceivers, especially those of the circumcision, 11 whose mouths must be stopped, who subvert whole households, teaching things which they ought not, for the sake of dishonest gain.

12 One of them, a prophet of their own, said, *Cretans are always liars, evil beasts, lazy gluttons.*

13 This testimony is true. Therefore rebuke them sharply, that they may be sound in the faith, 14 not giving heed to Jewish fables and commandments of men who turn from the truth.

15 To the pure all things are pure, but to those who are defiled and unbelieving nothing is pure; but even their mind and conscience are defiled.

16 They profess to know God, but in works they deny Him, being abominable, disobedient, and disqualified for every good work.

In the depth of a problem, do your actions toward resolution confirm to witnesses who hear you profess to know GOD that you truly do know GOD?

Repentance for _____?

Adjustment(s) planned? _____

DAY FIVE

DOUBT. Titus 3:6.

Graces of the Heirs of Grace

Remind them to be subject to rulers and authorities, to obey, to be ready for every good work, 2 to speak evil of no one, to be peaceable, gentle, showing all humility to all men.

3 For we ourselves were also once foolish, disobedient, deceived, serving various lusts and pleasures, living in malice and envy, hateful and hating one another.

4 But when the kindness and the love of God our Savior toward man appeared, 5 not by works of righteousness which we have done, but according to His mercy He saved us, through the washing of regeneration and renewing of the Holy Spirit, 6 whom He poured out on us abundantly through Jesus Christ our Savior, 7 that having been justified by His grace we should become heirs according to the hope of eternal life.

Grace. A wonderful gift!

As a joint-heir with CHRIST do you choose, daily, to be conformed to HIS mind and do your actions and words confirm this to be true to others?

Repentance for _____?

Adjustment(s) planned? _____

DAY SIX

UNBELIEF. Hebrews 4:2 (1-7).

The Promise of Rest

Therefore, since a promise remains of entering His rest, let us fear lest any of you seem to have come short of it. 2 For indeed the gospel was preached to us as well as to them; but the word which they heard did not profit them, not being mixed with faith in those who heard it. 3 For we who have believed do enter that rest, as He has said: *So I swore in My wrath,* *'They shall not enter My rest,'* **although the works were finished from the foundation of the world. 4 For He has spoken in a certain place of the**

seventh *day* in this way: *And God rested on the seventh day from all His works*; 5 *and again in this place: They shall not enter My rest.*

6 Since therefore it remains that some *must* enter it, and those to whom it was first preached did not enter because of disobedience, 7 again He designates a certain day, saying in David, *Today,* after such a long time, as it has been said: *Today, if you will hear His voice, Do not harden your hearts.*

Father prompted me to continue beyond **verse 2** due to the depth of message when viewed 'in context', beyond reminding us to hear the truth 'without faith' does not strengthen (profit) us. The true goal is to NOT harden our hearts or to speak or act in a way to cause others to harden their hearts. Hard to accept when I first heard our Father prompt me to 'stop praying' for a person or for a situation to change. To realize that we may continue to pursue a person or a matter when their hearts are already hardened, either a person or a decision maker in the midst of the situation we are praying for change. Important to share the gospel and leave the results in the hands of our Father for HE knows the condition of their heart.

Do others confirm the gospel and faith are evident in your life?

Repentance for _____?

Adjustment(s) planned? _____

DAY SEVEN

BLESSING. Numbers 6:24-26.
> *"The LORD bless you and keep you;*
> 25 *The LORD make His face shine upon you,*
>   *And be gracious to you;*
> 26 *The LORD lift up His countenance upon you,*
>   *And give you peace." '*

Blessings received: _____

Blessings shared:_____

Declarations/Testimonies: _____

<u>UNBELIEF</u>. **Hebrews 3:12-19.**

Beware, brethren, lest there be in any of you an evil heart of unbelief in departing from the living God; 13 but exhort one another daily, while it is called *Today,* **lest any of you be hardened through the deceitfulness of sin. 14 For we have become partakers of Christ if we hold the beginning of our confidence steadfast to the end, 15 while it is said:**

Today, if you will hear His voice,
Do not harden your hearts as in the rebellion.

<u>Failure of the Wilderness Wanderers</u>

16 For who, having heard, rebelled? Indeed, was it not all who came out of Egypt, led by Moses? 17 Now with whom was He angry forty years? Was it not with those who sinned, whose corpses fell in the wilderness? 18 And to whom did He swear that they would not enter His rest, but to those who did not obey? 19 So we see that they could not enter in because of unbelief.

Exhort one another, daily. To exhort means to strongly encourage to do something. **I Thessalonians 5:11.** *Therefore comfort each other and edify one another, just as you also are doing.*

Supporting each other to remain strong in the faith while gaining knowledge and understanding to not return to sin. After our Father did ALL while bringing the people out of Egypt, providing ALL each day for 40 years and yet, their fate was confirmed by their own rebellion. The result, at the border of the promised land, they died. They did NOT 'enter in' to HIS REST.

Each Sabbath, which our Father commanded to honor and keep holy as one of the ten commandments, we are to enter into HIS rest. When we enter into HIS rest, we hear HIS truth so clearly even when HE whispers. It is tearful to hear our Father exhort to us, about us!

Who will you exhort daily? Will you enter into HIS rest?

Repentance for _____?

Adjustment(s) planned? _____

FEAR. Hebrews 13:6 (1-6).

Concluding Moral Directions

Let brotherly love continue. 2 Do not forget to entertain strangers, for by so doing some have unwittingly entertained angels. 3 Remember the prisoners as if chained with them—those who are mistreated—since you yourselves are in the body also.

4 Marriage is honorable among all, and the bed undefiled; but fornicators and adulterers God will judge.

5 Let your conduct be without covetousness; be content with such things as you have. For He Himself has said, *I will never leave you nor forsake you.* 6 So we may boldly say:

The Lord is my helper;
I will not fear.
What can man do to me?

So many examples could be shared due to the days, weeks and months spent with hostesses and hosts families during the last three decades. This scripture is so powerful! We can 'be together' in a blessed environment for each other or not. Each word and action when we are together reveals character! It is not easy to witness a path people are on which is destructive and not be able to speak into their lives. To dust shoes off on the 'inside' of the threshold and depart is not an easy thing to do and sad to say, it is not typically understood until months later. GOD wakes people up 'when they are willing, when they are open to waking up to the truth'.

It is exactly the same experience of remaining open to 'reach a soul and bring the person to salvation in CHRIST', whether it takes 575 or 999 people, we may not see the results. Our Father does prompt people to contact me later, whether months or years. Then, the prayers become powerful because the path forward is clear and the price was already paid for the time of rebellion.

It is the same in the prayer lines. Father points out who is 'on assignment' to attempt to impact me or 'take me out'. Grateful HE does not confirm their 'intention' until AFTER the meeting and the people have departed from the venue! HE lets me know to NOT touch or pray directly for them. Instead, HE wants me to look into their eyes and BLESS THEM and that releases them to the Holy Spirit who will do a mighty work with them.

Knowing there is nothing 'mere mortals' can do to you, will you 'take on' what is before you, knowing you are not dealing with flesh and blood but, the spirits affecting the people in your life?

Repentance for _____?

Adjustment(s) planned? _____

DAY THREE

UNBELIEF. I Peter 2:7 (7-8).
Therefore, to you who believe, He is precious; but to those who are disobedient, *The stone which the builders rejected*
Has become the chief cornerstone,
8 and *A stone of stumbling*
And a rock of offense.
They stumble, being disobedient to the word, to which they also were appointed.

Powerful to realize they rejected CHRIST, the Chief Cornerstone. Since CHRIST resides in your heart, when you stand firm in truth and they battle against you, it is important to remember you are NOT causing them to stumble!

Does the rejection of CHRIST help you understand why some of the people will also reject you, because you are a believer, a joint-heir?

Repentance for _____?

Adjustment(s) planned? _____

DAY FOUR

UNBELIEF. I Peter 3:1.
Submission to Husbands
Wives, likewise, be submissive to your own husbands, that even if some do not obey the word, they, without a word, may be won by the conduct of their wives, 2 when they observe your chaste conduct accompanied by fear.

As the bride of CHRIST, this refers to all of us. Will your conduct always be accompanied by (reverential, in awe of the LORD) fear?

Repentance for _____?

Adjustment(s) planned? _____

DAY FIVE

<u>FEAR</u>. I Peter 3:6 (3-7).

Do not let your adornment be merely outward—arranging the hair, wearing gold, or putting on fine apparel— 4 rather let it be the hidden person of the heart, with the incorruptible beauty of a gentle and quiet spirit, which is very precious in the sight of God. 5 For in this manner, in former times, the holy women who trusted in God also adorned themselves, being submissive to their own husbands, 6 as Sarah obeyed Abraham, calling him lord, whose daughters you are if you do good and are not afraid with any terror.

<u>A Word to Husbands</u>

7 Husbands, likewise, dwell with them with understanding, giving honor to the wife, as to the weaker vessel, and as being heirs together of the grace of life, that your prayers may not be hindered.

Powerful. A special testimony from Bill McCartney, founder of ***Promise Keepers.*** He attended a meeting where the speaker challenged men by stating the status of the relationship is easy to see in the eyes of the wife. His book, ***Sold Out,*** and the impact on marriages through ***Promise Keepers*** are major contributions he has made to the body of believers.

How will you proceed so your prayers may not be hindered?

Repentance for _____?

Adjustment(s) planned? _____

DAY SIX

<u>FEAR</u>. I Peter 3:14 (13-17).
<u>Suffering for Right and Wrong</u>

And who is he who will harm you if you become followers of what is good? 14 But even if you should suffer for righteousness' sake, you are blessed. *And do not be afraid of their threats, nor be troubled.* 15 *But sanctify the Lord God in your hearts, and always be ready to give a defense to everyone who asks you a reason for the hope that is in you, with meekness and fear;* 16 *having a good conscience, that when they defame you as evildoers, those who revile your good conduct in Christ may be ashamed.* 17 *For it is better, if it is the will of God, to suffer for doing good than for doing evil.*

This was a major lesson to learn after crying out for so long: *Why does it hurt so much to stand in truth and faith and yet, be rejected?* It took a while to

240

realize what is important to our Father, SEED TRUTH. No matter what is going on or what people are saying, SEED LIVES WITH TRUTH. Even if you are sharing truth in faith, are you willing to pay the price of suffering for the sake of truth and souls no matter what it costs you in relationships or losses in your life?

Repentance for _____?

Adjustment(s) planned? _____

DAY SEVEN

BLESSING. **Numbers 6:24-26.**
> *"The LORD bless you and keep you;*
> **25** *The LORD make His face shine upon you,*
> *And be gracious to you;*
> **26** *The LORD lift up His countenance upon you,*
> *And give you peace."* '

Blessings received: _____

Blessings shared: _____

Declarations/Testimonies: _____

WEEK FIFTY

DAY ONE

REVERENTIAL FEAR. **I Peter 3:14-15 (13-16).**
Suffering for Right and Wrong
And who is he who will harm you if you become followers of what is good? 14 But even if you should suffer for righteousness' sake, you are blessed. *And do not be afraid of their threats, nor be troubled.* **15 But sanctify the Lord God in your hearts, and always be ready to give a defense to everyone who asks you a reason for the hope that is in you, with meekness and fear; 16 having a good conscience, that when they defame you as evildoers, those who revile your good conduct in Christ may be ashamed.**

Would the people in your life, family or observers, confirm your good conduct in Christ?

Repentance for _____?

Adjustment(s) planned? _____

DAY TWO

FEAR. 1 Peter 5:6-7 (5-11).
Submit to God, Resist the Devil
Likewise you younger people, submit yourselves to your elders. Yes, all of you be submissive to one another, and be clothed with humility, for

> *God resists the proud,*
> *But gives grace to the humble.*

6 Therefore humble yourselves under the mighty hand of God, that He may exalt you in due time, 7 casting all your care upon Him, for He cares for you.

8 Be sober, be vigilant; because your adversary the devil walks about like a roaring lion, seeking whom he may devour. 9 Resist him, steadfast in the faith, knowing that the same sufferings are experienced by your brotherhood in the world. 10 But may the God of all grace, who called us to His eternal glory by Christ Jesus, after you have suffered a while, perfect, establish, strengthen, and settle you. 11 To Him be the glory and the dominion forever and ever. Amen.

It surprises people when I say, *I am still in training.* The truth is the truth. The more I learn from our Father, the more I realize I do not know! The process of surrender and becoming an empty vessel to do and say what HE wants me to do and say is an hour by hour, each and every day, process. Conforming to CHRIST, after suffering a while, may the GOD of all grace perfect, establish, strengthen, and settle you. Are you willing?

Repentance for _____?

Adjustment(s) planned? _____

DAY THREE

DOUBT. II Peter 1:19 (19-21).
And so we have the prophetic word confirmed, which you do well to heed as a light that shines in a dark place, until the day dawns and the morning star rises in your hearts; 20 knowing this first, that no prophecy of Scripture is of any private interpretation, 21 for prophecy never came by the will of man, but holy men of God spoke as they were moved by the Holy Spirit.

People often wonder why I do not walk forward to get a word when a prophet is speaking somewhere in the area, or at a church. The truth is our Father will get the word to us if we are not hearing it direct from our Father or if a confirmation would help us continue the race! Important to remember the prophecy does not come by the will of man, but holy men of GOD. Will you rush forward in a meeting to hear a word from a prophet or wait for a true word spoken by a prophet moved by the Holy Spirit?

Repentance for _____?

Adjustment(s) planned? _____

DAY FOUR

FEAR. 1 John 4:18 (17-19).
The Consummation of Love
Love has been perfected among us in this: that we may have boldness in the day of judgment; because as He is, so are we in this world. 18 There is no fear in love; but perfect love casts out fear, because fear involves torment. But he who fears has not been made perfect in love. 19 We love Him because He first loved us.

Remembering our first love, knowing we are HIS beloved, will you pursue perfect love which casts out fear? Can you think of a situation where you showed or were shown perfect love?

Repentance for _____?

Adjustment(s) planned? _____

DAY FIVE

DOUBT. I John 5:13.
These things I have written to you who believe in the name of the Son of God, that you may know that you have eternal life, and that you may continue to believe in the name of the Son of God.

Will you continue to believe in the name of the Son of GOD?

Repentance for _____?

DAY SIX

FEAR. Revelation 1:17 (9-20).
Vision of the Son of Man
I, John, both your brother and companion in the tribulation and kingdom and patience of Jesus Christ, was on the island that is called Patmos for the word of God and for the testimony of Jesus Christ. 10 I was in the Spirit on the Lord's Day, and I heard behind me a loud voice, as of a trumpet, 11 saying, *I am the Alpha and the Omega, the First and the Last,* and, *What you see, write in a book and send it to the seven churches which are in Asia: to Ephesus, to Smyrna, to Pergamos, to Thyatira, to Sardis, to Philadelphia, and to Laodicea.*

12 Then I turned to see the voice that spoke with me. And having turned I saw seven golden lampstands, 13 and in the midst of the seven lampstands One like the Son of Man, clothed with a garment down to the feet and girded about the chest with a golden band. 14 His head and hair were white like wool, as white as snow, and His eyes like a flame of fire; 15 His feet were like fine brass, as if refined in a furnace, and His voice as the sound of many waters; 16 He had in His right hand seven stars, out of His mouth went a sharp two-edged sword, and His countenance was like the sun shining in its strength. 17 And when I saw Him, I fell at His feet as dead. But He laid His right hand on me, saying to me, *Do not be afraid; I am the First and the Last. 18 I am He who lives, and was dead, and behold, I am alive forevermore. Amen. And I have the keys of Hades and of Death. 19 Write the things which you have seen, and the things which are, and the things which will take place after this. 20 The mystery of the seven stars which you saw in My right hand, and the seven golden lampstands: The seven stars are the angels of the seven churches, and the seven lampstands which you saw are the seven churches.*

Will you remain in truth and not fear, knowing you are with CHRIST?

Repentance for _____?

Adjustment(s) planned? _____

DAY SEVEN

BLESSING. Numbers 6:24-26.
> "*The LORD bless you and keep you;*
> *25 The LORD make His face shine upon you,*
> *And be gracious to you;*
> *26 The LORD lift up His countenance upon you,*
> *And give you peace.*" '

Blessings received: _____

Blessings shared: _____

Declarations/Testimonies: _____

WEEK FIFTY-ONE

DAY ONE

<u>FEAR</u>. Revelation 2:10 (8-11).
<u>The Persecuted Church</u>
And to the angel of the church in Smyrna write,
'These things says the First and the Last, who was dead, and came to life:
9 I know your works, tribulation, and poverty (but you are rich); and I know the blasphemy of those who say they are Jews and are not, but are a synagogue of Satan. 10 Do not fear any of those things which you are about to suffer. Indeed, the devil is about to throw some of you into prison, that you may be tested, and you will have tribulation ten days. Be faithful until death, and I will give you the crown of life.
11 He who has an ear, let him hear what the Spirit says to the churches. He who overcomes shall not be hurt by the second death.'

As was the test for Job, will your soul remain with the LORD?

Repentance for _____?

Adjustment(s) planned? _____

DAY TWO

<u>REVERENTIAL FEAR</u>. Revelation 11:18 (15-19).
<u>Seventh Trumpet: The Kingdom Proclaimed</u>
Then the seventh angel sounded: And there were loud voices in heaven, saying, *The kingdoms of this world have become the kingdoms of our Lord and of His Christ, and He shall reign forever and ever!* 16 And the twenty-four elders who sat before God on their thrones fell on their faces and worshiped God, 17 saying:

We give You thanks, O Lord God Almighty,
The One who is and who was and who is to come,
Because You have taken Your great power and reigned.

245

18 *The nations were angry, and Your wrath has come,*
And the time of the dead, that they should be judged,
And that You should reward Your servants the prophets and the saints,
And those who fear Your name, small and great,
And should destroy those who destroy the earth.

19 Then the temple of God was opened in heaven, and the ark of His covenant was seen in His temple. And there were lightnings, noises, thunderings, an earthquake, and great hail.

Judgment. As it was for the thousands who died at the border, those who did not enter into HIS rest, the promised land. Will you be ready to enter in?

Repentance for _____?

Adjustment(s) planned? _____

DAY THREE

REVERENTIAL FEAR. Revelation 14:7 (6-7).
The Proclamations of Three Angels
Then I saw another angel flying in the midst of heaven, having the everlasting gospel to preach to those who dwell on the earth—to every nation, tribe, tongue, and people— 7 saying with a loud voice, *Fear God and give glory to Him, for the hour of His judgment has come; and worship Him who made heaven and earth, the sea and springs of water.*

Immediately after this proclamation, Babylon falls.

The moment of choice: knowing divine protection is only for those who honor and fear, stand in awe of the living LORD, and knowing the hour of judgment is coming, are you remaining in an attitude of worship?

Repentance for _____?

Adjustment(s) planned? _____

DAY FOUR

REVERENTIAL FEAR. Revelation 15:4 (1-4).
Prelude to the Bowl Judgments
Then I saw another sign in heaven, great and marvelous: seven angels having the seven last plagues, for in them the wrath of God is complete.

2 And I saw something like a sea of glass mingled with fire, and those who have the victory over the beast, over his image and over his mark and over the number of his name, standing on the sea of glass, having harps of God. 3 They sing the song of Moses, the servant of God, and the song of the Lamb, saying:

> *Great and marvelous are Your works,*
> *Lord God Almighty!*
> *Just and true are Your ways,*
> *O King of the saints!*
> *4 Who shall not fear You, O Lord, and glorify Your name?*
> *For You alone are holy.*
> *For all nations shall come and worship before You,*
> *For Your judgments have been manifested.*

ONLY the living LORD is holy. All nations (people) will come and worship HIM. Through it all, knowing HE is the first and last, and HE knows the end from the beginning for each of us, will you worship only HIM? Are you currently, worshiping ONLY HIM?

Repentance for _____?

Adjustment(s) planned? _____

DAY FIVE

REVERENTIAL FEAR; also FEAR. Exodus 20:20.
Moses said to the people 'Do not be afraid. God has come to test you, so that the fear of God will be with you to keep you from sinning.' (WEEK THREE)

Are you still in the same place as you were in week three? Can you name a notable change in your heart, mind or life?

Repentance for _____?

Adjustment(s) planned? _____

DAY SIX

DOUBT, also FEAR. Deuteronomy 20:1.
Principles Governing Warfare.

When you go out to battle against your enemies, and see horses and chariots and people more numerous than you, do not be afraid of them; for the Lord your God is with you, who brought you up from the land of Egypt. **(WEEK SEVEN)**

Are you still in the same place as you were in week seven? Can you name a notable change in your heart, mind or life?

Repentance for _____?

Adjustment(s) planned? _____

DAY SEVEN

BLESSING. **Numbers 6:24-26.**
"The LORD bless you and keep you;
25 The LORD make His face shine upon you,
And be gracious to you;
26 The LORD lift up His countenance upon you,
And give you peace." '

Blessings received: _____

Blessings shared: _____

Declarations/Testimonies: _____

WEEK FIFTY-TWO

DAY ONE

<u>DOUBT</u>, also <u>FEAR</u>. Isaiah 41:10 (8-10).
But you, Israel, are My servant,
Jacob whom I have chosen,
The descendants of Abraham My friend.
9 You whom I have taken from the ends of the earth,
And called from its farthest regions,
And said to you,
'You are My servant,
I have chosen you and have not cast you away:
10 Fear not, for I am with you;
Be not dismayed, for I am your God.
I will strengthen you,
Yes, I will help you,
I will uphold you with My righteous right hand.'
(WEEK TWENTY-FIVE)

Are you still in the same place as you were in week twenty-five? Can you name a notable change in your heart, mind or life?

Repentance for _____?

Adjustment(s) planned? _____

DAY TWO

<u>FEAR</u>. Psalm 56: 3-4 (1-4).
Be merciful to me, O God, for man would swallow me up;
Fighting all day he oppresses me.
2 My enemies would hound me all day,
For there are many who fight against me, O Most High.
3 Whenever I am afraid,
I will trust in You.
4 In God (I will praise His word),
In God I have put my trust;
I will not fear.
What can flesh do to me?
(WEEK FIFTEEN)

Are you still in the same place as you were in week fifteen? Can you name a notable change in your heart, mind or life?

249

Repentance for _____?

Adjustment(s) planned? _____

DAY THREE

DOUBT. Isaiah 42:3.
A bruised reed He will not break,
And smoking flax He will not quench;
He will bring forth justice for truth. **(WEEK TWENTY-SIX)**

Are you still in the same place as you were in week twenty-six? Can you name a notable change in your heart, mind or life?

Repentance for _____?

Adjustment(s) planned? _____

DAY FOUR

UNBELIEF. John 1:11.
He came to His own, and His own did not receive Him.
(WEEK FORTY)

Are you still in the same place as you were in week forty? Can you name a notable change in your heart, mind or life?

Repentance for _____?

Adjustment(s) planned? _____

DAY FIVE

UNBELIEF. Psalm 106:24 (21-27).
They forgot God their Savior,
Who had done great things in Egypt,
22 Wondrous works in the land of Ham,
Awesome things by the Red Sea.
23 Therefore He said that He would destroy them,
Had not Moses His chosen one stood before Him in the breach,
To turn away His wrath, lest He destroy them.
24 Then they despised the pleasant land;

They did not believe His word,
25 But complained in their tents,
And did not heed the voice of the Lord.
26 Therefore He raised His hand in an oath against them,
To overthrow them in the wilderness,
27 To overthrow their descendants among the nations,
And to scatter them in the lands. **(WEEK TWENTY-ONE)**

Are you still in the same place as you were in week twenty-one? Can you name a notable change in your heart, mind or life?

Repentance for _____?

Adjustment(s) planned? _____

DAY SIX

REVERENTIAL FEAR. Deuteronomy 4:10-11 (7-11) .
For what great nation is there that has God so near to it, as the LORD our God is to us, for whatever reason we may call upon Him? 8 And what great nation is there that has such statutes and righteous judgments as are in all this law which I set before you this day? 9 Only take heed to yourself, and diligently keep yourself, lest you forget the things your eyes have seen, and lest they depart from your heart all the days of your life. And teach them to your children and your grandchildren, 10 especially concerning the day you stood before the LORD your God in Horeb, when the LORD said to me, 'Gather the people to Me, and I will let them hear My words, that they may learn to fear Me all the days they live on the earth, and that they may teach their children.'
11 Then you came near and stood at the foot of the mountain, and the mountain burned with fire to the midst of heaven, with darkness, cloud, and thick darkness. **(WEEK FOUR)**

Are you still in the same place as you were in week four? Can you name a notable change in your heart, mind or life?

Repentance for _____?

Adjustment(s) planned? _____

DAY SEVEN

BLESSING. Numbers 6:24-26.

"The LORD bless you and keep you;
25 The LORD make His face shine upon you,
And be gracious to you;
26 The LORD lift up His countenance upon you,
And give you peace." '

Blessings received: _____

Blessings shared:_____

Declarations/Testimonies: _____

4th QUARTER: What is our Father revealing to you, about you?

_____

FEAR. Psalm 119:165 (161-168).
Princes persecute me without a cause,
But my heart stands in awe of Your word.
162 I rejoice at Your word
As one who finds great treasure.
163 I hate and abhor lying,
But I love Your law.
164 Seven times a day I praise You,
Because of Your righteous judgments.
165 Great peace have those who love Your law,
And nothing causes them to stumble.
166 Lord, I hope for Your salvation,
And I do Your commandments.
167 My soul keeps Your testimonies,
And I love them exceedingly.
168 I keep Your precepts and Your testimonies,
For all my ways are before You.
(WEEK TWENTY-TWO)

Are you still in the same place as you were in week twenty-two? Can you name a notable change in your heart, mind or life?

Repentance for _____?

Adjustment(s) planned? _____

DAY TWO

DOUBT. Numbers 11:21-23.
And Moses said, *The people whom I am among are six hundred thousand men on foot; yet You have said, 'I will give them meat, that they may eat for a whole month.' 22 Shall flocks and herds be slaughtered for them, to provide enough for them? Or shall all the fish of the sea be gathered together for them, to provide enough for them?*

23 And the Lord said to Moses, Has the Lord's arm been shortened? Now you shall see whether what I say will happen to you or not. (WEEK FOUR)

Are you still in the same place as you were in week twenty-one? Can you name a notable change in your heart, mind or life?

Repentance for _____?

Adjustment(s) planned? _____

DAY THREE

<u>UNBELIEF</u>. John 12:37-38.
Who Has Believed Our Report?
37 But although He had done so many signs before them, they did not believe in Him, 38 that the word of Isaiah the prophet might be fulfilled, which he spoke:
Lord, who has believed our report?
And to whom has the arm of the Lord been revealed?
(WEEK FORTY-TWO)

Are you still in the same place as you were in week forty-two? Can you name a notable change in your heart, mind or life?

Repentance for _____ ?

Adjustment(s) planned? _____

DAY FOUR

<u>REVERENTIAL FEAR</u>. Revelation 11:18 (15-19).
<u>Seventh Trumpet: The Kingdom Proclaimed</u>
Then the seventh angel sounded: And there were loud voices in heaven, saying, "The kingdoms of this world have become the kingdoms of our Lord and of His Christ, and He shall reign forever and ever!" 16 And the twenty-four elders who sat before God on their thrones fell on their faces and worshiped God, 17 saying:
"We give You thanks, O Lord God Almighty,
The One who is and who was and who is to come,
Because You have taken Your great power and reigned.
18 The nations were angry, and Your wrath has come,
And the time of the dead, that they should be judged,
And that You should reward Your servants the prophets and the saints,
And those who fear Your name, small and great,
And should destroy those who destroy the earth."
19 Then the temple of God was opened in heaven, and the ark of His covenant was seen in His temple. And there were lightnings, noises, thunderings, an earthquake, and great hail. (WEEK FIFTY-ONE)

Are you still in the same place as you were in week fifty-one? Can you name a notable change in your heart, mind or life?

Repentance for _____?

Adjustment(s) planned? _____

DAY FIVE

REVERENTIAL FEAR. Deuteronomy 6:13-15.
You shall fear the Lord your God and serve Him, and shall take oaths in His name. 14 You shall not go after other gods, the gods of the peoples who are all around you 15 (for the Lord your God is a jealous God among you), lest the anger of the Lord your God be aroused against you and destroy you from the face of the earth. (WEEK FIVE)

Are you still in the same place as you were in week twenty-one? Can you name a notable change in your heart, mind or life?

Repentance for _____?

Adjustment(s) planned? _____

DAY SIX

FEAR. Matthew 6:25-34 (22-34).
The Lamp of the Body
"The lamp of the body is the eye. If therefore your eye is good, your whole body will be full of light. 23 But if your eye is bad, your whole body will be full of darkness. If therefore the light that is in you is darkness, how great is that darkness!
You Cannot Serve God and Riches
24 "No one can serve two masters; for either he will hate the one and love the other, or else he will be loyal to the one and despise the other. You cannot serve God and mammon.
Do Not Worry
25 "Therefore I say to you, do not worry about your life, what you will eat or what you will drink; nor about your body, what you will put on. Is not life more than food and the body more than clothing? 26 Look at the birds of the air, for they neither sow nor reap nor gather into barns; yet your heavenly Father feeds them. Are you not of more value than they? 27 Which of you by worrying can add one cubit to his stature?

28 "So why do you worry about clothing? Consider the lilies of the field, how they grow: they neither toil nor spin; 29 and yet I say to you that even Solomon in all his glory was not arrayed like one of these. 30 Now if God so clothes the grass of the field, which today is, and tomorrow is thrown into the oven, will He not much more clothe you, O you of little faith?

31 "Therefore do not worry, saying, 'What shall we eat?' or 'What shall we drink?' or 'What shall we wear?' 32 For after all these things the Gentiles seek. For your heavenly Father knows that you need all these things. 33 But seek first the kingdom of God and His righteousness, and all these things shall be added to you. 34 Therefore do not worry about tomorrow, for tomorrow will worry about its own things. Sufficient for the day is its own trouble. (WEEK THIRTY-THREE)

Are you still in the same place as you were in week thirty-three? Can you name a notable change in your heart, mind or life?

Repentance for _____?

Adjustment(s) planned? _____

DAY SEVEN

BLESSING. Numbers 6:24-26.
> *"The Lord bless you and keep you;*
> *25 The Lord make His face shine upon you,*
> *And be gracious to you;*
> *26 The Lord lift up His countenance upon you,*
> *And give you peace."* '

Blessings received: _____

Blessings shared: _____

Declarations/Testimonies: _____

A Personal Note 'Just Between Us'

Grateful the Father guided each step of HIS plan for the devotional.

Everything about the process has been unique for me!

Prayers are with you for ALL our Father wants to reveal to you being made known to you as you take on each scripture, repent for anything which is in the 'in between' between you and the Father! Standing with you as you realize progress in your life while countering fear, doubt and unbelief each day.

Deep in our heart where Christ resides, we do know there is ONLY ONE WAY, ONE TRUTH, ONLY ONE NAME ABOVE ALL NAMES, ONLY ONE SAVIOR Jesus Christ of Nazareth, the ONLY Son of the Father, our LORD Almighty, the ONLY LIVING LORD, our Yeshua, our Yahweh, our Jehovah.

LORD thank you for Your promise!

Grateful to know Your hand is upon us and You will never leave us or forsake us! Thank you for providing Your truth in Your word and through Your prophets so we will be prepared to march with You before the SONrise!

Amen (Hebrew meaning, Our GOD is a Faithful KING!

To live from glory to glory, it is important to comprehend that our Savior, Jesus Christ, the Messiah, as confirmed in **John 17:22**, gave us the glory that we would be one, unite together 'In One Accord' as He and the Father are one. He gave us this truth, while He was with us! Blessings upon you until the next ONE MORE TIME* our LORD brings us together!

Sheila

Email: office@hisbest.org

Ephesians 2:19-22 *We are no longer foreigners and aliens, but fellow citizens... members of GOD's household, built on the foundation of the apostles and prophets, with Christ Jesus himself as the chief cornerstone. In Him the whole building is joined together and rises to become a holy temple in the LORD. And in Him you too are being built together to become a dwelling in which GOD lives by His Spirit.*

II Corinthians 12:14-15. (a) *"Now, I am ready to visit you...what I want is not your possessions but you...So I will very gladly spend for you everything I have and expend myself as well."*

II Corinthians 13:11-14. *Aim for perfection ... be of one mind, live in peace, and the GOD of love and peace will be with you. May the grace of the LORD Jesus Christ, and the love of GOD, and the fellowship of the Holy Spirit be with you all.*

* While in Ghana, West Africa for the coronation of a King, Bishop Duncan William's worship team sang a simple verse: ONE MORE TIME, ONE MORE TIME, HE HAS ALLOWED US TO COME TOGETHER ONE MORE TIME, and by the third time they shared this verse, pointing to each other, then, to each of us on the platform and then, to each of the participants speaking at least 13 Afrikaans dialects and nine foreign languages, there was not a dry eye in the house!

Books Authored by Sheila Holm

It's A Faith Walk!

Sheila Holm

GOD'S STOREHOUSE
PRINCIPLE

SHEILA HOLM

GOD'S STOREHOUSE
PRINCIPLE
WORKBOOK

SHEILA HOLM

God's Currency

Foreword by
Bishop George Dallas McKinney

Sheila Holm

A Wake Up Call: It's Restoration Time!

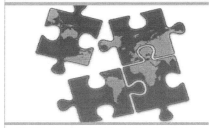

MYSTERIES REVEALED: HOW AND WHEN THE CHURCH WAS DECEIVED AND WHAT IS REQUIRED FOR FULL RESTORATION.

SHEILA HOLM

IN SEARCH OF WIGGLESWORTH

A JOURNEY WHICH SPEAKS TO THE VERY CORE OF WHAT IT MEANS TO BE A TRUE BROTHER AND SISTER IN CHRIST!

SHEILA HOLM

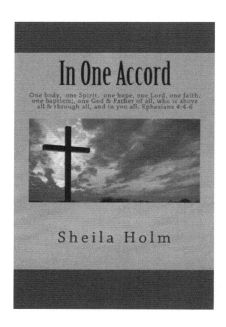

In One Accord

One body, one Spirit, one hope, one Lord, one faith, one baptism;, one God & Father of all, who is above all & through all, and in you all. Ephesians 4:4-6

Sheila Holm

A PECULIAR PEOPLE

A holy nation, a peculiar people.

We are not ashamed of the Gospel of Jesus Christ!!

DISCIPLESHIP OF PECULIAR PEOPLE BY PECULIAR PEOPLE

SHEILA HOLM

ALWAYS SPEAK LIFE

For the eyes of the Lord are on the righteous, and His ears are open to their prayers ... 1 Peter 3:12

SHEILA HOLM

CHRISTMAS

Mysteries Uncovered & revealed: Truth Regarding the Birth of The Messiah, Hidden Since 300 AD

SHEILA HOLM

FOR THE SAKE OF AMERICA

America is in Trouble The Root Problems and the Promises of the LORD are Revealed For The Sake Of America!

SHEILA HOLM

FOR THE SAKE OF AMERICA II

Ancient and Current Roots Revealed Repentance for Deeper Truth Required Then, the LORD's Blessings Will Flow As A Restoration Flood For The Sake Of America!

SHEILA HOLM

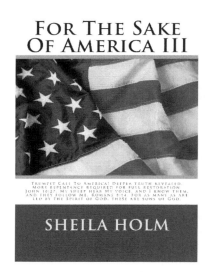

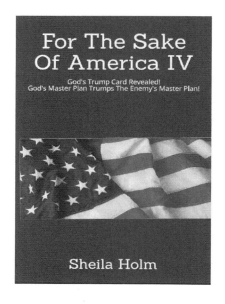

Releasing soon

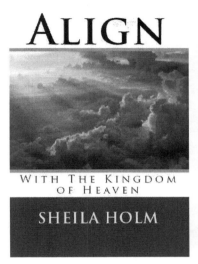

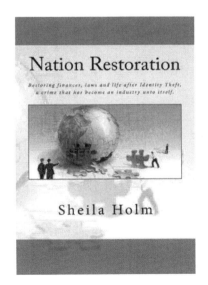

Nation Restoration

Published July 2014

Seven Step Business Plan

Published, 2007

Latin America edition:

Spanish Language

Published, 2009

ACKNOWLEDGMENTS

AFRICA

Ghana, West Africa

Pastor Sam,

"Truly, GOD has sent you to us with a strong word for our church."

Pastor Charles,

"It blesses my soul to hear of your faith & see the fruit of the ministry."

Johannesburg, South Africa

Pastor Jhanni,

"GOD is doing a good work through you and I pray with you and our church."

Coronation Ceremony

AMERICA

Bishop George Dallas McKinney, California

"Sheila is GOD's ambassador to encourage Christians, especially pastors, throughout the US, Africa, Australia and Europe. Without sponsors or any visible means of support, she has traveled the world sustained by the faithfulness of GOD.

Dr. Nancy Franklin, Georgia

"Thank you God for answering my prayers by sending Your apostle to (the region) to unite the believers ... "

Prophetess Nancy Haney, Alaska

"God has never given me this before. I see circles and circles and circles ... you drink and you draw from one circle to the other, and that's what you do, you drink and draw and you bring these circles together ... Pulling many groups together. All these groups need each other ... He can use you for you have ears to hear and you hear His deep truth. You are filtering what is nonsense and what is real ... because you have been in that circle, and because of what you say they are going to merge. It is going to expand, become bigger than you could imagine."

Pastor, Host of "Praise the Lord", TBN,

"...The fruit of the ministry is evident in your testimony..."

Man of God (Georgia), Requesting to be Discipled while attending the coronation of a King in Africa, Georgia

"...at my age, it is hard to believe I am learning so much in these few days about what I did not know...realizing what it is to know that I know how it is to live within God's word each day. Will you consider discipling me?"

International Prophet,

"You have remained steadfast to God's plan and God will continue to send you forth for His plan and purpose to be fulfilled, and for the thousands who have not knelt..."

President, Christian Publishing Company

"Only God could orchestrate such a grand plan..."

Prayer Director, International Prayer Center

"God is opening many doors for you..."

Christian Publisher, "God has given you a powerful voice and a sweet spirit..."

Pastor, Southern California

"God is raising you up and sending you forth to many nations..."

International Apostle

"God is doing a mighty work through you, for His righteousness precedes you, showers over you and follows you as a mighty wake. May it continue for each of your days…"

Prophetic Prayer Partner, Minnesota

"Only God could walk you through these days… accomplish so much through you, in the midst of your daily situations, the many blessings shared during each of your travels will continue to shower blessings upon each of the many households around the world…"

AUSTRALIA

Four Square Gospel Church, Aboriginal Cultural Center

Pastor Rex, "**GOD blessed us through your preaching on Easter Sunday. We will never forget that you were in our midst ... GOD brought new people to Jesus today and we thank GOD for what He has done because you answered His call.**"

Newcastle, New South Wales, Australia

Pastor Mark, "**...the staff and business leaders heard the message of Personal and Professional Life Management this week, so we are blessed you agreed to preach the word to our church this morning.**"

Prayer Team Meeting "**We know now how we will we be able to continue this mighty work when you are not in our midst...**"

ENGLAND

London, England

Pastor Vincent, Glory House, East London, "***...the honor is ours this Easter Sunday.***"

Associate Pastor, "***The Glory of our GOD Almighty shines upon you and through you in your speaking and your actions...we give Him praise.***"

Protocol Team,

"GOD has mightily blessed us by sending you into our midst."

Pastor Arnold,

"You have blessed the people of this congregation, and in His wisdom and timing, may He bring you back into our midst again, very soon."

Pastor, West London,

"We rejoice with you in hearing and seeing the mighty things GOD is doing."

Pastor, South London, **"Our GOD is evidenced in your life and your speaking, while we continue to thank GOD for the work He is doing through you…"**

High Commissioner, Kingdom of Tonga, serving in the Embassy in London, England; Ambassador Akosita, **"GOD's timing is always right…for you to be with us, prior to the Economic Summit, to meet and pray with us…"**

Sunderland, England

Anglican, Former Church of Pastor Smith Wigglesworth

Pastor Day, **"I thank GOD for sending you to our church this morning, for serving communion to me, and for renewing and restoring me for the call upon my life."**

Kingdom of TONGA

Pastor Isileli Taukolo, **"Our board and business leaders were fasting and praying and GOD confirmed He was sending someone to us. We are deeply touched by the message GOD sent to us, through you."**

Minister of Finance,Tasi, **"Our meeting was an answer to my prayers, and I thank you for providing the seminar for our senior staff members, and meeting with them individually for prayer and coaching."**

Government Office, **"Thank you for speaking today and for staying and praying with us."**

Interpreter, Sela

About the Author

The LORD fulfills upon His promises within the scriptures. He has equipped and trained Sheila while He:

- Places her feet on the soil of each continent,
- Sends her forth without an extra coin or tunic,
- Arranges flights and accommodations in each nation,
- Introduces her before she arrives,
- Lifts her up and encourages her,
- Seats her before governors and kings,
- Fills her as an empty vessel,
- Shares His wisdom and word of knowledge,
- Blesses and heals the people in her path,
- Comforts & re-encourages her to encourage pastors, prophets, apostles, believers, teachers & evangelists,
- Touches people individually in conferences/multitude,
- Speaks through her with power and authority,
- Takes people into gift of laughter when she preaches,
- Addresses situations the body of Christ is facing,

- Unites the people in the region,
- Confirms His word through her with each prayer & message shared,
- Speaks through her so people hear His words in their own language, especially when the translators also experience the gift of laughter and stop translating,

- Directs her path to <u>speak life</u> into each situation whether GOD sends people to her to be re-encouraged or he asks her to pray with a pastor, the church, or someone in a store or a restaurant, etc.

GOD has taken Sheila around the world, church to church, business to business, nation to nation, set her before governors and kings without an extra coin or tunic.

Many confirm Sheila walks in the five-fold ministry. She does not use a title because GOD does the work while He sends her as an apostle and prophet, and He orchestrates all arrangements for her to preach, teach, and evangelize.

People attending the conferences often say her segments are like watching someone walk out of the bible, share for a while and then, go right back in the bible, aka continue upon her journey in HIStory.

Made in the USA
Columbia, SC
29 March 2021